# YOUR DAD LOVES YOU!

## LIFE CONVERSATIONS WITH A DYING FATHER

Rob Stone

*"I once was blind, but now I see.*
*I once was dead, but now I'm alive!"*
John 9:25 and Luke 15:24

I am deeply in gratitude to my parents,
wife and children who have encouraged me in life
and in this work.

How I thank the Lord for you!

# CONTENTS

In the spring of 2005 I was losing my eyesight. After an emergency craniotomy, I could only see dimly in black and white. I could barely read using peripheral vision. inches from a computer screen. Welling with tears, the doctor read the news of my pathology. I had terminal melanoma. Twenty years earlier, God had broken into my proud, spiritually blind and dead heart with resolute authority and irresistible love. He redeemed this self-centered, small man. The gift of spiritual sight and new life is a miracle like no other, far greater than healing from cancer.  I pray that I can pass on rich stories and lessons to my dear children, grandchildren and other friends long after I am gone. May this very temporary, deteriorating body give glory to God and to others, life.

*Rob Stone*
SPRING 2018

# PRAISE FOR YOUR DAD LOVES YOU!

*"This is a beautiful love story, a story of God's love for Rob and his love for his children and all those who have lost a parent."*

Jack Herschend, Co-Founder Herschend Family
Entertainment and Silver Dollar City

*"Rob Stone in his book, Your Dad Loves You! from Life Conversations with a Dying Father, does an excellent job of putting Psalm 78:2-7 into practice. Those verses exhort fathers to communicate to succeeding generations how awesome the God of Scripture is and how wonderful are His works. As I read the manuscript, I felt I had been invited into a personal conversation between Rob and his kids. The wide ranging topics he addressed, areas critical to our children living the victorious Christian life, proved insightful. The last two pages were amazing. My most valuable take-away, however, was the strong desire to do something similar for my own children and grandchildren."*

Bill Jones, Chancellor, Columbia International University

*"Although my wife and I have known Rob for many years, we knew he had many and varied experiences, but not all the details in his book. "Wow," she said after looking over the manuscript, "What an interesting life he has had!" In these pages, he describes events and stories that illustrate the hand of God. Rob has done a service to believers and seekers alike by writing down the story of God's work in his life."*

Greg Parsons, Chancellor, William Carey International University

*"I have had the unique privilege of knowing Rob Stone, in various stages of life. I first met him at the time in which he was a young, single, Air Force pilot, and my wife and I were just starting our family. Through the years, Rob has been "uncle" to our three sons, and such an inspirational role model to them that two are now military officers, citing "Uncle Rob's" influence greatly factoring into selecting their career paths of service. When Rob transitioned from military to missions' ministry, it was a joy to witness him pour so much of himself into others, meeting the needs of so many people in so many parts of the world. As Rob became a husband and father himself, we celebrated the realization of a dream he had long held: to have a family. But just as it seemed that life had become incredibly sweet for a cherished, unique friend, a devastatingly grim cancer diagnosis rocked the Stone family's world.*

*I pray that as you read through this book, taking a journey laced with nuggets of hope and wisdom from Rob's miraculous bout with a life-threatening illness, you will find life-giving truth for your own journey."*

Kevin Weaver
CEO Network211/The Warrior's Journey

# SECTION 1

## LIFE AND DEATH

# A LETTER TO MY CHILDREN

*"All flesh is like grass*
*and all its glory like the flower of grass.*
*The grass withers,*
*and the flower falls,*
*but the word of the Lord remains forever."*[1]

My dear children,

What do people do when the doctor says they have only a few months left to live? Some react with fear. I've had a few close calls in cars and planes, so I know that feeling. Surprisingly however, when I was first diagnosed with terminal cancer, I was not afraid. Years ago, God burst in and radically changed everything. I had not been seriously looking for Him, but a buddy invited me to church. In one moment, God showed me what a mess I was, yet offered me forgiveness and a new life with Him. I knew beyond any doubt now that death meant being more fully alive than ever in God's presence. So cancer was no threat. My first real concern was for my young family. I was leaving you behind. Would you have enough money to live on? But I knew my parents and brothers would help. More importantly, God would care for your physical needs.

My overwhelming concern, one I couldn't shake, was that you, my children, would be left without a dad. This world is a hostile and difficult place to grow up. Although I knew your mother, my dear wife, would grieve for a season, she has a firm foundation in God. But there was no guarantee for you kids. Who would take my place to guide and protect you? Children lacking a father can suffer tremendously. They miss out on God's intended design for family which includes a father and a mother. Dads are unique. So are moms. Your mother is amazing. She loves, nurtures, and cares for you in ways I don't. But our complementary strengths and attributes give you a fuller foundation to thrive in life.

So this book was born. At first, I wanted to call it Saturdays with Grace and Sam. That was before Miracle and Joshua came along. As

---

1   1 Peter 1:24-25

a family trying to help others on God's path, Sunday was often too busy for us to have quality time at home. On Saturdays we could rest, play and talk to our hearts' content. As a child, I remember wonderful summer Sundays with my grandad when we would rest in the afternoon on the cool, living room floor. Grandma had just served lunch fit for a king. Grandad would tell stories about his youth. He told us he nearly gambled away all of his pay from Sears & Roebuck to some card sharks in Chicago back in 1920. The kindhearted matron of the home helped him recoup his losses and escape out the back door. His short career in gambling was over. Another time, Grandad boasted of a five-legged lamb born into his little flock of sheep back in Missouri. He was going to get rich from showing off that lamb! The next morning, that little lamb was stolen. It was another hard lesson, but I can testify I never saw my grandad boast. Over 50 years later, we were benefiting from his school of hard knocks. Grandad tickled us and popped our toes. His stories about life and his good nature helped shape our character in a profound way.

That's what I want to do for you. The lessons I got from my grandad, my dad and others came slowly over the course of many years. The love, experiences and wisdom of our fathers is a wealth far beyond money. With God's grace, it is the best we can pass on to our children.

_____

In the months and years after my terminal diagnosis, I met many people who had lost a mom or dad in their childhood. Rarely had the parent left some written advice or a letter of love. Others did not lose their dad, but he did not lovingly take part in their childhood. What advice would have helped? What could help soothe a broken heart? What would Dad say at my graduation? What should I teach my own kids someday? What is life all about?

I have great sympathy for both the child and parent in a life-threatening illness. Even in "normal" life we are usually too busy. Time feels more fleeting in sickness. Surgery, radiation, and chemo sap your strength and clarity of mind. Through tears, you try to finish important projects. In the fog of the moment, you don't always prioritize rightly. You try to write or rewrite your will, mend broken relationships, and say goodbye to many dear people. This book, including a hard drive crash, took over ten years, a luxury that terminal patients don't have. I trust for grace on some important topics I have surely left out. May God fill the gaps.

This might seem like a big book. I don't want you to try to read it in a few days. If you did, some of the things that took me a lifetime to learn would never sink in deeply and give you the roots you need. Did you know that fast-growing trees like banana or pine trees are weak or soft? Slow-growing hardwood trees like oaks or maples are strong and solid. You can't speed read advice. Ask your mom questions. Take time to look up some of the Bible verses. Check context. Most importantly, ask your Father in heaven what He thinks.

A note of caution: there are some topics that you may not be ready for, like a fuller discussion of sex. If your mom is reading to you, I'm sure she will filter out the parts you aren't ready for yet. On the other hand, if you are old enough to read, there is a great deal of "disinformation" on the hard issues of life from the media and certain friends, so I'd rather you hear it first from your mom or me!

I love you more than words can express and will wait for you. Remember that even when I am gone, we do not have to say goodbye forever. As you put your trust in Jesus, our parting is a very temporary one. I will wait and cheer until you come Home and tell me of the great exploits you have done by God's grace. We will have all eternity with Jesus to tell stories of great faith, eat royal meals, pop toes and laugh until our bellies ache.

*Dad*

# SECTION 2

## THE BIG PICTURE

# WHAT IS THE BIG PICTURE?

*GOD, the Lord, is my strength; he makes my feet like the deer's; he makes me tread on my high places.*[2]

Flying in an airplane as a passenger is fun. But nothing compares to actually sitting at the controls as the earth slips away beneath you. Puffy clouds on a warm spring morning seem untouchable standing on the ground. But then, they slide by your wings as you gently roll between the growing cotton balls that will become afternoon rain storms. Gradually they give way to an expanse of deep, clear blue sky that stretches as far as the eye can see. Looking down between clouds, cars are little dots moving on streets that look more like lines drawn by a thin marker. Houses and buildings get smaller and smaller until they blend together in a splash on a canvas. Even Tokyo, the first time I saw it, looked shockingly small against the backdrop of the vast ocean we'd just crossed. The famously populated city was enveloped by massive forests and hills. Mankind seemed so puny and insignificant. Mount Fuji[3] was the only visible character and appeared also small as she kept watch over the scene.

Beyond fun and simply beautiful, there is something very cathartic (a fancy word for "cleansing") about flying. On most of my longer trips in the Air Force, the last minutes were filled with packing, paying bills and leaving instructions with a good friend about feeding the dog and watering the plants. There were always things left undone and the stress that goes with it.

Then, the world slips away. Nothing on the ground came with me. (Thankfully, this was the day before email, internet and cell phones. Inconceivable, I know.) As soon as the landing gear was up, the stress, complexities and problems of this world fell away with every foot we climbed. Our "problems" and even egos that seem so big become terribly small when you view them from above and see how tiny we are on this planet. Sometimes I would look at the cars below while they were still visible and wonder what the occupants were thinking about as they raced along. "We're late to school! What will my boss say? I can't believe my girlfriend wants to break up with me." Did they see a contrail as we were leaving everything behind?

2  Habakkuk 3:19
3  Mt Fuji photo Alpsdake 1999, public domain Wikimedia Commons

Even if they did, it was probably only a fleeting glance and they were back on to the next task or concern.

What is the "big picture" for us in life? How can we get it when our lives are so filled with busyness?

One thing is for sure, God has the big picture always. Perhaps that's why He lives in heaven. At the same time, however, he can be everywhere from an insect battle in an Amazon jungle to a secret talk in the Oval Office or our bedroom. But He lives in heaven. With that kind of perspective, if He takes up dual residency in your heart, some amazing things can begin to happen inside of us.

Unexpectedly I lost my eyesight in a day. I could no longer fly. I couldn't read or drive. But God had so transformed my perspective that neither the loss of sight or flight stole my joy. It felt bizarre but so free at the moment. Paul, the apostle, also, was bound in a different prison, one bound by chains, but found the secret of soaring with God in heaven.[4]

*Rejoice in the Lord always. I will say it again: rejoice! Let your gentleness be evident to all. The Lord is near. Do not be anxious about anything, but in every situation, by prayer and petition, with thanksgiving, present your requests to God. And the peace of God, which transcends all understanding, will guard your hearts and your minds in Christ Jesus.[5]*

This section, in a sense, is intended to be an introduction to flight. Before a young pilot experiences the thrill of solo flight with God sitting in the empty seat, the student will study hard and fly many times with a human instructor. Even then, most students are like I was, sweaty and a bit

4  For an interesting reference to flying in the Spirit, see 2 Corinthians 2:2-3
5  Philippians 4:4-7 Keep reading this passage to learn how Paul found the secret of being content in every circumstance, whether rich or poor, well fed or hungry.

rattled by that first ride without someone visible and experienced to fix my mistakes. Let God take you on a flight. Departure time is anytime you choose to live by faith. Remember, you'll never go alone. God promises to always be with you and lead you as you trust in Him.

In this section I call "The Big Picture," you'll discover how God saved me. How He taught me to have joy in spite of hard circumstances. How you can have real success. How you can make the most important decisions of your life by putting Him at the center of everything. Have a fantastic flight!

THE BIG PICTURE

# A UNIQUE BUT COMMON STRUGGLE

*There is no one who calls upon your name,*
*who rouses himself to take hold of you;*
*for you have hidden your face from us,*
*and have made us melt in the hand of our iniquities.*
*But now, O Lord, you are our Father;*
*we are the clay, and you are our potter;*
*we are all the work of your hand.*[6]

Every person is made by God extremely unique, even identical twins like my wonderful nieces, Molly and Mady. Sure, almost everyone has two arms and two legs. But no two of us are alike. Even Molly and Mady have different fingerprints, freckles, hairs on their heads and, more importantly, separate dreams and thoughts. The way God saves each person is unique, too. Just like the endless variety of snowflakes, God delights in the kaleidoscope of His universe and deals with each of us in a very special way. When you hear someone speak about their personal encounters with God, try not to let yourself think, "I wish God would do it that way with me!" He will touch you with love in a way that no other person will experience.

On the other hand, people have much in common. We all want to be loved. We want to enjoy beauty, happiness, and believe there is life after death. But we are also born self-centered and inclined to do wrong whenever we think it is to our benefit. We resist God's guidance for our lives. With all that potential conflict, it is miraculous He has changed so many people for good.

Every story of God's transformation of lives has a few things in common. Almost everyone can look back and see when God touched them with a spectacular scene in nature or friends who spoke sincerely of God's love to them. At some point, each person is struck to the core with their own self-centeredness and desire do wrong. God removes our spiritual blinders. We can see the purity, love, and power of God. The grace of Jesus' sacrifice for our rebellion becomes our life and we long to be closer to Him. But similarities end as we learn about individual stories. They are like the bright

6  Isaiah 64:7

colors of God's paintbrush and palette that masterfully adorn His universe.

MY GOD STORY

My mom and dad raised their three boys to believe in God. We went to church most Sundays. We prayed before meals and learned to live by Christian principles: don't lie, don't cheat, don't steal. Treat others as you would want to be treated.

When we spent summer months with our grandparents in Oklahoma, we attended my grandma's church on Classen Boulevard every Sunday. That was the one day of the week we'd have to put on shoes (no flip flops or barefoot kids in church!) My brother Jim and I had to put on a shirt, tie and sweaty polyester suit. Yuck! Afterwards, we'd have lunch at a cafeteria like Adair's or eat Grandma's wonderful cooking at home. Then we'd lay on their living room floor and wrestle with Grandad who told us tall tales until we drifted off into an afternoon nap.

When I turned thirteen, my family moved from Virginia to Fort Lewis, Washington. We got involved in Youth of the Chapel and Sunday School, taught by a couple named Ray and Elizabeth. They were a fun couple who had gotten saved in their late twenties. They taught us Bible stories, took us bicycling on Anderson Island and organized retreats.

One day after Sunday school, they stopped me and asked, "Rob, are you born again?" Honestly, I felt insulted. After all, I was there each Sunday, knew all the songs and knew the answers to most of the questions they asked. I answered, "My family is Christian and I've just always believed in Jesus." I thought they were trying to impose their experience of being saved later in life on me. But Ray simply answered, "You know, Jesus said, 'You must be born again.'" I didn't have a response and left wondering if I was born again and what exactly did that mean?

The next year, I went through confirmation with Chaplain Schweitzer. He patiently met with me once a week to make sure I knew the most important doctrines of the Christian faith. After many weeks, confirmation day came. Sweating nervously in front of my family, I professed faith and took my first communion. During the entire oath, I almost screamed to myself, "How do I know this is true? If I had been

born in a Muslim country, I would believe in Muhammad! Who can say Christians are right and Muslims are wrong?"
The story of Doubting Thomas stood out and bothered me. Thomas said "Unless I see in [Jesus'] hands the mark of the nails, and place my finger into the mark of the nails, and place my hand into his side, I will never believe."[7] That made sense to me. How could I believe in someone I could not see or touch? Jesus' reply to Thomas perplexed and bothered me, "Put your finger here, and see my hands; and put out your hand, and place it in my side. Do not disbelieve, but believe." Once Thomas believed, Jesus continued, "Have you believed because you have seen me? Blessed are those who have not seen and yet have believed."[8] I was frustrated. That didn't make any sense. How could someone not have seen yet believe!

I remember moments sitting on the wooded bluffs behind our housing area at Fort Lewis, overlooking the neighborhood. Something there was so peaceful. Years later, I looked back on them and believed the Lord was making His presence known to me. He gave me a hunger to seek the peace and love only He can give.

In my high school, very few teachers or students openly believed in God. Classmates ridiculed the handful of other students who expressed faith in God. The ones who believed were nerds, rejects. I was probably a nerd, too, but I didn't openly show any belief in God. For several years, I thought that we were simply an evolved animal. We have just seventy or eighty years on earth and then we become simple matter again, a part of the dirt. There is no sense in being sentimental or losing sleep over the matter of eternity. This life is all there is. Or is it?

I love science. Just like Jesus' disciple Thomas, it seemed to me that someone should not believe in something that cannot be seen, heard or felt. Even so, I don't know why I didn't think about x-rays, electrons and photons. We accept them as real but cannot normally see or feel them. Sure, we can observe their impact described in books, but in truth, they remain invisible. We accept scientific explanation and theory with complete faith. Neutrons, protons and electrons are real, right? We experience electricity and see nuclear bomb explosions on video. But don't we see the impact of God all over the world around us? DNA, extremely complex design even

7  John 20:25
8  John 20:27, 29

in single cell life, incredibly diverse life on a fragile and finely balanced planet. Yet earth is resilient in the hostile and lifeless vacuum of space. God's fingerprints are everywhere. But I couldn't see them. In ignorance, I silently agreed with my atheist classmates. Belief in anything invisible like a story about God was probably just a fairy tale. Or so I thought.

THINGS TO THINK ABOUT AND TALK OVER:

- *Why do you think God makes snowflakes and fingerprints all different?*

- *Where do you "see" God in the world around you? What might you say to someone who doubts that God exists?*

- *Read John 3. What do you think being "born again"( or more literally "born from above") means?*

THE BIG PICTURE

# GOOD LIFE OUTSIDE, GNAWING KNOTS INSIDE

*[God] has made everything beautiful in its time.*
*He has also set eternity in the human heart; yet no one can fathom*
*what God has done from beginning to end.*[9]

As a teenager I rarely went to church except for Easter and Christmas. On those occasions when everyone was praying silently in church, I cried out in my heart, "God, if You're out there, let me know who You are before I die!" I thought the only way I would be convinced was if Jesus came to me like He came to Thomas or at least parted the skies on a cloudy day. But I didn't think anyone would ever know the truth until after death. Of course, then it's too late to change!

When I was 18, I flew out to the Air Force Academy and started basic training. That first night I sat in the arena with a new blue uniform and just a name tag on. I was topped with the first crew cut of my life and I looked out on a sea of other light blue shirts and wide eyes. I thought to myself, "I'm in prison!" That started my prayers again, "God, if You are out there, I could sure use some help!" In my freshman year, I visited chapel a few times, but nothing significant happened that I could see. I do remember a few classmates like Steve Groenheim would bow their heads and pray silently before meals. It seemed like a good idea, so I began to do the same, thanking God for the meal . . . and asking Him to save me.

In my sophomore year, I was in the dorms serving restrictions on a Saturday night for having done something wrong. In our hall there were two upperclassmen that I respected and liked. Having nothing to do, I stopped by their room and knocked. One of them cracked the door about six inches and said, "Yes, what do you want?" I replied, "I just wanted to know what you guys are doing." The terse reply came back, "We are having a Bible study. What do you want?" I remembered thinking with all my heart, "Well, I'd really like to come in and listen," but I didn't and quietly said, "Oh, okay. See you later." Years later I realized that they probably thought I wasn't interested. After all, I had centerfold pictures in my room and

---

9  Ecclesiastes 3:11 (NIV)

prided myself that I could belch and be heard from one side of the dormitory to the other.

At pilot training in Oklahoma, my roommate, Wade, was a patient friend. He was searching for God himself and invited me to go to find a church. I'm sorry to say that I declined and he decided not to go either.

I was thrilled at the end of pilot training to get my first choice of aircraft (the C-141) and base (McChord) in Washington State where I spent most of my childhood. My parents had retired nearby. Life could hardly be better. I was in my dream airplane, living in my hometown and flying all over the world to places like Hawaii, the Philippines, Japan, Korea and other tropical islands like Guam and Diego Garcia in the Indian Ocean. I'd just finished building a beautiful house with a three-car garage where one bay had a gorgeous red Mercedes. Life was good.

But I always had a gnawing sense that there must be more to life. I had a feeling of background noise that goes unnoticed most of the time. But if you're quiet for a few minutes, you can hear it. I had no clue, however, how radically my life was about to change.

THINGS TO THINK ABOUT AND TALK OVER:

- *Do you ever feel like God is trying to talk to you? Are you normally busy or do you have time to be quiet and hear the "background" noise? Do you have a gnawing sense that there must be more to life?*

- *Do you know anyone who lives a life others would like to live? Do you consider your life exciting or good in many ways? Do good things make people happy for long? Or is it only good for a little while and then you (or they) need to find something new? Where do you think people can find lasting happiness?*

- *Paul wrote in Romans 1:20 that God's divine nature and power have been plain ever since the creation of the world. Where do you see them? If the evidence of life and the finely tuned, enormously beautiful universe points to God, why do we suppress what seems to be obvious?*

# WALKING WITH GOD

*Enoch walked with God, and he was not, for God took him.* [10]

In our squadron there was an interesting, young navigator named Steve Brown. He was different than most of the other crew I flew with and he was a different Christian than I had ever met. He was athletic, well-spoken and asked great questions. I can remember one starry night we had an early morning alert. Steve said, "Look at all those stars! Do you think we are the only ones in the universe?" Most of the others I spent time with were talking about bars, not stars. When Steve invited me to church, I didn't hesitate. He picked me up and we went to a Wednesday evening service.

The pastor, Fulton Buntain, stood up to share a thought after a song. He said, "Imagine you are adrift in a boat without an oar or life jacket and can't swim. Jesus is standing on the shore and throws you a rope. For you to get saved, will you pull Him out to the boat to be with you? Or will He pull you and the boat to the shore?"

The obvious answer is, He must pull you to shore. Buntain explained that in our attempts to find God, we want our curiosity satisfied but we don't want Him to actually change us. We're telling Him, "I want to know if You exist, but come on over to my boat." That is no salvation at all.

I suddenly felt overwhelmingly "sinful." A flood of memories — many things I'd done wrong in my life (my boat) — filled my mind. Even though I knew much of what the Bible said and how we should live, my actions showed my stubbornness, default love for myself and evil. Later I realized that this was the conviction of the Holy Spirit — a very unpleasant but priceless gift of God.

In the next moment, I heard a question from the Lord that was clear and audible to me but not anyone around me. "You always asked Me to appear to you, just once. What would you do if I came to you right now?" He didn't say His name, but it was crystal clear: Jesus was speaking to me.

---

10  Genesis 5:24

All I could imagine if He came to me in that moment was that I would fall on my face and weep, asking His forgiveness. I felt the sins of my life had just been played like a movie on a big screen TV for anyone to see.[11] I was decimated. Utterly humiliated. Gone was any pretense of being "good."

Even more amazing was what happened next. I felt like He reached down and picked me up saying, "I don't want you to spend your life weeping before Me but to get up and walk with Me." As He picked me up to my feet, I felt so much love, all guilt and shame was completely gone. My reaction was to "hug" Him. As I "hugged" Him, I felt the wound in His side — something I hadn't thought about in probably ten years.

By this point, Dr. Buntain had already sat down and we were singing a song. Steve had no idea what was happening inside of me and I didn't tell him what happened for quite a long time. I walked out of church that night, wondering if I had been "born again" like Ray and Elizabeth had spoken about so many years before.

Maybe I was just hungry that evening? Maybe I just imagined the whole thing? It crossed my mind that if this was true (this encounter with God and Christianity in general), I would read the Bible for six months. It would then either hold out as true or it would become clear over time that it was false. Everything I ever tried in life that was exciting — a new girlfriend, flying airplanes or a new car — all grew uninteresting within six months. My suspicion was that this would bear out as true. In fact, what I learned far exceeded my expectations. I am so thankful that Life Center, the church where I was discipled, believed in the inerrancy and infallibility of Scripture. They brought in guest speakers who were gifted in medicine, biology, cosmology and other fields. It became abundantly clear to me that the Bible is trustworthy in all areas of life.

Tremendous things have happened since that day when I was twenty-four. Many of those stories are on the following pages. I have no doubt more have yet to happen!

---

11  Jesus said in Matthew 12:36, "On the day of judgment people will give account for every careless word they speak." So the idea of everyone seeing what you've said, thought and done in private isn't new! Who would not be completely destroyed by allowing the whole world see the worst parts of their lives? Our few good moments, granted only by God's grace, would seem like a pitiful plea next to the ugliness of our souls.

Jesus told me to "get up and walk with Him." Imagine my delight when I read in Genesis about Enoch, just one of two men we believe in history that never physically died. Elijah was the other one. The Scriptures say Enoch "walked with God and was no more." How do we walk with God? Talk to Him throughout the day. Quietly listen. If you hear directions, obey! Don't try to pull Him into your boat. Read, memorize and meditate on the Scriptures. Be God's hands and voice to others.

God's says to us every day, "get up and walk with Me." What an amazing privilege and joy God — the Creator of the entire universe — offers to be with us and share life together. All of this became possible because of what Jesus did on the cross to tear down the walls between us. I fervently pray that you will discover this abundant, rich life.

THINGS TO THINK ABOUT AND TALK OVER:

- *Someday you will "be no more," at least to those who see you on earth. Time goes by so quickly. Before then, how do you want to live? What do you think it means to walk with God? Have you ever had an experience when God has powerfully convicted you of your sin and you have had a sense of His absolute, perfect holiness? Was it followed by an overwhelming understanding of Jesus' love and plan to forgive you by His gift of the cross? Even if the answer is no, do you believe it's true? Remember, that you are not saved by an experience. The "proof" you are saved is a belief in those two elements: I am a wretched sinner and Jesus' love set me free to be forgiven and walk with Him. Like John Piper has said, the proof that you were born is not your birth certificate; the proof you were born is that you are alive.The proof that you are born from above (some say "born again") is not a baptism certificate or the fact that you can remember a powerful encounter with God; the proof is that you know you are a sinner but Christ has paid for your sin. I was spiritually dead. Now everything is new and I am alive to God.[12]*

- *If you don't think you've embraced these truths, what's holding you back? Specifically, can you say what your doubts or questions are? Tell someone. Tell your mom. Tell your best friend*

---

12  Piper, John. https://www.desiringgod.org/messages/gods-great-mercy-and-our-new-birth, Sermon Oct 10, 1993.

*who loves God. They won't make fun of you. They will either help you find answers or get someone who can help. Remember, God has no grandchildren. Don't ever take comfort, like I did, that I had Christian parents. No, faith that saves you must be personally yours. God only has children. He gives you the right to become one, too, if you'll believe and receive Him.[13] If you do pray right now and think you've started your journey with Christ today, tell someone! Let them rejoice with you.*

- *What's your next step? If you haven't already, start four important habits to grow in Him:*

  1. *Read your Bible daily*
  2. *Talk to God all the time*
  3. *Obey His commands, especially to love others*
  4. *Have regular times to hang out with friends who follow Jesus and good teachers of His truth.*

*Before you leave this earth, you can never say "I've arrived!" You're just starting to walk with God in a wonderful adventure of faith. You'll have many more questions, wonderful experiences, deep wounds and deeper healing to go through. Keep learning to rejoice and let the peace of Christ take you through every trial.*

13  John 1:12

THE BIG PICTURE

# WHEN YOU LOSE SOMEONE YOU LOVE

*"Where have you laid him?" They said to him, "Lord, come and see." Jesus wept.*[14]

You've been through one of the hardest things that anyone could experience. Losing your dad, your mom, or a good friend to death can make you feel like a shark took a big bite out of your stomach. The pain feels like it will never heal. There's an emptiness and a sadness that keeps you from eating, playing or sleeping very well. What will help you?

### REMEMBER, GOD LOVES YOU

The first thing that helps is to remember that God loves you. That may be hard to understand when you know that He was certainly able to keep me or someone else you loved from dying. (See note on divorce below.[15]) But keep in mind that God has a much bigger picture in view. He sees things from the perspective of not just one lifetime but of millions of years into the future. He sees how our lives should or shouldn't impact one another. If I hadn't gotten cancer, I probably would not have written this book. I trust this book will help you and hopefully some others. We never know how our sickness, suffering and even death — especially if experienced by grace with faith and peace — can greatly impact others for good.

God knows what it's like to suffer the loss of someone He loves. He lost His only Son Jesus to a terrible death on a cross. God also loses people He dearly loves every day to death, eternally separated from them. Through their whole lives God calls them, surrounding them with blessing and evidences of His love. Yet they continually reject Him throughout life. God can relate to our suffering and loss much more than we can imagine.[16]

---

14  John 11:34-35
15  Sadly, many children today have suffered the divorce of parents. It can feel like a death. If you know someone who has gone through divorce recently or even a long time ago, you might want ot share some of this chapter with them.
16  For we do not have a high priest who is unable to sympathize with our weaknesses, but one who in every respect has been tempted as we are, yet without sin. Hebrews 4:15

I'll say more about it later, but it's important to say something here. I shed a lot of tears thinking about leaving you — one of the hardest things I've experienced. Anyone with terminal cancer or anyone who loses someone close may question God's love. But there was one verse that put that question to rest, erasing all of my objections:

> *"If God is for us, who can be against us? He who did not spare his own Son but gave him up for us all, how will he not also with him graciously give us all things?"*[17]

We may not completely understand why hard things happen, but the fact that God gave His only Son to die for my sins puts to rest for all time any question that He loves me. God loves you, my dear children. If He took me to heaven, He will take care of you. God promises to never leave you or forsake you.[18] Trust in His love.

## CRYING IS NORMAL

When Miracle was four years old, her little goose, Glory, died. Miracle cried and cried. We could have said, "That's enough. It was only a goose." But tears are an important part of life, love and saying goodbye. They say in a way that words can't express, "I loved you very, very much!"

Did you know that there can be a good side to being very sad when you miss someone? We call that kind of sadness mourning. Jesus said, "'Blessed are those who mourn, for they shall be comforted.'"[19] Who will comfort us? God Himself will. When you were little and skinned your knee, I'd scoop you up and hold you tight. Even though your knee still hurt, I could tell from your crying that something was much better just knowing that your daddy cared. There is a peace from being held in Mama or Papa's arms.

God cares. He really cares. His peace and presence is like nothing else. God's comfort cannot completely be put into words. You can only experience it the moment you quietly say, "God I need You. Be the Daddy I need.[20] I give everything to You. Take me into Your arms."

---

17  Romans 8:21-22
18  Deuteronomy 31:6, Hebrews 13:5
19  Matthew 5:4
20  Romans 8:15

## GOD IS IN CONTROL

King David suffered a lot of hurt, attacks and victories in his life. With confidence he declared, "All the days ordained for me were written in your book before one of them came to be."[21] There are no surprises for God. He knows the day you were born and the day you will die. He ordained Joseph's sale into slavery so he could go to Egypt. God ordained Job's losses. In the end Job trusted even more in his Redeemer and Lord. God ordained Jesus' death on a cross in order to give us eternal life. He also has ordained my death. It gives me great comfort to know the God of love is in absolute control of the universe.

Some people try to explain away suffering and death by saying God is not in control. . . either by choice or by mistake. But that is of little comfort to us when we mourn. God has lost control? Not only is it not true, it would be absurd. If God is not in control, He is not God.

Jesus wept when His beloved friend Lazarus died. Both of his sisters reminded Jesus that if He had been there, Lazarus would not have died. Jesus even delayed two days during His ministry up north after He'd heard the news of His friend's serious illness. Perhaps you've felt the same way about me or someone else: "If God were here. . . if He really cared . . ." What did Jesus tell Martha and Mary? "Your brother will rise again."[22] Lazarus' death and, more importantly, his resurrection brought more glory to God than if Jesus healed him before death. Trust that God is in control of each of our lives and always acts to do what is right in the right time.

So much could be said here, but we will have to save that for later. But remember, the God who loves you is working out a plan for you — even in my death or someone else's death — for your good.[23] You probably cannot see it now. But wait. Trust Him and you will  see it someday.

## BRING A SACRIFICE OF PRAISE

This world is not our home. Along with our bodies, it is falling apart. Our hope is in God's love for us today and being with Him in a sure and better world to come. Only in this life, we can choose to honor, trust and praise Him even while our hearts hurt.

21  Psalm 139:·6
22  John 11:23
23  Romans 8:28, Jeremiah 29:11

*"Through him then let us continually offer up a sacrifice of praise to God . . ."*[24]

Anyone can easily praise God if life is going well. Praising or thanking Him[25] when we are hurting is a special sacrifice that honors God. Job had just lost all his wealth and all his children. Anyone would be devastated. Job was. But listen to what he did:

*"Job arose and tore his robe and shaved his head and fell on the ground and worshiped. And he said, "Naked I came from my mother's womb, and naked shall I return. The Lord gave, and the Lord has taken away; blessed be the name of the Lord."*[26]

Although you may not feel you can do it, find things to praise God for and give thanks. Be specific. You will find healing, joy and strength much deeper and faster as you do.

### THIS IS ONLY FAREWELL FOR NOW, NOT FOREVER

Will we see each other again? We can! That is one of the great promises of the Bible. For those who put their trust in Jesus, our separation will ultimately seem like just a blink of the eye before we are with one another for eternity.[27]

I remember many summers having fun at my grandparents' house, catching box turtles and horny toads. We rode horses, shot fireworks and ate too much watermelon and Grandma's homemade ice cream. The sad day always came to say goodbye and fly home. My brother and I would walk partway down the jetway, turn and wave goodbye to them one last time. I was filled with a terrible sense of grief. As I sat in my seat on the plane, I tried not to cry. They were so old. Would I ever see them again? Of course, we did see each other again many times. The previous summer's painful farewell was completely forgotten the moment we were together. You can be sure I am in heaven and I will be waiting for you! What a joyful moment it will be when we hug each other so tight again.

### GIVE YOURSELF TIME

Over many centuries people have said, "Time heals all wounds."

---

24  Hebrews 13:15
25  Leviticus 7:12, Psalms 107:22 and 116:17
26  Job 1:20-21
27  1 Thessalonians 4:13-18

While there may be exceptions, this is an important kernel of truth. The ache you feel inside from missing me or someone else you love will become less and less over time. You will eventually stop crying when you lay down at night and think about me or the one you recently lost. I trust you will reach the point where you will only smile or even laugh out loud as you remember the adventures we shared or the jokes we enjoyed together. But for now, it may help you to keep in mind that sadness fades in time and joy is waiting for you.

## DON'T PLAY THE BLAME GAME

Not everyone has a feeling they are to blame when someone close dies but sadly some people can have those thoughts. You need to know with total certainty my death was not something you could have changed. The devil has a trick to make you feel worse and wallow in some sense of sin. *If only I had done something different, maybe prayed more, he might still be alive. If only I'd been nicer, more loving and thoughtful while they were alive.* Have you had any thoughts like that? If so, there are at least two possibilities. One, there is no truth in your thoughts. Tell the devil and those dark thoughts to go to hell (which they will). Two, there may be some truth or half-truth in blaming yourself or having regrets.  Now what should you do?

Put those accusations to rest where they belong. God's Word tells us two important things. First, you should confess *any sin* to God and *know* He forgives you, cleanses you and will help you to change.[28] You can rejoice knowing that God has freed you from condemnation and is helping you resolve to live in love and holiness from this day forward. Just as  your sins are as far from you as the east is from the west.[29] For sure, you know I forgive you of anything you did or didn't do. When we are honest deep down with our faults, we become better people, better friends and better family. I've heard of many people who — after the death or near-death of someone close they took for granted — never let a day go by without telling their closest family and friends that they love them. We can't do anything about the past, but we can sure use it for good and make a different future![30] Our greatest defense when we feel like playing the "blame game" is Romans 8:1, *"There is therefore now no condemnation for those in*

28   1 John 1:9
29   Psalm 103:12
30   Philippians 3:13

*Christ Jesus!"*

God loves you so much. He hasn't given up or lost control but is working a plan far better than we can imagine. Keep trusting in Him and the time will come when your joy will return and you will even see something good coming from your hurt and loss.

THINGS TO THINK ABOUT AND TALK OVER:

- *One of the best ways to get over grief in a healthy way is to talk with someone mature you love and trust. Tell them how you really feel about God. Do you believe He loves you or do you honestly have some doubts? What might help you to trust Him more?*

- *Have you cried in a good way or are you shutting out tears? Maybe you've gone the other way. Do you feel like your sadness will never end and might be getting worse? It is super important to be open with someone who is wise and loves you. The devil wants us to keep secrets. Open up your heart to a good counselor (or just a good friend who loves Jesus) and put the devil in the dark. You may need to get more help from a pastor and that's a great thing.*

- *Can you make a list of ten things to praise and thank God for? More?*

- *Is there anything you feel like you blame yourself for in losing me or another person? What will help you get over that condemnation?*

# THE GREATEST JOY

*You make known to me the path of life;*
*in your presence there is fullness of joy* [31]

Do you want to be joyful? Do you want joy that can never be taken away?

When I first saw your mother, my heart skipped a beat. She was beautiful. She had love for life, an eagerness to learn new things, and a warm peace, She became a caring leader in church that drew many others into enjoying God's love. To behold her on her balcony from the courtyard below made me feel like Shakespeare intended when he wrote about Romeo and Juliet. When your mom agreed to marry me, no problem in life could affect me!

That's what love does. Old problems become insignificant in the face of joy-filled love. You had an argument with your roommate? Caught the flu? Who cares? Sometimes people have so much joy and love they would give their life to them. That's the kind of love and joy God has for you. He is crazy about you!

> *The Lord your God is in your midst,*
> *a mighty one who will save;*
> *He will rejoice over you with gladness;*
> *He will quiet you by his love;*
> *He will exult over you with loud singing.* [32]

Maybe you feel God should not be that excited about you. Do you want to know a secret? For sure, you and I are not very lovely or lovable. But it's not about you or me. It's about Him! God is love. Love courses through His veins. Love is His being. If the description of His Spirit flowing through us is first love then, joy,[33] God is the most loving and joyful being in the universe. That's how He can rejoice over His bride (us) when we are a mess.[34] He loves us like

---

31  Psalm 16:11
32  Zephaniah 3:17
33  Galatians 5:22
34  Even though God's joy over us in Christ is unimaginable, we must remember that our sin or acting in unbelief without repentance can cause God immeasurable grief and ruin our joy in Him. We can deeply grieve the Holy Spirit. (Ephesians 4:30) Don't block His joy. Be sensitive

He loves His own Son, Jesus.[35] Incredible! God sees the beauty of what we will become in Christ, not the mess we have made. When we realize that Creator of the Universe loves us with infinite delight, even with "shouts of joy," that should make us want to explode with happiness. This is joy that can never be taken away.[36]

### A COUPLE WITH IMPOSSIBLE JOY

Let me tell you about a couple who had impossible joy that no amount of suffering could steal.

In the 1930s a young Jew named Richard Wurmbrand experienced hatred by fascists in Romania. He and his wife, Sabina, came to faith in Jesus in 1938 and then experienced extreme persecution from the Communists since the young couple were now devoted Jesus followers. Richard joked about being in trouble as a Jew with the Nazis and later as a Christian, with the Communists. The serious truth is that he spent a terrible fourteen years in prison with unspeakable torture. Concurrently, Sabina was given seven years of hard labor. It was illegal for anyone to help the children of parents incarcerated for faith in God. Somehow, their young son, Michael, survived seven years without either parent.

Did they experience joy? Pastor Wurmbrand wrote that he was thankful to the Communists for providing them with free musical instruments. When they could be together, the prisoners sang and clanged their shackles and chains together like tambourines.[37] More than once, the guards interrupted a sermon and took the offending preacher away for a severe beating, he obediently marched off and after returning declared, "Now, where did I leave off?" Then they resumed their service! Hundreds got saved in prison. Even some of the worst prison guards came to Christ and then were sentenced to prison and torture. Years later, when Wumbrand was freed and

and turn from any sin.

35   John 15:9

36   If you want to read about how to keep the fire of your joy in God bright, read in the next section  the chapter, Practicing Joy. We all know that the glow of newlyweds can grow dim after the honeymoon ends and the challenges of married life begins. But it doesn't have to! To keep the fire, we need practical insights and practice.

37   "We, in prison, sang every day and every Christian in jail had a musical instrument. The Communists were nice: every Christian, when he entered jail, received a musical instrument. Not a guitar but chains on his hands and feet. Chains are splendid musical instruments. We could sing, "Onward Christian soldiers (clink, clank), marching as to war (clink, clank, clink, clank)." Lips are Given for Smiling,  Wurmbrand, Richard, http://richardwurmbrandbio.info/lips.html

found by other Christ followers, they couldn't believe he was the same man. 14 years of prison and torture could only leave someone broken, not full of joy![38] That kind of love and joy can't be faked.

What would enable the Wurmbrands to endure years of torture and imprisonment for Christ? What sustained them when the government would force their son to become homeless? Later in life, why would they risk death as frail seniors to continue traveling and speaking to others? The only answer is that their greatest joy was in God. Their unshakable confidence was in a better reward than what this world could offer.[39] That reward is the joy of being with Jesus, both in the present and more fully in the future.

### GOD'S ABUNDANT JOY

Jesus came, in part, to put His joy in us — abundant joy.[40] No one has greater joy than the Creator of the universe. He says that same joy can be ours. The condition to receive it is simply to abide in Him and to obey His commands by loving one another as He loved us, even to the point of death. Who can do such a thing? A rare person, indeed, unless they are filled with the Holy Spirit and give Him control of their lives.

Do you struggle with being joyful in Christ? Welcome to the struggles of walking with God — and really, walking in a relationship with anyone! The joy we have in any good friendship is proportional to the time we give to that person. In the second section of this book, you can read more about "Being Joyful." But let me leave you here with my best experience and understanding: the only fuel you can give to finding and enjoying the greatest joy of all, the joy of Christ, is to saturate your heart and soul with Him. If you find your flame of joy dying, look to Him. Remember, He rejoices over you with gladness and exults over you with loud singing, not because of who you are but because of who He is, the very essence of love. Lean into Him every day and your joy will burn brightly until the day He takes you home.

---

38   Wurmbrand, Richard Tortured for Christ, Voice of the Martyrs, Bartlesville, OK 1967 p. 54
39   For you had compassion on those in prison, and you joyfully accepted the plundering of your property, since you knew that you yourselves had a better possession and an abiding one. Hebrews 10:34
40   John 15

THINGS TO THINK ABOUT AND TALK OVER:

- *Do you know the most repeated command in the Bible? Is it not to murder, lie or steal? No! The most frequent command: "Have joy!"[41] What brings you joy? Does the joy last or fade over time? Have you ever experienced joy in God that feels deeper than anything offered by this world?*

- *Every analogy has its limit. For example, Mary is the earthly mother of Jesus but that doesn't make her the mother of God. God has given us marriage as a picture of of love and joy that can be very helpful. How can that comparison break down if carried too far? When a man and woman agree to get married in our culture, there is a high level of mutual attraction and admiration. Given our sinfulness, how is that different than the manner God gets His bride? How can that impact our joy?*

- *Do you think it makes sense to talk about joy in suffering like the Wurmbrands'? What do you think about the Wurmbrands' sacrifice? Do you think they should have simply stayed quiet and never have gone to prison? What about the sacrifice their young son had to make? (If you are curious, he has strong faith in the Lord today and has done much to help the cause of those who are suffering for Jesus.) If the Wurmbrands had stayed quiet, what would have probably happened to the hundreds who were in prison and turned to Christ through their ministry? Would the Wurmbrands have been able to inspire millions of Christians in turn, who have joyfully risked and sometime lost everything in order to tell others about the love of Jesus?[42]*

- *Do you feel like you are experiencing the full joy of God? If not, don't let busyness or "fun" but hollow entertainment fill your days. Get radical if you want to be saturated in lasting joy.*

  ⇨ *Make time for God by getting to bed early so you can pray and read the Bible. Take time to memorize verses so you can think about them during the day and night.*

---

41  John Bloom writes, "God tells us more than anything else, in different ways, to "praise the Lord," "do not be afraid," "rejoice," and "give thanks" — all of which are commands, in essence, to be happy. Nov 21, 2017 "The Most Repeated Command in the Bible." DesiringGod. org

42  Wurmbrand's first book, Tortured for Christ,  has been printed over 10 million times in at least 85 languages

⇨ *Clear out sin by specifically confessing them to Him.*

⇨ *Sing a new song to God. Find great worship by When our heart is full of other things - entertainment, work, sin, etc. - there is no time or space to let Him fill us with His joy.*

⇨ *Find excellent teaching or preaching that finds joy surrendering everything to God. If you are not sure where to look, ask a trusted friend or search the internet for "favorite sermons" or "preachers." If you are a reader, in addition to good contemporary books by authors like Lucado, Piper, or Sproul, you should consider classics by Edwards, Spurgeon, Oswald Chambers, and others.*

⇨ *Serve others, especially by sharing the good news of Jesus and what He is teaching you.*

# TIME IS SHORT . . . MAKE THE MOST OF IT!

*This is what I mean, brothers: the appointed time has grown very short . . . . the present form of this world is passing away.*[43]

What would you say and do if you had just one day left to be with people you love before parting forever?

### MISSILES IN SUDAN

"AL-la!" I said with surprise to my co-pilot, "What is that fire on the ground? Is that some kind of oil burn off?"

We were flying after dark into Khartoum, something we almost never did in Sudan.

"No," my friend replied. "We don't have oil in this area."

Both of us strained in our seats to see a couple of large fires burning north of the airport before we made our final turn to line up with the runway for landing.

A few minutes after landing, we saw firetrucks and emergency vehicles racing north on the perimeter road. We wondered if they were going to the fires we had seen several miles away. The air traffic controllers then asked us if we had seen any fighter planes that were reported as missing and may have crashed not far from a nearby military airport. That turned out to be a false lead. We left the airport, wondering what had happened.

As we were filling out paperwork in the empty UNICEF office thirty minutes later, the phone rang. I didn't normally pick up, but decided to answer since the office workers had all gone home. The caller was a frantic American English-speaking woman. "Is my daughter okay?" "Ma'am, who is your daughter?" Our mechanic's mother-in-law had been watching television in America and was desperately worried about the safety of her child. President Clinton had announced that

43  1 Corinthians 7:29 and 31

America sent cruise missiles against sites in Sudan owned by the increasingly infamous terrorist, Osama bin Laden. The missiles were retaliation for horrible attacks against American embassies in Kenya and Tanzania that left hundreds dead.

We had just gotten away from the airport in time. Once the authorities understood this was an attack and not an accident, the airport was on lockdown. I might have had a long stay in Sudan if they had known an American pilot was flying locally when cruise missiles were in the air flying invisibly through the country.

Demonstrations the next day were on the news channels in front of the American embassy. Although the rest of the city was calm and no one expressed hostility towards us, our headquarters thought it best to shut down the flight program temporarily and get our American team out of the country. Although I wanted to stay, they only gave us a few days to shut everything down and catch the first commercial plane out. (It was interesting that the Sudanese version of the attack story was that the "factories" hit were pharmaceutical factories. Our local friends, on the other hand, said they always suspected those sites were weapon factories. They also told us that the "demonstrators" at the embassy were from poor regions, given a dollar and a free bus ride to town to come demonstrate. )

## URGENCY

Knowing that our days were short, I felt great urgency to share the message of God's salvation with local friends with whom I had built close friendships.

One special friend was Abu (not his real name.) He was a local welder who had done some very good work for us and we had enjoyed many meals, gifts and tea during our time in Sudan. With a local friend translating, I said, "Abu, you have become a good friend and it seems we must leave soon. I don't know if I will see you again on this earth, but I would like to know I will see you again in heaven."

Abu replied, "We cannot know these things. Only God does. But inshallah (God-willing) we will."

"But I am sure I am going to heaven. Do you want to know how I am sure?"

"Yes, please, tell me," Abu said.

With careful attention, he listened to the story of Isa al Masih, Jesus the Messiah. He knew a little of what I told him and then interrupted, "But Jesus did not die on the cross. Our teachers tell us that God would never allow His Prophet to be killed like that. Allah substituted Judas the betrayer at the last minute and they killed him instead."

"Abu, that story is not in the Quran," I responded. "The Injil (the New Testament) says Jesus went to the cross for us. Let me give you an example. Imagine one day, I am standing in a road by a noisy bazaar. There is a big cargo truck racing down the road towards me from behind and I can't see it. Your son is yelling at me to get out of the way but I can't hear him over the crowd. At the last second, he pushes me out of the way to save my life but gets killed by the truck himself. Let's say I didn't see it happen but just felt the push and fell to the ground. I'm even upset that someone pushed me so harshly. Later in the day, you come to me in tears and tell me the whole story. Can you imagine if I responded by saying, 'No, Abu! Your son didn't die. I was just fine. Someone else pushed me in the market.' How would you feel?"

"I would feel sad," he naturally answered.

"How do you think God feels when He gave His best — His only — Son, and people say, 'No! He did not! A dirty pig died instead?'" Muslims think of pigs like we think about rats.

Abu agreed that would certainly be sad and insulting to God. Although it was the first time he had heard the full story of Jesus' sacrifice for us, Abu believed it was true and prayed to follow Isa that day.

### WHY NOT LIVE FULLY FOR GOD TODAY?

Some days feel more urgent than others. But it is not every day that cruise missiles hit near us or we are told we have terminal cancer. Most days feel pretty mundane. But truly, life is like a wisp of smoke or the dew in the morning. In a moment, it is gone. Only what we've done for Jesus will be important to us. C.T. Studd penned a great poem about this. Here is the last stanza:

*"Only one life, 'twill soon be past,*
*Only what's done for Christ will last.*
*And when I am dying, how happy I'll be,*
*If the lamp of my life has been burned out for Thee."*

Studd was certainly inspired by these words in the Bible, *"What I mean, brothers and sisters, is that the time is short. From now on those who have wives should live as if they do not; those who mourn, as if they did not; those who are happy, as if they were not; those who buy something, as if it were not theirs to keep; those who use the things of the world, as if not engrossed in them. For this world in its present form is passing away."*[44]

We may have things and enjoy relationships but should not make them the focus of our lives. God and His kingdom are the only worthy pursuits. One of my first pastors said, "Show me your checkbook [or last month's credit card usage] and I'll show you where your treasure is." Is it God and His kingdom? Or do we spend most of our money on ourselves (or even others) but for insignificant, non-eternal things?

Paul told his young friend, Timothy, *"Preach the word; be ready in season and out of season; reprove, rebuke, and exhort, with complete patience and teaching."*[45] What can be more important than telling others about God's truth and love? Paul goes on to tell Timothy that people's hearts are not always open. We must let them know the truth while we can.

What if you find yourself working in a very mundane job with little human interaction? You can still do your work as if you were doing it for God. Your boss and coworkers will see your joy and commitment to do your best. The time will come when someone will ask you why you are so different or you can initiate a conversation during a break or lunch. Of course, pray that the Lord may open up employment that will give you more opportunities to talk freely with others. But don't be resentful or discouraged if He has sent you to work in a salt mine. He may have a very specific mission for you to reach the heart of the toughest supervisor or coworker that no one else would.

44  1 Corinthians 7:29-31
45  1 Timothy 4:2

Live life knowing your time is short and God is with you. If you do, you can live with great joy, no regrets and receive a rich welcome into heaven.

- *Have you ever had a time when you thought your living situation or life would end soon? If you had three days left to live in your town, what would you do and what conversations would you seek out?*

- *What are some distractions of the "world" in your life? What would help you to be free from them?*

- *Do you feel a sense of urgency? What might help you to maintain that sense? How do we balance urgency and the peace of God (Philippians 4:6-7)?*

THE BIG PICTURE

# HUMILITY

*Whoever exalts himself will be humbled,*
*and whoever humbles himself will be exalted.* "[46]

"Aim at nothing and you'll hit it every time!"[47] The first time I heard that saying I was in the Air Force. They weren't talking about bombs or bullets. Any organization or person either clearly knows their purpose and goals or they cannot be successful. When you get to the end of life, will people say, "That was a life well lived"? More importantly, what will God say? Adjustments can certainly come later in life, but what you decide to aim at in your youth will be a foundational key for a lifetime of success.

How does the world measure success? Lots of toys. Popularity. Power. Prestige. An early retirement with a sailboat. A big home and luxury car in the garage. Muscles. Eye-popping fashion. Do any

of those make your heart skip a beat? Be honest, and welcome to humanity! The lie, however, is that these things will bring lasting happiness or real joy. All of them are fleeting. Toys break. Boats rust. Bodies sag.

46  Matthew 23:12
47  Quote usually attributed to Zig Ziglar

What should you do?

Humble yourself, and reject personal dreams of success that are self-serving, shallow and short-lived. Get a God-sized dream of success that is bigger than you and will count for all eternity. It shouldn't surprise us that our Creator knows exactly what will make us happy. Why not start with God's view of the end goal? Our world is filled with people who chased a mirage. Saul of Tarsus was a young man who was going places. He was a student zealous for faith in God and knew scriptures probably better than most teachers. Paul had respect and the trust of the highest religious leaders of the land. That all dramatically changed when he met Jesus face to face. Paul said he considered all those accomplishments and accolades to be garbage in comparison to knowing Christ.[48] Humble yourself before God and then He will have full reign to direct your footsteps to true success.

If you are not convinced, consider King Solomon. In one sense, he was the ultimate example of mirage chasing.[49] Solomon's fame was so great that Ethiopia's head of state, the Queen of Sheba, traveled over 2500 arduous miles[50] to see his kingdom and hear his wisdom. It literally took her breath away to see Solomon's court, his lavish banquet table, servants, ministers, their clothes and the procession he led to God's temple.[51] He built his nation's first navy and brought back exotic animals and treasures from the far corners of the world. He built pools and gardens, houses, cities and the magnificent temple of God overlaid with gold. He wrote books and was a great patron of music and art. Peace, unprecedented prosperity and justice marked much of his reign. Solomon denied himself no pleasure. He had 700 wives and 300 concubines. Most men then and today drop their jaws with foolish envy. Did all these things make Solomon happy?

This is Solomon's summary of all his efforts: "Vanity of vanities! All is vanity."[52] What is vanity? Charles Allan Gilbert drew a picture in 1894 of a young lady fixated on her own beauty titled, "All is Vanity". Another word for vanity is "meaningless" In fact, many

48  Philippians 3:8
49  If you haven't read Ecclesiastes, take some time to read it. Solomon tried everything from luxury to deprivation, drunkenness to sobriety. In the end, it all proved meaningless.
50  Assuming Sheba's caravan went by land from Addis Ababa, today's capital of Ethiopia, they traveled over 4300 kilometers each way, over forbidding mountains, jungles, swamps, burning deserts and certainly hostile enemy territories
51  1 Kings 10:4-5
52  Ecclesiastes 1:2

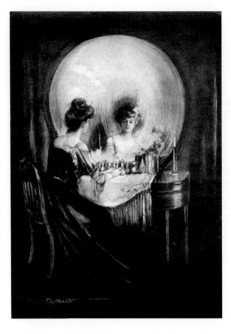

people find Solomon's book of Ecclesiastes so depressing that they never read it again! Solomon tried everything from pleasure to self-denial. In the end, every pleasure or pain, success or discovery, was ultimately meaningless or vain.

Sound depressing? Consider this: Jesus gives us the ultimate insider secret to real success. Humbly change your earthly focus. Follow His advice and you will be truly rich[53] and successful. He said, "Do not lay up for yourselves treasures on earth, where moth and rust destroy and where thieves break in and steal, but lay up for yourselves treasures in heaven, where neither moth nor rust destroys and where thieves do not break in and steal."[54]

You probably already have a good idea of what those real treasures are. In the next chapter, we'll look more closely at them.

THINGS TO THINK ABOUT AND TALK OVER:

- *Do you have some examples of characters in history who chased after "vain" things? Do you know anyone like that today?*

- *How do you think God would define true riches? What about true success?*

- *What would protect you from making the mistake of pursuing vanity?*

- *If you haven't read Solomon's conclusion after his life of trying*

---

53  Before you might think "rich" = "lots of money," read Jesus' warning in Revelation 3:17: "You say, I am rich, I have prospered, and I need nothing, not realizing that you are wretched, pitiable, poor, blind, and naked.'"
54  Matthew 6:19-20 ESV

*everything from self-denial to hedonism, read Ecclesiastes 12:13-14. How might he adjust his conclusion if Solomon lived after Christ walked the earth, died and rose again?*

THE BIG PICTURE

# ETERNAL TREASURE

*"The kingdom of heaven is like a merchant seeking beautiful pearls, who, when he had found one pearl of great price, went and sold all that he had and bought it."[55] -Jesus*

What are the treasures Jesus says to lay up for heaven that will last for ever and ever? Paul gives one excellent answer: the souls of people who will be glad in God forever because we shared Christ with them. *"For what is our hope, our joy, or the crown in which we will glory in the presence of our Lord Jesus when he comes? Is it not you? Indeed, you are our glory and joy."[56]*

The crown Paul is talking about here is not like Burger King's or the Queen of England's, but a wreath given to a victorious Olympic athlete in ancient times. The joy and glory on Paul's head were the

lost slaves of sin who came to faith by God's grace and our labor in love. What a wonderful way to cross the finish line of life: to have a multitude of friends who love Jesus with us! People are ultimately transformed, at least in part, when we live by faith and love, as we are not ashamed to share the good news of Jesus ← our treasure is eternal, not temporal.

Of course, ultimately all the glory belongs to Jesus. Only by His grace and the power of the Holy Spirit do we have any hope of watching anyone become saved. I believe this is why the elders gathered around Jesus' throne in heaven and cast their crowns at His feet.[57]

Here is another treasure: Paul tells us, *"Godliness with contentment*

55  Matthew 13:45-46
56  1 Thessalonians 2:19-20 NIV
57  Revelation 4:10

*is great gain."*[58]

What does godliness mean? Not just purity and avoidance of sin. It means being like God. You were made in God's image. Did you ever wonder what that means? God is spirit, so it doesn't mean He physically looks like you or me. Paul wrote twice that we are being transformed into Jesus' image.[59] Should we put on a robe and grow a beard to look like Jesus? Of course not. Godliness means that we let the power of God's Holy Spirit transform our character into something that looks more like the character of God. The first thing that God is, according to John, is love.[60] How do we learn to love? Study the Bible. Memorize and think about God's truth. Let His Holy Spirit take control of your life as you obey what you read and hear from Him. As you do, not only love, but joy, peace, patience, kindness, goodness, faithfulness, self-control,[61] and a whole host of treasures will fill your life. You will look more like your Lord every day.

I admire and love my dad more than most men I have known. Imagine my joy when someone says, "You remind me so much of your dad." Imagine my dad, who loves me very much, hears someone else say, "Your son is so much like you." What a joyful statement to hear! Seek a character like your heavenly Father's. He will rejoice and you with bless countless others.

Two great treasures you can seek are sharing Christ with others and becoming more like Him yourself. In the third and final chapter on success, we will look at the greatest treasure of all, being with Him.

THINGS TO THINK ABOUT AND TALK OVER:

- *Read in the appendix a letter from my great-great-great grandmother to her son in 1854, the future Dr. Joseph T. Scott. Do you think she would define his success in life by his anticipated degree or profession? He has been dead now for over 100 years. Do you think today he would define his life accomplishments by his profession?*

58  1 Timothy 6:6
59  Romans 8:29, 2 Corinthians 3:18
60  1 John 4:8
61  Galatians 5:22

- *If a friend of yours were asked to describe you, would they include that you love to share the good news of Jesus with others? Would they say your character reminds them of Jesus? Of course, we all struggle to be who God wants, but if neither of those descriptions has any place nor increasing importance to you, you should take a hard look at what is important to you in life. If you want to change, how can you make a shift to begin to focus on those treasures? Would it help you to know from Philippians 1:6 and Hebrews 12:2 that the main Person working for those two treasures is Jesus Himself? Yes, we have to submit and strenuously work, but it is ultimately God's energy at work in us (Colossians 1:28-29). Do you know anyone who actively shares their faith in love? Can you spend time with them to learn how they do it?*

- *You may not think you can explain the good news of Jesus to someone, but what are the most important parts? Can you tell someone what He did for you? If you were the best speaker to ever live and could convince almost anyone to believe, would their faith rest in God or in your silver tongue? (First Corinthians 2:55 says, "My message and my preaching were not with persuasive words of wisdom, but with a demonstration of the Spirit's power, so that your faith would not rest on men's wisdom, but on God's power.")*

- *What do you think it looks like to become more like the image of Jesus? "And we all, with unveiled face, beholding the glory of the Lord, are being transformed into the same image from one degree of glory to another. For this comes from the Lord who is the Spirit." 1 Corinthians 3:1*

THE BIG PICTURE

# ULTIMATE SUCCESS

*"Better is one day in your court than a thousand elsewhere."*[62]

In our first year at seminary, our theology professor asked an interesting question, "What are two things God wants you to do on earth that you can't do in heaven?" Think about that question for a minute. What would you say?

These were his answers:

1. To know Christ and make Him known
2. Worship God under duress (while suffering)[63]

We've already talked about the first treasure. The second — worshipping God while suffering — is something I'll talk more fully about in another chapter. But think about this: in heaven there will be no more suffering or pain. Worshipping God there will be like diving into a beautiful pool on a warm summer day. Nothing could be more natural or fulfilling.

To worship God under extreme difficulty, we must have a treasure that so captivates our hearts that present pain seems minor in comparison. Even better, the pain can make our highest treasure shine more brightly in comparison. What is that treasure?

The greatest treasure of all can only be God Himself. The writer of Psalm 84 sang beautifully, *"My heart and flesh cry out for the living God. . . . better is one day in your courts than a thousand elsewhere."*

The Old Testament is filled with writers declaring that God is "my portion." What does my "portion" mean? Imagine this: your rich uncle just died. His lawyer has gathered everyone together who will receive part of his enormous estate and everyone is buzzing with excitement. Everyone gets a very special and meaningful gift. You are last in line and now it's your turn. All eyes are on you. As the words are read from your beloved uncle, everyone gasps that you get the whole of the estate. This is your portion. When you get God,

---

62  Psalm 84:10
63  Brad Mullins, CIU 1993

your portion is everything. He is the best anyone could have.

We've looked at the extraordinary life of Solomon. Jesus mentioned the Queen of Sheba's arduous journey to meet Solomon and then told His listeners that she would condemn them because, "One greater than Solomon is here."[64] Who? Greater than even Solomon? They had been accusing Jesus of healing through the power of the devil. But we know Jesus as the One through whom everything was created and is held together. [65] The One who set us free from slavery at the cost of His own life.[66] The One who rules from heaven with perfect love, perfect justice, blinding beauty — the author and finisher of our faith.[67] When you have cast your crown of a victorious life at Jesus feet, there will be one Treasure remaining that outshines the sun. Jesus will be your joy and you will never grow tired of enjoying His presence, love, beauty, and breathtaking universe.

What should our target be? Aim high and set your eyes on Jesus. Throw off everything that keeps you from Him, whether sin or simply empty pursuits.[68] Success is helping others know and love God more. Success is running hard after God. We want reflect His image and character — for His glory, not ours. Ultimate success is a life that increasingly and consistently enjoys Christ above all things.

### THINGS TO THINK ABOUT AND TALK OVER:

- *We only have one opportunity to live for God in this broken world. Would you add anything to my professor's list — what does God want us to do on earth that we cannot do in heaven? What would help you to keep your joy when a time of testing or fire comes into your life?*

- *What is your definition of success in life? Paul wrote thirteen letters of the New Testament. He was a scholar of scholars. He was beaten, stoned, maligned and shipwrecked while serving God. Did he boast of those things? If not, why not? (Read 2 Corinthians 11-13 and Philippians 3 for help.)*

64  Matthew 12:42
65  John 1, Colossians 1
66  Romans 5:7-8, 7:24-25
67  Revelation 4, 21; Hebrews 12:2
68  Hebrews 12

- *What are your skills, gifts, and interests that bring you joy? How might you use them for God's glory? What changes, if any, do you need to make to maximize your gifts and your preparation to be successful in God's eyes?*

THE BIG PICTURE

# HOW SHOULD WE LOVE GOD?

*"Love the Lord your God with all your heart and with all your soul and with all your mind and with all your strength."*[69]

How should we love God? What a strange question. In the same moment it seems both too simple and too complex to ask. Simple, in the sense that you would probably not need to ask two young people in love how they should love each other. They would probably look quizzically at you and say, "We don't know; we just do!" However, the answer becomes much more complex if you say, "Well, what happens if one of you is in a car wreck and your beauty is gone in an instant? What if one of you develops a serious disease and your brain doesn't function normally? What will your love look like then?"

The day we come to Christ, we may be amazed at His beauty, His incomparable holiness, His matchless love. We are probably speechless to think that He would choose us and even die for us. We love Him. The intensity and emotion defy description.

But after the first few days or weeks pass, the reality of competing loves surface. Jealous parents or friends may not be so enthused about our newfound love for God and desire to give Him our lives. Some old sins we quickly jettison, but others don't give up so easily. Their tentacles have wrapped deeply around our souls, perhaps for many years. What do we do when God puts His finger on those and says, "That stinks! It needs to go!" The "honeymoon" may end abruptly and we will have some important decisions to make. Even our lifelong dreams and aspirations may need radical adjustment as we think about loving the King of the universe.

One teacher who was genuinely drawn to Jesus asked a famous and helpful question, *"Of all the commandments, which is the most important?"* Jesus answered by quoting scripture, *"Hear, O Israel: The Lord our God, the Lord is one. Love the Lord your God with all your heart and with all your soul and with all your mind and with all your strength."* Then Jesus threw in a tremendous and challenging

---

69  Deuteronomy 6:5

addition: *"The second is this: 'Love your neighbor as yourself.' There is no commandment greater than these."*[70]

The first command is from a very famous Jewish passage called the Shema. Jesus tells us to love God with all of our heart, soul, mind, and strength. Not to love Him with just part — but all — of those things. That's pretty complete! You might think that's impossible, and you'd be right except that all things are possible with God.[71]

## HEART

Jesus used the Greek word *kardia* from which we get the English phrase cardiac arrest to refer to the heart. When our hearts pump blood well, we feel great. When our heart beats irregularly or suffers a blockage, most people are suddenly struck weak and immobile. No wonder the heart was seen and felt to be where our affections and sense of well-being are found. Paul prayed for the Ephesians that Jesus would live in their hearts[72], not because blood pumps there, but because of the sense that the heart is where our deepest passions and longings are felt. Interestingly, some scientists are now calling the heart and intestines our second and third brain because they are learning that those areas actually do process and influence emotions.[73] Regardless of what you might think about the science of hearts, God is calling us to love Him with all of our passions, dreams, and desires.

## SOUL

Next, Jesus tells us to love God with all of our soul (*psyche*). Our soul is the essence of who we are. Long after our hearts, brains, and other organs have died, our souls will continue. The Bible teaches us that everyone's soul will continue to exist, either in a new body in heaven with God or separated from God forever tormented in

---

70   Mark 12:28-31, Deuteronomy 6:4-5, Leviticus 19:18
71   Philippians 4:13
72   Ephesians 3:17
73   Did you know your intestines and liver contain over 100,000,000 neurotransmitters and your heart has 40,000? Both areas can send powerful messages to our "main" brain about how we feel or even who we are. Hadhazy, Adam. online Scientific America article, Think Twice: How the Gut's "Second Brain" Influences Mood and Well-Being Feb 12, 2010 https://www.scientificamerican.com/article/gut-second-brain/ Liver transplant patients often have an inexplicable complication of depression. Heart transplant patients report memories and passions they've never had before like a sudden love for classical music or infatuation with sports. - "Woman dies 21 years after heart-lung transplant that gave her a taste ...." 19 Aug. 2009, http://www.patriotledger.com/article/20090819/NEWS/308199597. Accessed 14 Feb. 2018.

hell. What we decide to do with our soul on earth has much to do with our joy in life for eternity. If the very core of our being delights and rejoices in God, imagine the joy when our soul is fully in His presence! Why not start worshipping Him now?

## MIND

God wants not just our passions and the core of our being, but all of the intellectual and analytical abilities. He set us apart from animals by giving us minds. Jesus uses the word dianoia, related to our word diagnosis, to refer to our minds. God wants us to use our math skills as architects and engineers to build great buildings for Him and as pilots to fly airplanes safely for His glory. He wants us to diagnose patients as doctors and nurses and analyze what treatment will bring them back to health, as an extension of God's hands of love. The application of our mind in love for God has limitless possibilities for every profession and pursuit from playing chess and parenting to computer programming and care for our environment. Paul wisely advised His friends, *"Whatever you do, whether in word or deed, do it all in the name of the Lord Jesus, giving thanks to God the Father through him."*[74]

## STRENGTH

Lastly, Jesus tells us to love God with all of our physical ability, forcefulness, strength, and might. The first quality Paul gives to love in his beautiful and famous definition of love is *long-suffering.*[75] It is impossible to love without physical suffering. Jesus said, *"Greater love has no one than this: to lay down one's life for one's friends."*[76] The next day, He suffered on the cross and died for them. Jacob labored fourteen years to get to marry his beloved, but it seemed to him like only a few days. When I dated your mother, I was happy to stay up late or get up early just to see her for a few minutes in the midst of our busy schedules.

The exact opposite is true of the Greek myth, Narcissus. He loved himself so much that he couldn't stand those who loved him. Eventually he ended stuck at a pool that showed his reflection and he could never tear himself away. We all find the story repulsive. But, if we are honest, most of us can relate to Narcissus in some way. We

74 Colossians 3:17
75 1 Corinthians 13
76 John 15:13

pathetically love ourselves so much we do not take the time, energy, and emotion to love God and others the way we should. If only we could understand the person who keeps their life to themselves will lose it, but the person who gives their life for the love of God will get it back forever.[77]

So what should you do when you fall short of loving God and your neighbor? Jesus has strong, caring advice, *"You have abandoned the love you had at first. Remember therefore from where you have fallen; repent, and do the works you did at first."*[78] Think about when you first fell in love with Jesus, what He did, what you realized about yourself, and what beauty and love you saw in Him. "Repent!" He says. That means turn around and confess what you've done wrong. God wants to forgive us and draw us back. Then *"do the works you did at first."* If you spent long hours listening to praise music, reading your Bible, and listening to sermons, go back to those things! If you were telling others about Christ and teaching the Bible, do those again! At the same time, ask God to show you where you went astray in loving Him with all your heart, soul, mind, and strength.

God is the One who started this great love story and faithfully will be with you to complete it.[79] You just need to jump on board to enjoy the journey. I heard Josh McDowell speak at a conference, Jesus Northwest. He said that the way teens spell "love" is T-I-M-E. We can't say we love someone without giving them time. The same is true for God. If you want your love for Him to grow (or return), give Him your time and the best part of your day.

Does it discourage you or seem impossible to you to meet God's command to love Him with all your heart, soul, mind, and strength? I am left gasping at the impossibility, knowing how self-centered and sinful I am. *But thankfully*, God does not leave this kind of joy beyond our reach. A certain young, rich ruler left Jesus in great sorrow because 1.) The young man couldn't give up his riches to follow God and 2.) He was seeking perfection and eternal life by his own means, instead of by faith in Jesus. "What must I do to inherit eternal life?"[80] Although Jesus tells him clearly that there is none good but God alone, the Lord shakes the young man's perception

77  Matthew 16:25
78  Revelation 2:4-5
79  Philippians 1:6
80  Matthew 19:16

of his own goodness by saying, *"If you want to be perfect, go, sell what you possess and give it to the poor . . . and come follow me."*[81] Who then can love God with all his being and possessions? Answer? No one! That is, no one without God's miraculous intervention.[82] Our place is to acknowledge how far we fall short of God's rightful expectations, embrace His merciful love, and surrender to Him. His power will then fill your heart and soul to do the impossible.

### THINGS TO THINK ABOUT AND TALK OVER:

- *If you had a friend struggling to love God, what advice would you give them? How would you explain loving God in the four areas Jesus mentioned? How can God's power make up for our weakness in loving Him?*

- *Is your love for God where you want it to be? What would it take for it to be better (or even great)? Although Peter was the only disciple brave enough to walk on water, he still denied Jesus three times just before the crucifixion, but then Jesus affirms Peter after the Lord's resurrection. You might take time to read that story in John 21. What helped Peter? What did Jesus tell Peter to do? You may want to look further by reading about the power of the Holy Spirit in Acts 1 & 2. Peter becomes extremely bold, even squaring off with the religious court that executed Jesus in Acts 4. What do you think transformed Peter?*

81  Matthew 19:21
82  Matthew 19:26

THE BIG PICTURE

# FRIENDS

*"Greater love has no one than this, that someone lay down his life for his friends."*[83]

"I never met a man I didn't like," said Will Rogers, a well-loved humorist from Oklahoma.[84]

Most of us are not like Will Rogers — neither so witty, nor so friendly. If we're honest, even the most outgoing of us have a shy streak that we have learned to overcome or hide. I was so shy throughout high school that I could hardly talk to a pretty girl or present a speech to my class. The first time I remember meeting my dad's boss, I was in sixth grade and Dad was being promoted to colonel. The commander was very nice and came over to meet our family. I remember looking at his nice shoes and that's about all. I couldn't tell you what his face looked like because I didn't look up or get up. I don't think I said anything, not even "Hello." When I think back, I can imagine my parents were probably very embarrassed and realized they had missed imparting some important points of etiquette. We did get a short lesson on the spot, and thankfully dad was kind in his instruction.

So how do we make friends, greet strangers, and communicate well? How might other people influence us? How do we influence them? In short, how do we interact with people outside of our family? Here is some helpful advice:

*"Whoever walks with the wise becomes wise, but the companion of fools will suffer harm."*[85]

"Dad, I have a new best friend!" Everyone I've ever known longs to have a best friend they can share deep secrets, crazy dreams, love, and hurts with. One of my four children (unnamed, of course!) especially longed for a best friend. Anyone that gave a little extra time, kindness, or laughter had immediate and high potential to become "my best friend." Your mom and I would always say,

83   John 15:13
84   Will Rogers photo from Melbourne Spurr 1922, public domain Wikimedia Commons
85   Proverbs 13:20

"Woah! Get to know that person first. It takes time to become best friends." Indeed, probably all of us have experienced hurt on several occasions as kids when someone we trusted and thought of as a close friend gave away our secrets to embarrass or gossip about us. Ouch! Not only is there a risk of getting hurt, but even worse, the proverb above tells us that foolish friends can lead us into a great deal of harm. Wise friends, however, sharpen us to become better than we could ever be alone. How can you choose? How do you make a good friendship? I'll give you my "list" first (which you can add more to) and then help you understand each point in more detail.

### PUT GOD FIRST
Serve sacrificially. Be joyful and trust in God.

### LEARN TO BE FRIENDLY
For some, this is natural. For most, we need to learn from others who are good at it.

### LIVE IN THE JOY OF FORGIVENESS
Forgive offenses knowing Christ has forgiven you of the worst sins. Be quick to ask for forgiveness.

### LIMIT OR ELIMINATE TIME WITH UNWISE FRIENDS
Be wary of spending too much time with those who have no interest in God or tempt you in an area of sin that you are weak in. Of course, you are called to love unbelievers even to the point of death. But you are not called to let their influence pull you into sin.

### SEEK REGULAR FELLOWSHIP
Seek regular, open times with mature Christ followers. Find a Bible study, coffee time, workout, or meal at least once a week (if not several times a week) where the real goal is knowing and loving God more. Pray, serve, and debrief ministry together.

### RELEASE GOOD FRIENDS WHEN IT'S TIME
When God calls you or your closest friend (or child) to a new phase of life and ministry, don't hold back. We belong first to the Lord.

PUT GOD FIRST

If you seek God's kingdom first, as Jesus advised many of His friends in Matthew 6:33, God will take care of you and make you rich. Not rich with money necessarily, but in blessings, joy, and true friends. After falling in love with God, I can say I feel like a rich man every day. My life is filled with His love and with close friends.

When I first went to Kazakhstan, I was wisely told by experienced Americans to be careful not to quickly call new acquaintances "friends." This was probably the result of life under Communism. One hint to a "friend" that someone is critical of the government could mean ten years in a Siberian labor camp or disappearing forever. Most people could count on one hand the people they would call "friend" in their lifetime. *Friend* meant that you would die for the other person. *Friend* meant you would never give away secrets that would endanger them. Perhaps that is how we *should* be a friend and think of friendship. However, in America, some people "friend" others on Facebook even though they've never met. Perhaps they are friend of a friend. You can see the dangers here even though we are not at risk of the secret police.

As you seek God first in friendships, that doesn't mean you won't naturally enjoy being with friends that like activities that you do. Several of my closest friends are pilots. A few others like to keep in shape. Many like to travel to other countries. But the most common element and powerful in our friendship is Christ. If you find your closest friends prefer talking about football, cars, music, or movies, but rarely talk about Christ, you don't need anyone to tell you that God is not put first! Although you may really enjoy hanging out with this friend, how deep is your friendship, really? How much are either of you thinking and growing in the most important things of life and eternity? You may not need to stop being friends, but wisdom would certainly tell you that your time would better be spent with someone passionate and serious about God first and hobbies second.

## LEARN TO BE FRIENDLY

Here's a good saying that may seem obvious (but too many people don't practice it): "If you want to have friends, learn to be friendly." Most of us think about one person nearly all the time — ourselves! "How do I look? How can I make some more money? How can I get that new, cool cell phone?" A true friend thinks about the other person first. "How can I help him to get into shape or have more self-confidence? How can I help her make more money? How can I help my friend get a better phone?" That is not an easy shift, but a seismically good one. There are lots of ideas about how to become less shy, initiate friendships, and put others first. Look for someone who is good at these things and try to imitate them. I always remember one friendly captain I flew with. Every time he called someone on the phone, he wrote down their name on a notepad and would use their name several times during the conversation. "Hello. This is Captain Ulrich. With whom am I speaking? — Hello Sergeant York! How are things at the inflight kitchen? —Great! Can you help me? I need to order seven box lunches for our crew tomorrow. — Fantastic. You've been very helpful. Have a great evening, Sergeant York!"

You won't master the many ways of being friendly in a short time. But take them one at a time and perhaps focus on that for a week or two until you think you've mastered it.

### ENCOURAGE

Meet new people and compliment them on something. What can you do to make their day brighter? One lady at a hotel looked at my name and said, "Robert Scott Stone? That is such a cool name!" She really meant it and I still smile when I think of that short conversation.

### LEARN NAMES

When meeting someone new, ask their name and practice it several times during your conversation. You may even have to keep saying their name in your head, "Paul, Paul, Paul, Paul, Paul . . ."

### MAKE EYE-CONTACT

on't look down or off into space. If that seems hard at first, look at their nose. They can't tell the difference. Of course, you can go overboard, so be natural. Blink normally and look occasionally at something else.

### LEARN TO ASK GOOD QUESTIONS

Questions that can be answered with a simple yes or no usually won't go far in making a rich conversation. Here are some ideas: "What's your favorite movie? Music? If you could be an animal for a day, what would it be? How about being a certain famous person? Where would you like to travel?" Give them plenty of time to think and answer. Don't jump in too fast with your own answer. Be interested and ask more probing questions like, "Why? How did you first get interested in that?" Find more good questions online.[86]

### BE AN INTERACTIVE LISTENER

Say to yourself, "This is the most important person in the world to me right now." Don't be distracted by thinking about the movie you want to watch tonight or needing to call your mom.

### LEARN SOMETHING ABOUT BODY LANGUAGE

For most people, slouching, folding arms, yawning, or having your hands in your pockets tells them you are bored or do not care. Sitting forward in your seat, appropriate facial gestures and interjecting related questions or comments like, "Wow! I would have been so nervous," will help enormously when you are making friends.

### LEARN TO TELL INTERESTING STORIES

If you haven't done this before, practice with your family or friends. Try telling parables. Try telling personal stories. Then try them on a stranger: "Can I tell you an interesting story?" Most people love stories. Again, ask questions to keep them engaged. "What do you think? What would you have done? Can you identify with any of the characters?"

### LEARN MORE FROM A PRO

Steve Saccone has some thoughtful material on "Relational Intelligence."[87] Go online to find out more.

---

86  One article of many: http://www.mantelligence.com/good-questions-to-ask-to-get-to-know-someone/
87  https://sed-efca.org/wp-content/uploads/2013/05/Relational-Intelligence-by-Steve-Saccone.pdf

## LIVE IN THE JOY OF FORGIVENESS

Sadly, as you know, people get hurt in friendships and can become shy or withdrawn as a result of a bad relationship. That's never God's will! Although it may take time and a lot of effort to forgive and heal, God created us to love Him. One of the best ways to love Him is to love others, even though we certainly risk getting hurt. Whatever someone has done to hurt you, you have done worse to hurt Christ! If He has forgiven you, how could you not forgive someone He loves? Do you remember what Jesus called Judas as he kissed Jesus, betraying him in the garden? Friend.[88] I have a strong sense that there were tears in both men's eyes. Even facing betrayal and a brutal execution, Jesus did not "unfriend" Judas.

On the flip side, if you've done wrong, ask others for forgiveness. Don't delay! You mother has taught me this: even if you don't think you've done something wrong, be quick to ask for forgiveness about any part of a conflict you are involved in. If you didn't cause the situation, you can apologize for your reaction. Surely it could have been better. Maybe you could have spoken more clearly at the beginning of the problem. Ask forgiveness for that. Usually both people are set free by just one person breaking down to ask forgiveness first.

*Limit your time with unwise friends who show no interest in God. Run from those who tempt you in an area of sin that you are weak in.*

Clearly God wants us to love and be involved in the lives of people who are living very hard lives. Jesus was known as a friend of sinners and was insulted by self-righteous people for it. He had harsh words in return for the second group. We want to be helpful to those who struggle with sin but be realistic about their potential influence on us. Jesus may have been impervious but we are not! Paul has good advice for his friends who lived in Corinth, Greece, a very immoral city:

*"I wrote to you in my letter not to associate with sexually immoral people— not at all meaning the sexually immoral of this world, or the greedy and swindlers, or idolaters, since then you would need to go out of the world. But now I am writing to you not to associate with anyone who bears the name of brother if he is guilty of sexual*

---

88  Matthew 26:50

*immorality or greed, or is an idolater, reviler, drunkard, or swindler..."*[89]

I can tell you stories of several friends who were in prison for years. Fortunately, they either met God or grew close to Him again while there. They promised the Lord that they would go straight once they were free. For a while, it went well. They found a church and were so happy to be with God, be free, and have a whole new life. But old friends have a way of finding out where their buddies are. Sometimes, the newly freed prisoners thought they were stronger than they really were. They had a healthy desire to help their troubled friends know Christ. Unfortunately, the influence went the wrong way. Spending too much time together led to a little drinking. A little drinking led to more. More drinking led to drugs. Sadly, several of these men ended up back in prison. But not all. Some realized their weaknesses in time, cut their ties with old friends, and even moved to completely new locations. As they grew stronger in faith, they did have success in reaching old friends with the hope of God's kingdom.

### SEEK REGULAR, OPEN TIMES WITH MATURE CHRIST FOLLOWERS

A diamond purchaser looking for the best gems will go the most reliable stores or even to the source where they are mined. The best friends I've ever found have been at church, a shared desire for prayer, accountability or ministry. Be intentional. If church services don't have time to get up close and personal (most don't) then invite someone you've met to lunch or coffee. Find or create a Bible study where you people feel safe to open matters close to their heart. If you jog, invite a Christ follower and agree to shape your time together around Bible memory work, prayer or accountability.

Truthfully, I'm amazed at the many and incredible friendships God has given me over the years in the places I went to worship, study the Bible or serve. There is something in genuine love of those who are passionate about Jesus that allows friends to go deep quickly. Some quickly come to mind: Steve, Marty, Mark, Jerry and Krista in Washington. Sisters Weenie and Cris in the Philippines. Jon, Karen, Hubert and many others in Korea. Brian, Heather, Eric, Ceci and Charlie in Panama. Saul Paul from Cambodia. Tim, Doug, Peter,

---

89  1 Corinthians 5:9-11

YOUR DAD LOVES YOU!

Ed, Sam, Thilak, Liny and others during seminary in South Carolina. Constantine in the Republic of Georgia. Bill, Larry, Jill, Edison, Susan, Ev, Steve, Diane, Tim and Chris in California. Aliya, Seydula, Eset and Olzhas in Kazakhstan. I can't list them all. Are you getting the picture that I feel like a very rich man? Some of these friends have already gone to be with the Lord. But we enjoyed deep friendships in Christ. A small handful have even caused me deep pain. I'm sure I've done the same. But that is the risk of any true friendship and the glory of Christ when we can forgive and move forward.

### RELEASE FRIENDS WHEN IT'S TIME

The time will come when every friendship on this earth will end. Sometimes death is the reason, but more often, God will call you or your friend to another assignment. Of course, the time to say goodbye may be very painful, but we belong first to God. Don't let others' expectations keep you back from a call God which put on your life. You might think to yourself, "How can I leave them in the ministry? They are depending on me!" That may be true, but God has others waiting for your arrival at a new location that depend on your message of truth and love. If God calls you away from one location, won't He fill the place you are leaving?

On the other hand, if a close friend (or maybe even one of your kids) is feeling called to ministry at a new location and you don't feel called to go with them, release them with your blessing! Our goal should always be to see God glorified and others drawn to see His beauty and love, even if it costs us our very best friend. Don't make it hard on them by being selfish. Your joy and theirs will be so much greater when God graciously blesses them in a new phase of life. You will have all eternity to share stories, more than enough to make up for any lost time on earth.

### THINGS TO THINK ABOUT AND TALK OVER:

- *Is there anything that keeps you back from making friends (like being shy)? What would help you overcome that?*

- *Do you have any friendships that have gone bad? What can you learn from them? Can you still go back and ask for and/or offer forgiveness?*

- *How can you tell if you are close to crossing a line from reaching sinners to falling back into sin with them? What options do you have if you feel you may be going that direction?*

- *Is there a minstry or change in life you feel God may be calling you to that would mean saying good-bye to some close friends? Are you hesitating to say "yes" because of them? What would help you to be free to do anything God wants and not be held back by friendships?*

THE BIG PICTURE

# THRILL AND DANGER: DATING

*"Behold, you are beautiful, my beloved, truly delightful.*
*Our couch is green;*
*the beams of our house are cedar;*
*our rafters are pine."*[90]

The lover and the beloved lay on verdant, thick grass under a canopy of endless deep blue with cedar and pine trees shading them from the heat of the sun. God provides those whom He favors with joy and unspeakable passion in a setting no craftsman could match in beauty. Solomon is unequalled among Bible writers as he paints a picture of passionate, deep, genuine love between a man and a woman — which is designed to help us embrace, in some small measure, God's love for us.[91]

When you bloom as a godly young man or woman, I wish I could take you on your first date. If you go to the prom, I dream you would ask me to chaperone. I have a vision you come to your mother and me one quiet evening and say, "I believe he or she is the one for me. What do you think? Would you bless our marriage?" I want to be there. If it's a match from heaven, I long to say enthusiastically with your mom, "We do!" Truthfully, I've already been there a hundred times in my mind, even when you were a baby. I've prayed for God to give each of you just the right spouse, if it is His plan for you to be married.

Falling in love is one of the most thrilling, exhilarating, and joyful experiences of our journey on earth. It can also be one of the most scary, heart-rending, and dangerous ventures at the same time! Thankfully, God promises to help us, be with us, and give us wisdom every step of the way . . . if we trust and choose His way to navigate uncharted waters.

When you listen to other kids talk about dating and parties, you might get the idea that they are experiencing the most exciting, fun life while yours is dull and uninteresting. Truthfully, there are moments that those kids have a certain amount of fun, but their

90  Song of Solomon 1:16-17
91  Revelation 19:6-9

lives are often empty and devoid of real love and meaning. I love those kids. I used to envy them. But now I understand so much more and feel sorry for their circumstances. Many will carry the scars of their youth for life: rejection, abuse, sexual diseases, and even abortion. Consider Neil Warren's warning from Falling in Love for All the Right Reasons, "One in three teens who date will experience violence in a dating relationship."[92] The temptation, pressure, and danger for premarital sex today is overwhelming. When I was a boy in the 1960s, there were only two major sexual diseases of real threat: syphilis and gonorrhea, both curable. Now, because of the cultural revolution and "free" sex, there are twenty-five major diseases you can get, nineteen of which have no known cure.[93] Of course, by grace, God can turn those sad experiences and even diseases into something good, but why go through such devastation if you don't have to?

One more note about "kid dating." As you listen to kids boasting about their latest date or boyfriend/girlfriend, note how many other kids aren't saying much about their dating. That would be most of them. Over 80% of seniors in high school aren't dating and almost half of kids don't date at all in high school![94] We often miss the silent messages of good friends while paying attention to the noisy minority.

What is the purpose of dating? As with everything we do, it should be for God's glory.[95] We are kidding ourselves if we try to believe dating is "just something fun to do. I'm just hanging out with a friend." That's not dating. That's simply friendship. "Dating" involves some level of romance, deeper feelings and revealing our secrets and dreams. Those are things that are best done in the safety and security of an unbreakable bond of love that we call marriage. Otherwise, bonds broken after dating or a fragile marriage can wreak havoc on our soul, scarring our hearts for future relationships. I've seen many friends who find it hard to be genuinely open or fully trust their spouses because of past wounds from previous romantic relationships. No, dating originally had its roots in courtship, a more noble and safe undertaking. Courtship is a protected and magical time to explore potential marriage between two people who have

92   Warren, Neil Clark. 2005. Falling in Love for All the Right Reasons. New York, NY: Center Street
93   Josh McDowell, The Bare Facts: The Truth about Sex, Love Relationships
94   Child Trends' original analysis of the Monitoring the Future Survey, 1976 to 2013.
95   Colossians 3:17

passed through loving observation and careful consideration for compatibility. Marriage is ultimately a picture of God's love for His people,[96] so dating or courtship should not be treated casually or for self-gratification. Read the next chapter to learn more about courtship.

I often tell my single friends, that when you date, realize this person very likely will not be your spouse. Picture yourself giving your date to another person at their future wedding. Would you feel ashamed? Or would you feel you have honored both your date, their future spouse, and God? Ideally you should feel that both of you have become better people. What kinds of things would you do to date someone like that? Kiss and hold hands? Or serve homeless people a meal? Would you "make out" but not go "all the way?" Or would you go to a Bible study and grow deeper in God together? Would you spend as much time alone as you could with your date and go to an offensive movie? Or would you help friends clean a disabled neighbor's yard and spend time getting to know each other's families?

Getting to know someone special of the opposite sex is a thrilling and joyful time of life. Keep it that way by staying far away from the hurt of both physical and mental sex before marriage.[97] Waiting for physical and mental sexual intimacy creates the most fertile ground for love to fully bloom in God's time.

God has a different priority than most of us do for a committed guy-girl relationship. As you've already read, God's greatest desire is that intimate relationships — and ultimately, marriage — should be a picture of His love for us. Can you imagine that God "tries out" many different people, different generations, and different ethnic groups, only to cast them aside for someone else more attractive? Never! He has taught us that love is a commitment higher than life or death.[98] If God has such a high view of marriage, surely our starting point should also be extreme value.

In the next chapter, we will examine smart, healthy dating "God's

---

96  Ephesians 5:22-33, Revelation 19

97  "Mental sex" is fantasizing about your date in a sexual way. This is defaming, turning your date into an object. It also powerfully sets you up for falling into premarital sex and is the sin of lust. Jesus said lusting is the same thing as adultery in Matthew 5:28, so don't fall for the devil's trick that if we don't "do" an act, the thought isn't a sin!

98  "For I am convinced that neither death nor life, neither angels nor demons, neither the present nor the future, nor any powers, nor height nor depth, nor anything else in all creation, will be able to separate us from the love of God in Christ Jesus our Lord." Romans 8:38-39 NIV

way," a tremendous foundation for a great marriage. Before we do, however, let's look at one more important and wonderful consideration in the big picture of marriage: the gift of singleness.

## DO YOU HAVE THE GIFT OF SINGLENESS?

Before you make any decision to date or marry, carefully read through chapter seven of Paul's first letter to the Corinthians. He wrote a very practical section on singleness, marriage, separation, divorce, and even re-marriage. So, how can you know if you have a gift to remain single? Paul gives a clear and simple test to a church living in a city that was crazy about immoral sex of all kinds. Do you burn with a passion to have sex? If not, you're special and there should be no shame or pressure if you don't have that strong desire. God's gift of singleness is a great gift and should be received by the few who have it.[99] If you do have the gift, you'll be happier and more fulfilled if you choose not to marry, but to serve God without the concerns of married life.[100] On the other hand, if you are single but don't believe you have the gift of singleness (in other words, the desire for physical intimacy is never far away), God knows your heart. When the time is right, He will lead you to a spouse that suits you best. In the meantime, as you walk closely with Him as single person, He will also keep you pure! Just because you are single now and don't have the gift of singleness, that is also no license to sin, lust,[101] or have sexual contact[102] before marriage. God will always give you greater strength than any temptation and provide a door of escape.[103]

---

99   Matthew 19:10-12
100   1 Corinthians 7:40
101   Pornography and/or masturbation are no cure for quelling a burning desire for sex. In fact, these activities will "feed" the fire and create an insatiable desire for more and can also hurt future marital sex. More on that in a later chapter.
102   Many young people ask, "How far is too far in physical contact? I know intercourse is wrong before marriage, but what about holding hands, kissing, or more?" That partly depends on the individual, but only in this way: caressing, hand-holding, and kissing are designed by God to move us towards intimacy, trust, and bonding. The most intense and powerful bonding is intercourse. If you hold hands or even touch a shoulder, and that touch begins to cause sexual arousal, you are crossing a line that will pull you towards further intimacy. If you are committed to keeping your heart pure for marriage, why would you want to go to the brink and possibly fall off? If you walk to the edge of a tremendous cliff, would you stand with your toes over the edge, wiggling in space? Or would you back up at least three feet? Just because it's possible to be so close to danger and not fall, does it make sense? Likewise, I cannot strongly encourage you enough to put up safe barriers. You will still have plenty of thrills and your joy will be even greater in marriage. Keep physical contact safe and honoring to each other and to God.
103   1 Corinthians 10:13

The thrill to finding a lifelong mate that has almost no equal, which is perhaps the main reason marriage is compared to the joy of finding the love of God.[104] But the danger that we will trade true love for a deception is equally great, a mirage that can sadly cause a lifetime of pain. Fortunately, God is for your joy, which means you can navigate these waters with confidence and happy expectancy when you keep your heart set on Him.

THINGS TO THINK ABOUT AND TALK OVER:

- *Did you catch my long footnote on physical contact in dating or courtship on the previous page? I started by asking, "How far is too far in physical contact?" What do you think about my advice? What would you say to a younger brother or sister asking for advice in the same subject? Remember, your words can strongly influence them towards a lifetime of safety and joy or a lifetime of regret. Would you protect yourself or someone else you are dating with the same advice? How does a passionate love for God help us in the question of physical contact with the opposite sex?*

- *What do you think that healthy dating or courtship might look like? What about unhealthy dating?*

- *Read the book of Ruth in the Bible. It's only four short chapters. How do you see God leading in Ruth's life? Ruth didn't "date" like we do. How did she honor God, her mother-in-law Naomi, her new people, and Boaz while still making her feelings clear? Besides finding a great husband, how did God ultimately bless Ruth? (Hint: she lived in a little town of Bethlehem and had a great-grandson named David.)*

- *The Bible says adultery (married people being intimate with someone beside their spouse) is wrong. Most non-religious people probably agree. But what about sex between unmarried people? Do you know any Bible verses that talk about that? (Hint: do a word search for "fornication.") Also, Josh McDowell tells a story about a friend who was active sexually before marriage. He was very distressed that those memories of other women were always in his mind when he was intimate with his wife, whom he loved dearly and considered the most*

104  Ephesians 4:25-32

*beautiful woman he ever knew. He confessed to Josh that he was "never in bed alone" with his wife.[105] Hebrews 13:4a says, "Let marriage be held in honor among all, and let the marriage bed be undefiled." Do you see how even single people can defile their future marriage bed? If you have already had sex, stop, confess to someone you trust, commit to wait for marriage and find healing in good counsel. Read the chapters "When You Fail" Parts I & II and "Set Free" to find more help.*

105   Josh McDowell, The Bare Facts: The Truth about Sex, Love  Relationships, 2010, p 23

THE BIG PICTURE

# SMART COURTSHIP

*Rebekah lifted up her eyes, and when she saw Isaac, she dismounted from the camel and said to the servant, "Who is that man, walking in the field to meet us?" The servant said, "It is my master." So she took her veil and covered herself.*[106]

Many people have gone down the road of falling in love with someone they barely knew, only to discover a terrible truth after the wedding. Their spouse was a fake. It's fairly easy to hide character flaws when you are alone together and date only a short time.[107] How can you choose a mate in a smart way? One of the best ways to get to know someone you have a romantic interest in is not fanning the flames of blinding romance (secret notes, special gifts, a beautiful smile, and laughter), but by spending time together around *other* friends and family, especially in difficult circumstances. Non-romantic friendship and time spent learning about the other person in a social setting also makes it much, much easier to back away from someone who still needs to grow in character.

I remember one very attractive girl at our seminary in South Carolina. She was a flirt and drew the attention of several guys as she checked each one out. One day, it was my turn. We enjoyed sitting over a meal in the cafeteria and talking about common interests. As we stood in line to give our trays to the dish crew, a friend of mine named Jerome walked up and greeted us. Jerome has cerebral palsy, walks with a severe limp, and can be hard to understand when he talks. He is also one of the most gentle and loving souls you might ever meet. My budding and cautious romantic interest in this young lady was suddenly severed when she rudely said to Jerome, "Hey, we're talking here! What do you want?" That was perhaps the fastest dose of reality and memorable cold shower I had ever received. Thank you, Jerome. Thank you, Lord. Anyone who excuses poor behavior, ("She'd never do that to me!") will have a rude and well-deserved awakening when the honeymoon ends.

---

106   Genesis 24:64-65
107   Please, be smart, and  ignore the rare exception of a foolish couple who dated briefly or without their parents' blessing, yet enjoys a good marriage by God's grace. That's like listening to the guy who never changes his car oil, but boasts he has 200,000 miles on his car. If you blow up your engine trying to do the same thing, no one will look at you with sympathy!

No one is perfect, but to discover deeper character traits (both good and bad) takes time. The crucible of life's pressures and other relationships — especially with parents and difficult siblings — will give you a much better picture of how this person will be as a spouse and a parent. Listen to how they talk about a challenging brother, sister, or friend. Are they exasperated and critical? Or are they genuinely concerned and trying to help?

Here's helpful advice for deciding if you should continue dating someone who has irritating traits or habits. *If those bad habits were ten times worse, would you marry the person?* The truth is that those bad habits will seem ten times worse after years of marriage and without the rose-tinted glasses of romantic dating.

Take time to see how the person of your interest treats his or her parents. One of the most compelling traits I saw in your mom when I considered marrying her was something that took a while to discover. Her father, although kind to me, was a very hard man to his family. He was as rough of coal miner and alcoholic as you could imagine. He was mean to his wife most of their married life. He was critical and harsh towards your mom. But you know, I always saw something amazing in your mom. As a forgiven Jesus follower, she loved her dad. She tried to tell him about God and His love. Thankfully, George came to faith in Christ a few years after we married due to your mom's faith and others. He changed a great deal, becoming a much more tender man. I knew that if your mom genuinely loved her father when he was cruel, she would be forgiving, committed, and loving to me on days when I would not be very lovable.

## CONSIDER SMART COURTSHIP

Not so long ago, when I was born, modern dating — inviting a relative stranger to a romantic time alone — was rare. *Courtship* was the main way to meet a possible mate. In courtship, the young man leads the way as a gentleman, ready to lay down his life for the young lady, following the example Jesus left in the way He loved us. A godly courting man respects the young lady's father (or her God-given authority if Dad is not in her life) and asks for his permission to court. During courtship, a caring adult is always with them so that physical or undue emotional intimacy doesn't happen. Any touching, caressing, or graphic words intended to arouse the other person during courtship is defaming and distinctly unloving. An extra set of caring eyes and ears in conversations is a very helpful protection of hearts for both guys and gals!

So how do you find a quality person to court? The best place for a genuine God-follower is in church or in ministry. Spend time with people who share your passions and standards. The best place to discover someone you like is in a group setting. In groups, it's easier to see what people are really like and you can safely tell if someone is genuine or fake, encouraging or critical. You can be friends with them without being overt about your growing interest. Let God work in their heart, as well, as they consider you.

If a young man has expressed interest in you, my daughters, ask him if he knows what courtship is. If not, explain to him that your dad is your authority and if he's interested, he'll need to go through me to spend serious time with you. I promise not to embarrass him, but to ask important questions like what ministry or work he is involved with, his views on marriage and family life, how he fights temptation, etc. I'll also provide a chaperone when you want to spend time together.

Why is this "smart" courtship? My precious daughters, here's a spoiler alert but one you need to know! Boys[108] are first attracted to external beauty and primarily want something different than you do. Even a godly young man is driven by powerful forces he probably doesn't completely understand. He wants sex and sooner is better! Committed young men, faithful to God, know they need to wait for marriage but are never immune from temptation. A smooth young man, however, may deceive you and even your father. But as soon as he tries to get you alone without a chaperone, you know he's fake, no matter how dreamy his eyes and kind his words are. Run away from a young man like that! True love can wait, even though it's hard.

## TEMPTATION

*Can a man carry fire next to his chest and his clothes not be burned?*[109]

---

108  I use the terms "boys" and "girls" or "young man" and "young lady" but mean them to be interchangeable. You might even find yourself single late in life and these principles are still the same. We are all young if we see life with joy and each day as a new experience — a time to learn and grow. "Old" people have everything figured out. I hope you never get old!
109  Proverbs 6:27

How can we be kept from temptation?[110] Of course, smart courtship
and chaperones are a tremendous help. But unintended time alone
can happen by accident. Your first line of defense needs to be prayer
that takes place well before temptation comes. That's why Jesus put
that petition into the "Lord's Prayer, "Lead us not into temptation
but deliver us from evil."[111] God is always the unseen Chaperone!
Follow His lead and He will guide you on excellent paths of
righteousness.[112] The second line of defense is really an offense.
Keep your thought life under control. Paul wisely said to "take every
thought captive for Christ."[113] When you find your mind wandering
into unhealthy territory, replace those thoughts with wholesome,
noble thoughts. This is where Scripture memory is extremely helpful
(like *Let marriage be held in honor among all, and let the marriage
bed be undefiled.*" Hebrews 13:4).

Hopefully you'll never be cornered by someone on a date (or in
courtship) that will pressure you to have sex. However, our enemy
rarely comes when we are alert. He also uses sly arguments that may
not be easy to refute if you aren't ready. Consider the following (or
similar) tempting words. What will you do? Here are some helpful
responses suggested by Josh McDowell[114] and others.

"Well, everyone is doing it!"
"Well, it shouldn't be too hard for you to find somebody else who is.
I'm not!"

"If you loved me you would!"
"If you really loved me, you wouldn't ask."

"Why wait for marriage? It's just a piece of paper."
"If it's just a piece of paper to you before marriage, that's all it will
be to you after marriage. Marriage means more to God and to me."

"We need to see if we're compatible."
"Anyone can have sex. That doesn't make them compatible. Love
that waits for marriage is someone compatible for me."

110   This section is mainly on temptations you may face in courtship or dating. Read further
for a whole chapter on temptation in general.
111   Matthew 6:13
112   Psalm 23:3
113   2 Corinthians 10:5
114   Josh McDowell, The Bare Facts: 39 Questions Your Parents Hope You Never Ask About
Sex, 2011

"You'll become a real man."
"Dogs have sex all the time. Is that how they can become men?"

"If you don't do it, you don't love me."
"If you loved me, you wouldn't ask. You're telling me you don't love me. You're just in heat."

Finally, memorize scripture *before* you get into the heat of a strong temptation. If that's how Jesus did it and overcame satan, do you have a better idea? Here is an excellent verse for memory:

*"No temptation has overtaken you that is not common to man. God is faithful, and he will not let you be tempted beyond your ability, but with the temptation he will also provide the way of escape, that you may be able to endure it."*[115]

Smart courtship is a recipe for a happy marriage. Your parents and God are on your side. Follow His lead to steer clear of temptation or mistakes and you will be blessed beyond all you can ask or imagine.[116]

### THINGS TO THINK ABOUT AND TALK OVER

• *Re-read the scripture below the temptation subsection. What do you think the proverb means about holding fire to one's chest? Also, look again at the chapter verse. For what reasons do you think Rebekah covered herself when she met Isaac for the first time? (She was not covered with her non-relative escort, so it cannot simply be cultural covering around men.) What do you think about "smart courtship"? What do you think it should look like? Consider issues like dress, who should initiate courtship, where you might go or what you might do while you get to know each other more and seek God's direction.*

• *What kinds of strategies do you have to keep yourself from temptation?*

• *What are the qualities you would like in a spouse? Write them down in a list, starting with the most important. Put an asterisk (\*) by the ones you will not compromise on. Share your list with*

115  1 Corinthians 10:13
116  Ephesians 3:30

*your parents.*

- *Look at the list you made and consider the characteristics that are mutually admirable for both men and women. How well are you doing on becoming the person someone else would like to marry? After making your list for your potential spouse, grade yourself on each area from 1 to 10 (1 = doing very poorly, 10 = doing very well here). What steps can you take to grow in the areas you need to?*

# DECIDING ON MARRIAGE

*But seek first the kingdom of God and his righteousness, and all these things will be added to you.* [117]

Marriage is a picture of God's love for His people.[118] Because of that tremendously important image, your expectations for your future spouse and your ability to be a good spouse should be extremely high. At the same time, grace must be an essential foundation of a lifetime commitment. The decision of if and whom you will marry is second in importance only to your decision to let God lead your life or not. The kind of person you marry will largely determine where you will live, what kind of peace (or strife) you'll experience at home, kids and grandchildren you will enjoy (or be frustrated by), and how you will serve God (or not). Your spouse's family and friends will also be a tremendous influence on you, so include them fully in your picture of what life will look like as a married couple. Because marriage is so important, this chapter will be longer than most. I hope you'll let these ideas soak into you long before you ever have a first date.

As you wrestle through the decision to marry another very imperfect person like yourself, I think it is helpful to ask several questions. Answer them honestly, not just as you think they should be answered! There is too much at stake to not separate truth from fiction.

As in every important decision — especially regarding your decision to marry or remain single — put God's Kingdom and His righteousness first. If you do, no matter what you decide, you can move forward with confidence and joy.

### AM I TRUSTING GOD TO GUIDE THIS DECISION? WHAT DO I THINK THE HOLY SPIRIT IS SAYING?

*If any of you lacks wisdom, you should ask God, who gives generously to all without finding fault, and it will be given to you. But when you ask, you must believe and not doubt, because the one who doubts is like a wave of the sea, blown and tossed by the wind.* [119]

117  Matthew 6:33
118  Revelation 19:6-9, Ephesians 5:25-33
119  James 1:5-6

Your Father in heaven cares for you far more than I ever could, and I love you like crazy! If you came to me to ask my opinion about your potential marriage, there's no doubt I would do my very best to help you decide. How much more will your heavenly Father help! Don't doubt He will lead you if you approach Him with an open heart and an intent to put Him first.

Have you heard God speak on the matter? I felt that even before I dated your mother (this was before I learned much about courtship), I heard God say, "Have you considered my servant, Luda?" Well, I had, but not seriously since she had been dating someone else. Once I felt the Lord's direction, I asked her out. As we got to know each other and I felt she would be a great wife and mother, I asked God if we could or should marry. Although I didn't hear a clear voice, my sense was that His blessing was on our union. Finally, as we were going through a rough time after I'd proposed, I didn't hear a voice, but felt a strong conviction from the Holy Spirit that I was the "chief of all sinners."[120] This great sinner was saved by grace. How much more should I embrace your mother, even though she had failures, as well?

As you can see, the Lord "spoke" in different ways as I felt Him lead us to the altar. Indeed, marriage is an altar where you need to learn to die to yourself if you are going to worship God with your life. If you want to learn more about recognizing God's voice, jump forward to the chapter "Hearing God's Voice."

Of course, to hear God's voice, you generally need to find a quiet place where you will not be distracted for an extended time. Even if you believe the answer is going to clearly be "yes," consider that your life is about to radically change. Reflect and ask questions. Where God has led you in passion to serve? Where are your strengths? Where are your weaknesses? Does the person you are courting or dating complement those areas well or poorly? (Be honest!) What unique vision He would want us to embrace as a new family? Take a weekend to go camping or find a remote retreat and leave your cell phone and computer in your car or at home. Tell a few close friends what you are doing and ask for their prayers. Consider fasting for a day or more, as fasting sharpens your ability to hear God's voice. Remember Jesus fasted for forty days before He embarked on His public ministry. Your marriage — if God leads

120  1 Timothy 1:15

you into it — will be one of the most important ministries you will have in this life. Your love for your spouse should reflect the same love God has for His people, which is forbearing, sacrificial, and unending.

If you've read this book to this point, you clearly know that God unconditionally and immeasurably loves you. He created the entire universe and sustains everything by the power of His word.[121] He knows more about you than you do and still loves you.[122] If you have any anxiety, especially a decision about if or whom to marry, listen carefully to Jesus' words:

*"...do not be anxious about your life . . . But seek first the kingdom of God and his righteousness, and all these things will be added to you."*[123]

When He says, "All these things" Jesus is referring to worries about clothing, food, or drink. How much more must God care about something like your choice of a husband or wife! So don't be anxious.

As you pray (and I hope fast) about this decision to marry someone special, are you willing to hear "No" or "Not yet" from God? If not, why are you asking Him? If you are really going to let God be God in your life, you must be willing to accept the answer "No" or "Wait."

Another spoiler alert: If God is not the center of your life, you *should* be very anxious. Although God can be gracious to you, most people who choose to walk outside of God's love, advice, and protection often make decisions that they regret for years — and sometimes will for the rest of their lives. My best advice would be not to get married before you've given Him control. That may sound harsh, but if you read on, I think you'll understand. If your life isn't controlled by the love of God, you cannot help but pull someone whom you care for (and your future children) into your brokenness.

---

121  Hebrews 1:3, Colossians 1:15-17
122  Before a word is on my tongue you, Lord, know it completely. Psalm 139:4
123  Matthew 6:25 and 33

Is that what you really want for someone you love enough to marry? First, give your life *completely* to Christ. Then He will enable you to give yourself fully to the people you love, just as Jesus did.

Here's another question you may want to ponder regarding the possibility of marriage as you seek to put God first: *Will our union glorify God more than if we stay apart?* Think and pray very carefully through the answer. Remember God is for you and wants your highest joy for all eternity. That kind of joy can only be found in Him and is completed by putting Him first.

## DOES THIS PERSON WHOM I WANT TO MARRY LOVE GOD MORE THAN ME OR ANYONE?

For many people, if the answer were "yes" they would run away as quickly as possible. "I want to be first in my husband's life!" The problem with a husband (or wife) that puts their future wife (or husband) above God is that eventually there will always be friction, frustration, or boredom between spouses. Where does the husband then turn for his counsel, relief, or escape? Will it be his guy friends, work, sports, or another woman? You will have little security when you fall from your pedestal. If he puts you above God in your dating life, you have become a little god to him. We don't make very good gods. On the other hand, if you know his life is built on his relationship with God, he should love you as he has been loved — unconditionally and lavishly with grace, sacrifice, and ready forgiveness. With that kind of husband you know that when you let him down, lose your temper, or even just grow old, he will always be with you because God is his rock.

One of my favorite stories of courtship comes from our friends Erik and Amber. They met at a graduation party for a friend and immediately liked one another. Amber said she was especially drawn to Erik's servant heart as he went around the party cleaning up cups and plates. Their fondness grew as they spent time together but the biggest obstacle was that Amber felt called to a different ministry focus. She was torn but wanted to put that call first. Because of her strong feelings for Erik, Amber went to her godly father, David, to seek his advice. David loves the Lord, is incredibly joyful, and is a fitness enthusiast. He wisely said, "Amber, you run your race for God. One day, you will look around to see who is running with you. If there is a young man there by your side, he will be the one for you." It was a challenging couple of years as Amber ran after God, prayed for God's will and His kingdom. Erik was also honorably and independently seeking God in his life. In the end, Amber felt released from her ministry focus. Sovereignly and powerfully, the Lord led them back together. As I'm writing this, they have an excellent marriage with four wonderful children.

Paul wrote, "Do not be unequally yoked with unbelievers."[124] Can you picture a farmer trying to plow his fields with two cows yoked together, pulling a plow? One is listening to his master, trying to pull straight and strong. The other keeps pulling right or left and sits down when he gets tired. That field will look like a preschool drawing! Truthfully, I know that neither you nor the person you are considering for marriage has a perfect love for God and puts Him first in all things. But is the general direction of life for you and your beloved to put God first? Do you have a vision of ministry together — how you will pour out your lives for others and for God's glory? Or is your dating life more about each other?

One last thought on being equally yoked. I believe this goes beyond just matching up two believers. Picture, if you can, ministry in married life where you are always by yourself. Your spouse either has her own separate place to do ministry or isn't interested in yours. Picture yourself in a vibrant church or Bible study, but your spouse doesn't go because the people there ask too many personal questions, the music is too loud, or they want to stay home to catch the football game. Go further in the future and imagine the Sunday morning struggle of where to take the kids. You want to go to a vibrant church with teaching from God's Word. Your spouse wants the kids to go to his or her church where there is nice psychology and "inclusive" teaching that there are many ways to God besides Jesus. Your bar of being "equally yoked" should be set well above the test of simply, "Is he a Christian?"

If the person you are dating loves God more than they love you, paradoxically, you've found the best potential spouse of all! A person who loves God most of all is the one who is able to follow Jesus' footsteps and pour their lives out for others, even to the point of death. Of course, you want to be that kind of person, as well, if you want to marry that kind of person.

124  2 Corinthians 6:14

## AM I CONTENT AS A SINGLE?
## OR DO I FEEL PERSISTENTLY LONELY?

Many people have tried to escape feelings of loneliness by getting married. Here's what I've observed:

1 Lonely Single Person + 1 Lonely Single Person
= 2 Lonely Married People

1 Contented Single Person + 1 Contented Single Person
= 2 Contented Married People

Some of the most lonely and discontented people I know are *married* people. They are frustrated with themselves, regret their decision and feel "stuck" with someone who doesn't talk or talks too much, has gas, got fat, isn't interested in sex, is too bossy, or doesn't spend much time with the kids! Sound like anyone you know? If you want to become content, God will teach you how.[125] Once you become content with God in every circumstance, you will find consistent joy and will be much more likely to attract the same kind of person for marriage.

I've had several friends jump out of singleness because they feel lonely, and many of them quote God from Genesis, "It is not good that man should be alone."[126] But remember, this was at a time when there were no humans on the earth, except Adam. If singleness were bad in general and promoted loneliness, Jesus and Paul were sad men, indeed, not to have married! I can tell you that at no time in my life, after Jesus broke through my dead heart, have I ever been lonely. First, He gave me a whole new family — more brothers and sisters than I ever could have dreamed of. Second and best of all, He gave me Himself. No matter where I go on earth, He is always there and with me.[127] I am never alone. That is the great joy of Immanuel, "God with us."[128]

### WHAT DO YOUR PARENTS THINK?

Sometimes you may think that your mom and dad are out of touch. And that may be true! However, the commandment to honor parents didn't come with the condition that they be perfect or that honor

---

125   Philippians 4:11-13
126   Genesis 2:18
127   Psalm 139:9-10
128   Matthew 1;23, Isaiah 7:14

stops at a certain age. They are the parents God gave you. Trust the Lord to work through them (unless they tell you to do something unbiblical). Proverbs tells us, *"The king's heart is a stream of water in the hand of the Lord; he turns it wherever he will."*[129] If God can direct the heart of a king wherever He wants, can't He direct your parents' hearts? Even if one or more parents are not Christ-followers, God can and will direct their advice. Blessing will follow if you honor them. That may be easier said than done when the moment comes.

When I was dating my first serious girlfriend as a young believer in God, I asked my parents what they thought about us getting married. They were reluctant to say anything, but I asked. They felt we weren't a good match. I didn't like their reasons but followed their advice and held off from asking her to marry me. In the end, I did see that we had some challenging differences and I don't think we were so well-suited. I'm glad I followed their advice, because it allowed me to meet your mother!

Let me give you another wonderful example. I had a close roommate at seminary who was from Cambodia, Saul Paul Kes. He was dating a phenomenal young lady from another culture, something generally taboo from her background. At that time, Alison's parents were not believers and weren't happy to hear any talk about marriage plans. They couldn't freely give their consent and blessing. I shared my story and Proverbs 21:1 with Saul. He agreed and, by faith, decided to wait. They waited *two years*. In the end, her parents gave their approval enthusiastically because this young couple had not only respected her parents' wishes, but he had taken the time to get to know them. Today, he is even closer to them in friendship than perhaps their own daughter. They are not yet believers, but became open to the Lord because of how their daughter and future son-in-law showed restraint, love, and respect. They have a great testimony because they chose to walk by faith as they believed God's Word.

### WHAT DO YOUR SPIRITUAL LEADERS, SIBLINGS, AND JESUS-FOLLOWING FRIENDS THINK?

*"Where there is no guidance, a people falls, but in an abundance of counselors there is safety."*[130] Who knows you best? God has given us

129 Proverbs 21:1
130 Proverbs 11:14

pastors, brothers, sisters, and friends in Christ to help us. I've known many relatives and friends who have held their tongues when they had a strong opinion about the poor marriage choice of someone dear to them. They didn't want to risk any future relationship by being critical. You may have to be the one to initiate the conversation with a trusted counselor. "What do you think? I love Johnny, but do you think he is a good choice for me?" Listen carefully and don't show frustration if their answer is not the one you want to hear! Of course, you may face a myriad of opinions and various motivations from pure to putrid. God will help you sort through them. But you should hear a consistent positive message from your most trusted confidants before pressing on to lifelong vows.

### CAN I SEE MYSELF GROWING OLD WITH THIS PERSON?

It's one thing to be excited about a vibrant and handsome young man or a beautiful, energetic woman in her youth. But look at the one you love and try to picture them in sixty years with wrinkles, a hunched back, and getting around the house with a walker. Remember, you will look the same! Will you love each other then? Hopefully, you will have a lifetime of memories, a quiver full of children, and more grandchildren than you can count (Lord willing).

Marriage should be one of the most wonderful experiences of life, a precious gift from God. You may feel some fear and that is probably healthy. More than anything, remember that God is for you and His plans for you are good. As you seek his kingdom first, trusting in His love, you can be sure He will guide your footsteps.

### THINGS TO THINK ABOUT AND TALK OVER:

- *Would you add or remove any questions in my list for marriage? Would it be more helpful to think about these things before you ever begin dating or courting someone?*

- *Our friends' children in the Petersen family made a promise to each other that they would not marry someone unless their siblings agreed it was a good match. Would you make that vow to anyone? If so, to whom?*

THE BIG PICTURE

# KNOWING GOD'S WILL

*"Delight yourself in the LORD,*
*and he will give you the desires of your heart."*[131]

Decisions, decisions! The last chapter was about one of the toughest decisions you may ever make: whom you will marry. If you are like most people, making a decision is tough. I'm not talking about what to have for breakfast, although some people really struggle with simple decisions like that. I am talking about questions like: *Where should I go to college or should I go at all? Where should I go to church? What kind of work should I look for?* Of course, if you are in love with God, you'll want Him in every conversation and desire to follow His leading. But how can you know what He wants?

ONE OF THE BEST PIECES OF ADVICE I COULD EVER GIVE YOU, NOT ONLY FOR KNOWING GOD'S WILL, BUT JUST FOR LIVING LIFE TO THE FULLEST, IS TO DELIGHT YOURSELF IN HIM.

If you remember the chapter on "The Greatest Joy of All," I tried to show you that there is no greater joy than being in love with God Himself.

THERE'S A CLEAR LINE CONNECTING THAT PASSION AND JOY FOR GOD TO KNOWING HIS WILL.

The italicized scripture above from Psalms 37:4 blew that truth deep into my soul.

You might think, "Okay, delight myself in the LORD and I can get anything I want? Like a mansion or a new car?" But if your delight is truly in God, will you place a premium on getting a swank house or a hot car? Probably not! If you are delighting in God, your delights will align with His delights, like sinners turning to Him for life, embracing righteousness and holiness, living in love and sacrifice for others, laying up treasures in heaven rather than on earth. In fact, I believe this Psalmist is telling us that God will actually give or put into people the desires we *should* have when He becomes our delight. When that happens, it's easy to understand the following verse:

131  Psalm 37:4

*"Commit your works to the LORD and your plans will be established."*[132]

The person who commits their plans fully to God from their heart (not for their personal gain) is someone who deeply loves God. Their plans will be ones that they hope will bring honor and joy to Him. Will not their Father in heaven see to it that this kind of person succeeds in their efforts? Of course, we know God may redirect the footsteps of His children in their effort to serve and love Him. James tells us to always qualify our plans with "if it's the Lord's will, we will live and do this or do that."[133] God is the only one with the "view from above" that is eternal in perspective. Even if we misstep in our limited perspective, God can still give and establish the unique plans we dream of for His sake and our joy.

In God's grace, He has prepared special works for us even in advance of our knowledge of Him.[134] Those works and the path to them won't be hard to find if we seek God and keep growing in love with Him. How can we tell if we are keeping on track? In the last chapter, we thought about how to make a good decision on a mate for life and asked questions that you can generalize for other major decisions:

- *Am I trusting in God to guide and give me wisdom?*
- *Is my goal to love and honor God by the outcome of my decision?*
- *Am I willing to hear "No" or "Not now" from God?*
- *Am I content in God and delighting in Him today?*
- *What do wise people tell me, particularly those who are close to God and me?*

If the answers to any of the first four questions is "no," then take time today to make it right. If you are not delighting in God, it may take time to change; however, you can start now. Talk to God. Ask forgiveness. Open His Word, perhaps to the Psalms or the book of John. Listen to some good worship music and sermons about drawing close to God, His amazing love, and His plan to finish the good work He started in you before the first day you believed.[135]

---

132  Proverbs 16:3
133  James 4:15
134  Ephesians 2:10
135  Philippians 1:6

If the answer to the last question about wise advisers is "I don't have any," don't move another inch forward before you get good counsel (unless the biblical answer is clear). Then intentionally set about cultivating some relationships with mature Christians.

As you seek advice, be completely honest. I knew a Christian in her late teens who was seeking advice from a pastor but she wasn't totally open with him. She wanted his blessing to marry. The pastor's first question was, "Have your parents given their blessing?" Her answer was a vague "yes." The second question was, "Is he a believer?" She hesitated, indicating he was a cultural Christian but open to more. After further discussion, the pastor advised her not to marry. However, she did not tell him that she was pregnant with the young man's child. How could the pastor give her sound advice without the full picture? The pressure of a pregnancy does not require marriage. Regrettably, they married, the young man turned completely away from God and became very abusive. They divorced after only a few years. Yes, mercifully there are a few examples of marriages starting with an unpromising foundation which become good over time. Those are rare exceptions. However, the point of this story is that this young lady could have spared herself much sorrow if she had been completely honest and open while seeking help.

If you are ever living in opposition to God or hiding sin, don't make any critical life decisions! It's not even enough to repent, as important as that is. You need to find the root of how you got to where you are. You need heart surgery and and recovery. That takes time. I would never encourage a couple who have gotten pregnant or engaged in sex while dating to go ahead with marriage. Without deep repentance, followed by a significant season (six months or more) of self-control and seeking God, they are very likely to multiply their pain by pressing into marriage. The reasons are many, but these stand out: first, they are immature, and show a weak faith in God. Both are recipes for a difficult marriage. Second, the lack of self-control before marriage can easily translate into a lack of trust after marriage. "If we weren't faithful to God before we got married, why do I think my spouse is faithful to me now?"

Likewise, be cautious about putting yourself into any position where others will depend on you if you have demonstrated unfaithfulness in some other areas of importance in your life. That doesn't mean you shouldn't stretch yourself when God and others encourage you to. However, keep in mind that others will depend on you if you step into a position that requires experienced maturity and commitment. More importantly, God's reputation expressed by your faithfulness (or lack of it) is also likely on the line. Don't bluff. Be faithful in small areas before stepping into larger ones.[136]

## DON'T LOOK BACK

Once you've made your decision based on your best understanding of God's will, try not to look back. In the Air Force, hard lessons learned from aircraft accidents taught us that pilots who vacillate between one course of action and another during an emergency can often end up in disaster. Only rarely is it wise for pilots to change their decision: when it becomes *extremely obvious* they chose the wrong course of action. But the Scriptures warn us not to put our hand to the plow of God's work and look back[137] or doubt His provision of wisdom.[138] I believe that even if you didn't make the best possible decision, if you did it with the intent to glorify and honor God, He will honor and bless your path.

## AFTER PRAYER, COUNSEL, AND LEADING, MOVE FORWARD!

Many, if not most, decisions in life are time sensitive. That is, a window is only open for a time — occasionally, a short one. Don't let fear paralyze you into putting off a timely decision out of concern that you may make a wrong choice. But equally, don't enter important decisions on impulse, without using the above questions to assess your best choice.

## FINAL ADVICE: BE INTIMATE WITH GOD'S WORD

We must make choices every day. Some of them are critical and require careful consideration. Many others, even some critical ones, may take no thought at all if we are daily reading God's Word. A temptation to sin sexually, cheat financially, or steal doesn't require much thought for a young man or woman who is soaked in God's truth. Most of our words and decisions probably come without much forethought. Our instinctive reaction to the opportunities that

---

136  Luke 16:10-12
137  Luke 9:62
138  James 1:6-7

present themselves may seem random. However, they are usually the overflow of where we have spent the most time. May the majority of your reflective time be found in God's Word and in His presence.

*"God's Word is a lamp unto my feet, a light unto my path."*[139]

A dear friend, Elizabeth Wietholter, gave me good advice when I was at an important juncture in my life. I remember an intense struggle trying to guess what was at the end of either road I might choose if I left my life of twelve years in the Air Force either for cross-cultural ministry or to stay in for retirement and then pursue vocational ministry. She said, "Looking at God's will is a little like looking through a long tunnel where you can see a small light at the end. The light shows the direction but doesn't give details. If you could actually go there and see what the end looks like, you would probably do one of two things. You'd be so excited to get there that you'd miss all the important stops of ministry and learning along the way as you tried to quickly get there. Or, the end could be so frightening or unpleasant (like a slow death from brain cancer) that you might refuse to take the path God is leading you on."[140] In the quote above from Psalm 119, the author is writing about lights for traveling at night in ancient times on Roman roads. Each ankle had a small oil lantern that would light about three feet or one meter in diameter around a walker's foot, just enough to help them take one more step without falling into a hole or tripping on a rock. God's Word is like those oil lamps. As we prayerfully memorize and meditate on His truth, His Word, God will lead us one step at a time until we safely get to the destination He desires.[141]

If you remain unsure of a right decision (or maybe are not sure what the right question is!), do what you know to be right from God's Word for now and wait on Him. Paul gave his friends three specific actions for everyone: *"Rejoice always, pray continually, give thanks in all circumstances; for this is God's will for you in Christ Jesus."*[142] Even before you ask God for a specific instruction, work on fulfilling His "general" instructions clearly revealed here and in other verses. Do you see how insulting to God this can be if we are

---

139  Psalm 119:105
140  In an unusual exception to the "end rarely revealed by God," Peter was told that his life's end would be an unpleasant execution. But Jesus had become everything to Peter. Although his own strength was too small to embrace the cross, God could and would enable Peter to go through it. (Matthew 26:75, John 21:18-19)
141  "Safely" means "in the center of God's will," which may include martyrdom!
142  1 Thessalonians 5:16-18

not walking in general obedience but are asking for wisdom and direction in specific areas? Imagine coming to me, urgently wanting advice for a college choice or a dating situation after you had been disrespectful to your mother. Would I be inclined to carefully help you work through an intricate, thoughtful decision when you were clearly in the wrong with someone I love?

Walk intimately and joyfully with God. Your decision-making process will be so much easier and more peaceful. Rest in God's great power, love, and presence. He is crazy about you and will not only show you the way but will take you there Himself.

THINGS TO THINK ABOUT AND TALK OVER:

- *How are you fulfilling your daily "will of God" from 1 Thessalonians . . . rejoicing, praying continually, and giving thanks always? What would help you improve?*

- *What do you do to discipline yourself in order to hear God better? If you haven't yet, do you think God would say to add fasting, scripture memory, and meditation to your life?*

- *What general advice would you give to a friend seeking God's direction in life?*

- *What can you do in advance to prepare yourself for coming decisions in life that you may know little or nothing about?*

THE BIG PICTURE

# GOD'S CALLING

*"For we are God's handiwork, created in Christ Jesus to do good works, which God prepared in advance for us to do."*[143]

In 1993 I was tremendously enjoying life in Panama. I was assigned to be the check pilot for all American Embassy airplanes in Central and South America, a job I could hardly have imagined existed, let alone have conceived of actually doing it myself! I'd learned enough Spanish to share the love of Christ everywhere I traveled. I was enjoying deep friendships in our singles group and many others at Crossroads Bible Church and in the community. Other than wishing to be married, I couldn't have dreamed of a better life.

Seven years earlier, I'd felt "the call" to missions during a church service at Life Center in Tacoma.[144] We listened to guest speakers like Mark and Huldah Buntain living in Calcutta, who shared the joys of caring for others and bringing the good news to people who had never heard of Jesus. I was excited to feel God was calling me to be a missionary. Since I loved flying, other cultures, and Latin America in particular, I dreamed of becoming a missionary pilot in a Spanish-speaking country. However, in 1987 I still "owed" the government five more years of service for my education. So I found myself in a situation similar to Paul, who made tents while serving the Lord. Instead of making tents, I was flying airplanes in lands from the Strait of Magellan to Mexico City.

Once my Air Force commitment finished, I was at a distinct crossroads. Should I stay in the Air Force, where I was very thoroughly enjoying serving both my friends in Panama and others throughout Latin America? Or should I go to Bible school to become a missionary pilot?

What about you? Is God calling you to a specific, highly focused ministry? Of course, everything we do should be for God's glory, but is there an area He wants you to concentrate on?[145] The possibilities

---

143  Ephesians 2:10
144  "Missions" is from a Latin word that means "sent." Because a minority of missionaries have poorly conducted themselves, the world has gained some negative connotations. It's also not very descriptive. I prefer "cross-cultural ministry" instead.
145  1 Corinthians 10:31

are endless: the abolition of global slavery, reforming politics, ecology, helping deaf people, child evangelism, or Bible translation for an unreached group. I believe all of us are commanded to play some role in reaching those who have never heard the good news of the Messiah, but maybe He wants you to use your gifts to reach a distinct, untouched group.

"CALLING" IN THE BIBLE

There are two different ways in the Bible and in English we use the word calling. In the first way and generally how use it in English, Americans mean a specific ministry based on gifts, passions, and usually a sense of God's leading. It may be your primary vocation (source of support), like a nurse caring for the sick in Calcutta. Sometimes our primary ministry calling may be separate from vocation, like a man who leads an excellent Bible study for 20 years but he works as an accountant. More often when the Bible translates God's call or calling, it refers to God's bidding to be or become His children, both to the Jewish people as a whole or individuals responding in faith to Christ.[146] This chapter, however, is primarily about first kind of calling we usually understand as a vocational, ministry assignment. Even though not often translated that way, the concept is throughout the Bible. Don't let that distract you. Words like *trinity, omniscience, omnipotence*, and *missions* are not in the Bible at all, but they are very helpful to describe what is clearly there. Examples of an individual, specific "calling" from God are everywhere in the Scriptures from Noah and Moses to four certain fishermen by the Sea of Galilee.[147]

Our calling may change over our lifetime several times. It goes without saying that we are all called to fulfill God's "general will," walking foremost in love with Him and loving others.[148] But most of us rightly ask, "How can I best do that with the gifts and passions I believe God has given me?" What does God Himself want me to do at this time in history? Let's look at what the Bible says about this kind of calling.

Paul tells us that God has prepared "good works" for us to do. *"For*

146  e.g. Romans 11:29, 2 Thessalonians 1:11, Hebrews 3:1, Philippians 3:14, 2 Peter 1:10
147  I found it interesting as I thought about this subject that the book of Numbers (normally considered "dry") had details about the specific calling of thousands of Levites to care for particular aspects of the temple.
148  1 Thessalonians 5:16-18, Matthew 22:36-40

*we are his workmanship, created in Christ Jesus for good works, which God prepared beforehand, that we should walk in them.*[149] Notice Paul adds the words *"which God prepared beforehand,"* showing that He had something specific and good for us to do before we even came to know Him as Savior. Should that surprise us? God is the most creative Being in the whole universe and beyond. Would the pinnacle of His creation — human beings made in His likeness, each one unique — not have been created for a special purpose during their time on earth? Paul draws a picture for us in Romans of God as an artist, a potter.[150] Every potter makes many different kinds of pots, depending on what he wants and needs, some perhaps as fine china and some for flower pots. Switching roles from what the potter intended would seem silly or even insulting (picture a waiter at an expensive restaurant putting salmon into a clay flower pot for a distinguished guest!)

Paul told his friends in Galatia that he was called before he was born to preach to non-Jews (Gentiles). *" . . . . He who had set me apart before I was born, and who called me by his grace, was pleased to reveal His Son to me, in order that I might preach him among the Gentiles . . . ."*[151]

A young Jeremiah heard something very similar from God about his calling as a prophet, *"Before I formed you in the womb I knew you, and before you were born I consecrated you; I appointed you a prophet to the nations."*[152]

David, whose highest calling was arguably to be the best king of Israel before Jesus, had very similar words. *"You formed my inward parts; you knitted me together in my mother's womb. . . . Your eyes saw my unformed substance; in your book were written, every one of them, the days that were formed for me, when as yet there was none of them."*[153] Without considering important questions of predestination right now, notice that David says by the inspiration of the Holy Spirit that all the days formed for him were written in God's book before David was even born. Those days included his unlikely anointing as king in spite of being a boy and the youngest son in his family, his victory over Goliath, David's righteous

---

149   Ephesians 2:8
150   Romans 9:20-24
151   Galatians 1:15-16
152   Jeremiah 1:5
153   Psalm 139:13 and 16

suffering under Saul's persecution, and finally David's installation as king.

Of course, our Lord Jesus had several, very specific callings, one as the firstborn among many brothers (i.e., "us" or all born-from-above Christ followers).[154] For us, probably Jesus' most important calling was *before the birth of the world* to be the Lamb slain — for our sins — so that our names would be written in His book of life.[155] If that is how God mapped out the life of Jesus, would it not make sense (like David said in Psalm 139) that God has mapped out our lives before one of them came into being? If we walk in step with God's Spirit, sacrificing everything for His glory, we can joyfully know we will discover His amazing plan for our lives.[156]

### INNATE GIFTS AND DESIRES

After the cross, the Bible reports that when Jesus *"ascended on high he led a host of captives, and he gave gifts to men."*[157] Some of those gifts enabled people to become *"apostles, the prophets, the evangelists, the shepherds and teachers."* [158]

Most of us love exchanging gifts at Christmas. The best gifts are those from the people who love us the most. Imagine what your gifts from God are! We will look at discovering your gifts in another chapter. But for now, consider the things you enjoy, whether it's writing, singing, building Legos, playing violin, reading to your baby brother, building robots, or helping at Sunday School. What else gets you excited that you haven't tried yet? Flying airplanes, making movies, fixing teeth, or scuba diving? Without getting overly concerned about differentiating the definition talents, desires, skills, dreams or spiritual gifts, know that all of these things blend with your growing experiences will shape your calling when the Holy Spirit leads.

Consider two guys in the Bible you've probably never heard of: Oholiab and Bezalel.[159] They were two slaves working for Pharaoh about 3,400 years ago. God made them intelligent and very skilled in

154  Romans 8:29
155  Revelation 13:8
156  Romans 12:2
157  Ephesians 4:8
158  Ephesians 4:10
159  Exodus 31

all kinds of art from ornate wood and stone carving to working with metals like gold, silver, and bronze. You might ask, "What does all that have to do with God's calling?" Oholiab and Bezalel probably asked the same question as slaves! But once they were free, God filled them with His Holy Spirit. After wandering in the desert for some time, God gave Moses some instructions about building a place to worship. Now all of their training, skills, and passions made perfect sense. God told Moses that He called Oholiab and Bezalel by name and said, "*I have filled [them] with the Spirit of God, with ability and intelligence, with knowledge and all craftsmanship*" so that they could make some of the most important art for worship that the world has ever known.[160]

Your journey to that sweet spot where God is using your gifts, skills, and passions in a powerful way for His glory and your joy may take a while. For now, pray for direction and pursue learning about the things you enjoy or dream of.

## GET EXPOSURE AND PRAY

A wise person once said, "You can't steer a ship that isn't moving." Once you get moving forward, God can direct your path. Your grandpa showed up for studies at West Point in 1951. All of the freshmen or "plebes" were ordered to try out for choir. The choir director listened to each one and declared after a few notes, "You, sing in the choir!" or "You, sing in the shower!" Grandpa got to sing in the choir and eventually got to hear a young Billy Graham in New York City because of it. Many years later, I went to a different academy. I was told singing in the shower was the best place for me! So you will try and either succeed or fail at many things in life before you discover what you are gifted in and what you enjoy. Don't let course corrections make you feel like you are a failure. God is most likely helping you not to waste time in a certain area.

I can remember after I got saved that I had a voracious appetite to read God's Word and talk to people about what I was learning. Our singles pastor took note and asked me to lead a Bible study. I was a little apprehensive, but agreed. Every time I taught, although I was shaking nervously, I felt the power of the Holy Spirit fill me. I felt certain He was directing both my preparation and during our discussions. The members of our group were enthusiastic and

160   verse 3

affirmed that they felt like they were growing and understanding so much more during our times together. My ship was moving and I could feel the wind of the Lord's direction and pleasure.

Lastly, the most important part of discovering your calling is prayer. I was terribly torn about possibly leaving the life and ministry I had known in the Air Force. I filled two pages of notes with the potential positives and negatives of either path, but couldn't discern which would be better. I was praying in earnest one day and felt like God told me, "There are over one billion people who go by the name 'Muslim' and they don't know Me. I am returning soon and want them to to come to Me." Based on my passions and my experience of life in Iran and around the world, I made the decision to launch into the unknown, leave the Air Force, and get more schooling at Columbia Bible College and Seminary (CBCS).

CBCS, which later became Columbia International University (CIU), was known as a school focused on discipling and missions. In my first year, I was getting plenty of exposure to things I'd never known before and there were many opportunities for prayer. Two people groups were promoted on campus by the student missions group for prayer: the Kazakhs and the Javanese, both of whom I'd never heard of. One day, I was praying for the Kazakhs and felt the Lord say to me, "I don't want you just to pray for them but to go." I thought to myself, "How can I go?" But there was an English team going that summer from campus, so I went to talk to the director of the TEFL department, Dr. Nancy Cheek. She was polite but doubtful that I would have a place on the team. After a week or two (and some research on who this young man was who was asking to join the team), she said, "If you would like to go, you may." That summer was one of the most amazing times of my life. We went to over five countries that were completely closed just a few years earlier. Many, many people from kids to grandparents were open to the good news of Jesus, more than I had seen anywhere in my lifetime.[161] I came back and knew this was where I wanted to live and

161   In my first interview with Dr. Cheek, she asked what I could do. I said in jest, "I can fly airplanes." She quipped back, "I don't think we need any of those." I answered, "I can also carry luggage." She raised an eyebrow, said, "We'll see," and told me later that she began to research to decide if it was worth the risk to take me. Her husband, Ed Cheek, was a prayer warrior and met with several students — including me — weekly for some intense times of intercession. During our first week in Kazakhstan, my fellow teammates who were conducting English classes were busy testing their students for placement. Ed grabbed me to go with him on a survey of Central Asia to see what God might open up. Without visas or any specific plan, we managed to go to Uzbekistan (Tashkent and Samarkand), Turkmenistan, and Tajikistan.

serve God for 20 to 25 years. If brain cancer hadn't been ordered into my life by our loving Father, I would probably still be there. But God in His perfect will knows how long a calling will last.

For most people God's calling is an evolving, lifelong process. Keep praying and seeking opportunities to serve. If you live to be 80, your calling will look different than when you were 25 or 50. Joy is found in the journey if you don't look at a calling as *yours*. Ministry is not primarily about you. *God's purpose in your ministry assignment is to build up others for their lives of service to God to bring Him glory.*[162] He will be with you, guide you and give you tremendous joy as you help other people in their journey with God.

### THINGS TO THINK ABOUT AND TALK OVER:

- *If you could do anything in life, what would you like to do? What kind of subjects do you want to study? What kind of work? Where do you want to travel? What kind of ministry do you want to do? If you can, list those for which you have the strongest passion. What do you think you need to do to get ready?*

- *Talk to some adults to help you get more exposure in areas you are interested in. They may help you find work, a class, a summer internship, or a time to talk to someone in a career you have an interest in.*

- *What do you think your spiritual gifts are? How can you try them out? Would you be okay to find out that you don't have a gift in one of those areas? Are you content to walk in lifelong holiness and do the hard work to develop and use a new gift you may discover in ministry? How does Jesus' instruction to His disciples, "take up your cross daily," apply in your preparation and calling? What waits for those who choose this path (see Luke 9:23-24)? What waits for those who refuse?*

---

Because of that trip, another team went the following summer to Dushanbe that led to another long-term work and many others going and sharing the love of Christ.

162   see Ephesians 4:12

# SECTION 3

## YOUR HEART
## THE FOUNTAIN OF LIFE

# YOUR HEART
# THE FOUNTAIN OF LIFE

*"Above everything else guard your heart,
because from it flow the springs of life."* [163]

When I lived in Sudan, I noticed that a few houses had large clay jars set in front of their homes beside the dusty road. Some of them had a shaded roof over the jars. I asked what they were for and my friend said, "Oh, because we live in the desert, some people put out clean drinking water as an act of kindness for travelers and workers." We decided to do the same, and many responded with great warmth to such a simple act of caring that made sense in their culture.

Can you imagine walking through a blazing desert, the dust and sand filling your nose and mouth so that they feels like they're filled with a thick, sticky paste? Everything in you yearns for a cup of water. Then you see it! There's an oasis in the distance with a cool pool of freshwater. As you get closer, you realize the oasis is just a mirage, dissolving from reality with every nearing step. Our hearts are like that. We yearn for living water that can only come from God. When we find Him, there is no greater joy and satisfaction. On the other side, the world tells us we can find that water in a physical relationship with someone or in money. We can find it in a prestigious job, a comfortable new home, or a sparkling new car. But the world is filled with people who will tell you that those cisterns were a mirage at best or poisoned at worst.

Has Jesus captured your heart? This section will make little sense to you if He hasn't. Stop and take time to talk to Him.

### HOW DO WE GUARD OUR HEARTS?

In his last known letter on earth, Paul wrote to his dear friend Timothy, *"I have fought the good fight, I have finished the race, I have kept the faith."* [164] What kept Paul fighting well for many years and from losing faith? This is his advice to his young friend:

---

163   Proverbs 4:23
164   2 Timothy 4:7

*"Now in a great house there are not only vessels of gold and silver but also of wood and clay, some for honorable use, some for dishonorable. Therefore, if anyone cleanses himself from what is dishonorable he will be a vessel for honorable use, set apart as holy, useful to the master of the house, ready for every good work. So flee youthful passions and pursue righteousness, faith, love, and peace, along with those who call on the Lord from a pure heart."* [165]

Paul is saying that in your home, you might find some fine china and crystal. You'll also find porcelain for the toilet. Would you like to be china and crystal in God's hands, or the commode? It depends on you! Step one: get the junk cleaned out. Nobody wants to eat a nice meal on a china plate caked with dry food and mold. Confess your sins to God and let Him cleanse your heart. Keep short accounts with God and others regarding your sin. Paul says elsewhere that we should "take every thought captive to obey Christ." [166] You will have plenty of opportunities every day to practice keeping a clean heart.

To be used for honorable purposes isn't an easy path. Paul says you'll have to run away from youthful passions . . . entertainment like late night parties, video games, and movies; fashions like the coolest shoes, pants, or jewelry; controlling your tongue and pride by not gossiping and not "proving" and arguing that you are always right.

You may say, "That is really hard!" I would say, "The end of a life unguarded and controlled by God's love is a *much* harder life. You will die a selfish, lonely person, haunted by the memory of what could have been."

Here's an illustration that might help. If I've not been faithfully exercising, I feel sluggish and unable to do some of the things I like. I don't like the bulge in my belly and I'm more irritable. Getting going again is tough. My best motivations are: one, I love my family and want to be as active and healthy as I can be for you in your youth. Two, I know my body is God's temple. It doesn't show Him much love when I don't take care of the gift He gave me. When I get back into running and exercising regularly, I feel more at peace. I sleep better. I'm more alert mentally and physically. What happens when we don't take care of our physical hearts? Our whole body suffers. Our fingers and toes may tingle. Our head gets dizzy and our

165  2 Timothy 2:20-22
166  2 Corinthians 10:5

chest tightens. Our legs feel weak. I think you'd agree that this kind of life is not the easier one!

What will keep your spiritual heart clean and ready to be used for good? Paul says *"pursue righteousness, faith, love, and peace, along with those who call on the Lord from a pure heart."* Love is the greatest fuel to doing what is right. People will do impossible and crazy things for love. Love never fails.[167] Paul says we have to run after righteousness, faith, love, and peace. They don't fall into our laps from the sky. That kind of pursuit comes from deep study of the Scriptures, keeping your eyes on Jesus, suffering, service, and sacrifice as the Spirit of love leads.

Don't miss one important last point Paul has for us. Do this *"along with those who call on the Lord from a pure heart."* You'll need some good friends and mentors who want the same thing as you do. The times I've been in my best shape physically have been the times when I've had a dedicated partner to workout with. My Christian friends and teachers have been key in my joy and challenge to grow deeper in God. God doesn't normally plan for us to guard our hearts alone.

Keep close guard of your heart, your passions, and desires, my dear children. Wrap them around the truth of God's Word and His heart. If you do, you will live a life of great joy in the midst of great challenge.

THINGS TO THINK ABOUT AND TALK OVER:

- *Be honest. Does God consume most of your passion? (For example, does He occupy most of your thoughts? Do you enjoy talking about Him? To Him?) If so, how can you guard your heart so you won't lose your fire? If not, what happened? Do you need to make some radical changes to guard and protect your heart?*

- *What advice would you give to a friend that is just now starting their life in Christ? How can they guard their heart to stay close to Him? If they fail, what should they do next?*

---

167  1 Corinthians 13:8

# MUSCULAR JOY

*"Rejoice in the Lord always. I will say it again: Rejoice!*
*Let your gentleness be evident to all. The Lord is near."*[168]

Does it seem a bit strange that Paul commands us to be joyful? Keep in mind, Paul was in chains when he penned those words. How could he make such a strange order? In order to understand, let's consider how most people think about happiness.

If you can, picture some of your happiest moments in life. Were they in a field with sunshine and flowers? Or were you riding with your best friend on a roller coaster? For me, some of my best memories would include summers in Oklahoma at my grandparents: enjoying a gully washer in their back field, riding a horse by myself to the Cowboy Hall of Fame, or laughing at my friend, Tom Cotton, who would tie a thread on a horse fly in the milk barn, making him into a flying pet on a leash. Whatever your moments were, wouldn't you like to hold onto those feelings of joy and peace? Unfortunately, those great moments end. Grandma calls us in from playing to eat dinner. People get really sick. A bully says something mean.

Some people might make a distinction between the words *joyful* and *happy*. Although I think they mean just about the same thing, it is helpful to understand there is a temporary kind of shallow happiness and another kind of joy that is a firm part of your character. The first is usually produced by a situation or momentary pleasure. The second deep or abiding happiness includes a peace that is unshakable in times of trouble. Everyone experiences the first kind of happiness. Far fewer get a firm hold of the second, more enduring joy. Let's look at how to get it and keep it.

In the Bible the word *blessed* generally means *happy*. But Jesus says some peculiar things about being happy. In the beginning of Jesus' famous Sermon on the Mount is a part called The Beatitudes. What kind of person does God want you to be? What kinds of "attitudes" does a person have who is blessed or joyful? I'll substitute the word *joyful* for *blessed* in Jesus' words below and you may be surprised:

168  Philippians 4:4-5

*Joyful are the poor in spirit (the humble), for theirs is the kingdom of heaven.*

*Joyful are those who mourn, for they shall be comforted.*

*Joyful are the meek, for they shall inherit the earth.*

*Joyful are those who hunger and thirst for righteousness, for they shall be satisfied.*

*Joyful are the merciful, for they shall receive mercy.*

*Joyful are the pure in heart, for they shall see God.*

*Joyful are the peacemakers, for they shall be called sons of God.*

*Joyful are those who are persecuted for righteousness' sake, for theirs is the kingdom of heaven.*

*Joyful are you when others revile you and persecute you and utter all kinds of evil against you falsely on my account. Rejoice and be glad, for your reward is great in heaven, for so they persecuted the prophets who were before you.*[169]

Doesn't that sound a little crazy to you? You should be joyful if you are humble, mourning, hungering for righteousness in the middle of injustice, and even persecuted? At each point, Jesus follows with the word "for" or *"because"*. Wouldn't you be happy *because* you will get to inherit the kingdom of heaven *and* earth? That's a pretty sizable inheritance! You should be joyful *because* you will get to see justice finally come — complete, full, and absolute everywhere. You should be joyful because you will see God for yourself and are now called His own son or daughter. What if you will be honored for eternity because you are considered through faith to be in the company of great prophets like Moses, Elijah, Isaiah, and Jeremiah? Those are some reasons to be happy forever in spite of the challenging price of entry.

Ultimately, we can enjoy an unmovable happiness and peace when our faith is sure in a mighty, present, and loving God. Joy in hardship comes when we have unshakable confidence in the

169  Matthew 5:3-12

knowledge that He is with me and will work all things together for good.[170] But, like most spiritual strengths, that confidence is initially a small muscle that needs to be exercised if you want to have power when you need it. Most of us would like to be a world-class champion athlete in some sport. But victory doesn't come without a lot of training and exercise. We start with small steps. Let me give you an example of how to exercise your muscle for happiness.

When you were small, we taught you from 1 Thessalonians 5:8 to "give thanks in all circumstances." It's easy to be happy and give thanks when the weather is beautiful and everything is going your way. But what happens when an accident happens or cancer comes? Are you still supposed to thank God then? Sure! That's when you need to do it the most. Your heart may not feel like thanking God. But when you do, you are saying that in spite of the circumstance, you know God has a better plan. I have no doubt that God planned for my cancer to be an opportunity to see genuine joy and trust in God, even when my skull was screwed to a bracket for radiation.

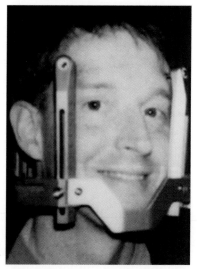

Almost anyone can be happy when life is going well and they have good health. But if finances, health or other supports are destroyed, joy will give powerful authenticity to your speech.

But a joyful reaction of trust requires exercise and obedience to your Coach (God) and fans (family and friends). For example, you kids would chime in when our car wasn't working right or I was frustrated at being lost and late for a meeting, "Dad, remember: 'Praise the Lord!'" It usually took me a few seconds of being cross-eyed and silently considering an excuse or two as to why this was an exception to the rule. I knew God was telling me to respond with trust and joy. I had to smile and say, "You're right! Praise the Lord! God, I don't understand why we are lost right now. Forgive me that I didn't make sure we left sooner. We love You and know that You have a reason that we can't find the right road. Would You please help us?" You know what? Very often we found out there was a good reason for the unexpected change in plans and

170  Romans 8:28

I was sure glad you helped me out of my stupor. You helped my joy muscle get a bit stronger.

Do you want muscular joy? Someday you may experience total destruction of everything that you thought was good in your world. Maybe you have already. The kind of joy we are talking about in this chapter which can hold you firm in that kind of storm is not like giddy laughter after a funny joke. When the muscle of your trust in God has been built by years of seeing Him work, you may be tested to the breaking point (but not beyond your limits.[171]) Even if you are still young, God can give you more than you need to simply trust in Him — He can give you peace even while your tears flow. Your friends might even see a gentle smile on your face. How can that be? Start when you are young and your faith is new. At disappointing moments that come every day, choose to praise God and trust in His love, ability and will to use them for good. When reach the point in life when all seems lost, you will have Jesus and He is enough!

> *How lovely is your dwelling place,*
> *O Lord of hosts!*
> *My soul longs, yes, faints*
> *for the courts of the Lord;*
> *my heart and flesh sing for joy*
> *to the living God.*
> *Even the sparrow finds a home,*
> *and the swallow a nest for herself,*
> *where she may lay her young,*
> *at your altars, O Lord of hosts,*
> *my King and my God.*
> *Blessed (joyful) are those who dwell in your house,*
> *ever singing your praise!*[172]

THINGS TO THINK ABOUT AND TALK OVER:

- *What kinds of things or experiences make you feel happy? Why do those feelings usually go away so quickly? What kind of joy or happiness stays with you much longer?*

- *Is it reasonable for God to command us to have a certain kind of emotion? Have you ever heard someone say, "Cheer up!" or*

171   1 Corinthians 10:13
172   Psalm 84

*"Shake it off?" We may not have perfect control of every emotion, but we can do a lot to influence our feelings and reactions.*

- *If we make "joy" or happiness alone our goal, what might happen to us? What goals or habits do you think produce lasting happiness? How can you strengthen your "joy muscle" today?*

- *Go to the appendix for a visual presentation of the different levels of happiness that can help you understand where lasting happiness is found.*

# FACING A FIERY FIGHT OF FAITH? NEVER, NEVER, NEVER GIVE IN

*"Count it all joy, my brothers, when you meet trials of various kinds, for you know that the testing of your faith produces steadfastness. And let steadfastness have its full effect, that you may be perfect and complete, lacking in nothing."*[173]

Winston Churchill, the leader of Britain during World War II, was known as "Bulldog," not only because of his good looks, but because he was such a tenacious fighter. In October of 1941 — six weeks before Pearl Harbor — Britain was going it alone against Germany in Western Europe. Everyone else had been overrun or cowed into peace. Churchill told students in his old school during those difficult days, "Never give in, never give in, never, never, never — in nothing, great or small, large or petty — never give in except to convictions of honour and good sense."[174]

173  James 1:2-4
174  Photo Wikimedia Commons

Somehow, those words came to me in the hard days of my cancer in 2005, in the middle of operations, radiation, chemotherapy, and my deep concern over leaving you without a dad. As badly as the illness and treatments hurt, I couldn't give up on life or on God. As Peter said, "Lord, to whom shall we go? You have the words of eternal life."[175]Where is your strength? What is your source of courage? What will keep you free from powerful temptations or free you from the grip of despair on hard days?

In addition to Jesus and Job, Joseph the son of Jacob is one of my favorite examples in the Bible of someone who never gave in and never gave up. If you haven't read his story, you might take the time to put down this book and pick up the "Good Book" and read his story from Genesis chapters 37 to 50. Here is a very short summary of his amazing journey:

Joseph's account picks up when he is just seventeen, the great grandson of Abraham. He is born to Jacob's first love, Rachel, after many difficult and barren years. Joseph becomes the favorite son of old Jacob, and as a result, he is hated by his ten jealous half-brothers. His father gives Joseph the famous multi-colored coat. Jacob sends him to check on his brothers in the fields and the report is not good. Two dreams that Joseph's family will bow to him put his brothers over the top with anger. The next time the "dreamer" is sent to spy on them, his own brothers nearly kill Joseph. However, they end up selling him into slavery at Reuben's suggestion.

Instead of being a menial, depressed slave, Joseph learns the language in Egypt and rises to the top of an influential family. He becomes second only to the wealthy master of the home, the captain of the king's guard, Potiphar. We are told that Joseph's success is because "the Lord was with him." Unfortunately, his master's wife tries to seduce Joseph. He refuses out of respect for his master and love for God. To cover her tracks, and doubtlessly for spite, she defames Joseph, accusing him of attempting to seduce her, which gets him thrown into prison.

Again, instead of falling into depression, Joseph rises to the top of the prison because "the LORD was with him." He interprets two more dreams  a pair of the king's servants had. Although forgotten for two more years, one of those servants finally remembers about

175   John 6:68

Joseph and tells the king. Joseph interprets the king's dream. God will bring seven years of good harvest, then seven years of drought. The king appoints Joseph as vice regent (second only to the king) to save the country. That was a pretty impressive instant promotion following thirteen years of slavery and prison!

Of course, Joseph's family is hit hard by the famine and his brothers travel two weeks on foot in hopes of buying food. They don't recognize their brother after twenty-two years, who is dressed in Egyptian garb and speaks the local language. Unwittingly, they bow down and fulfill the dreamer's dream which they so vilely hated. Joseph saves his family, who move to Goshen in Egypt. This fulfills a prophecy that Abraham's descendants would ultimately live in Egypt under slavery for 400 years because a future king would forget that through the Jews, God saved all of Egypt.[176]

What was the key to Joseph's fiery fight of faith so that he never gave in? The first thing that jumps out is "the LORD was with him." As a Christ follower, you have an amazing promise that Jesus is with you always, even to the end of the ages.[177] My Muslim friends do not believe that God is ever with them. He is spirit — "other" — and although they believe we can pray to Him, there is no sense that God communes with people.[178] In fact, Muhammad's revelations come through an angel, not by God Himself. In contrast, the Bible portrays God as walking with Adam and Eve in the cool of the day in the garden, meeting with Moses face to face, and communing with Abraham under the starry skies. Isaiah prophesies that a baby named Immanuel — "God with us" — would be born to a virgin as a sign of God's deliverance.[179] Matthew the tax collector writes that this is a prophecy about Jesus.[180] John the fisherman tells us that the Word of God became flesh and "dwelt" with us.[181] If you want to be confident and filled with joy, remember this fact: if you have repented of your sins and trusted in Christ for your righteousness, God is for you and will be with you always.

The second key to Joseph's life was that he never gave in! He never compromised and was faithful in both small and big things. Was

---

176  Genesis 15:13
177  Matthew 28:20
178  This would be true of roughly 95% of Muslims. One notable exception would be the sufis.
179  Isaiah 7:14
180  Matthew 1:23
181  John 1:14

God with Joseph because he was faithful or was Joseph faithful because he saw that God was with Him? Genesis 39:2 emphasized it was because God was with Joseph! Jesus told His disciples, "You did not choose me, but I chose you and appointed you."[182] A homeless, starving orphan who is adopted by a good king should only be filled with gratefulness, joy, and faithfulness. How much more should we? "One who is faithful in a very little is also faithful in much, and one who is dishonest in a very little is also dishonest in much."[183]

Do you wrestle with always being faithful? The great news of the Kingdom of God is that the King is here and your heavenly Father is always ready to help you. Are you struggling with a family relationship? The King's got it! He will intervene as you trust in Him. Are you struggling with sin? The King can defeat it! Are you worried about money? The King can cover it! Do you deserve it? No. That's why we need love and grace.

If you haven't already, you will face similar hard circumstances like Joseph did. The possibilities are endless — a lost job because of a false accusation, gossip that ruins your reputation, a car accident with a crushing lawsuit. When you feel alone, never give in. When the odds are completely against you, never give in. When you are utterly discouraged, never give in. God is with you.

Where do we draw a line in the sand? Jesus said it best many times, "It is written." That means we cannot compromise our character based on what is written in Scripture. The world will often pull you to give in. Many people and movies say, "Trust your feelings." Nike had an advertisement, "If it feels good, just do it!" Many young people don't get married but live together. "We love each other. How can we know if we are compatible? This feels so right. How can love be a sin?" But what does God tell us? Joseph knew. If he went by his "feelings," we would probably not have his story in the Bible. A more difficult example of things we should not give in to are immoral laws. You might even be told, "Isn't it written in the Bible to obey those in authority?" Just because the government says abortion is legal, it isn't right. Germany said helping Jews escape their death machine was wrong. In cases of immoral law, don't give in and don't compromise biblical convictions that you know are

182   John 15:16
183   Luke 16:10

right. Ultimately, the final authority of what is right and wrong rests with God, clearly given to us in the Bible.

A special warning about Bible knowledge: there are people who know the Bible well, obey every part they possibly can in great detail, and are very unpleasant to be with. They are often self-righteous and care more about their image than they do about important issues like mercy and grace. In Jesus' day, they called these people Pharisees. They were Scripture experts who missed the Messiah. Paul said later that even if you have knowledge of all mysteries, give everything to the poor, and are so "right" that you even suffer death by fire but don't have love, you gain nothing.[184] Nothing? That's right. Because without love, holding tightly to the right thing is ultimately about you, not about God or helping others.

So how do we fight, stay pure, and not give in? Love God and love others. Joseph made two points in his resistance to the advances of Potiphar's wife. One, he couldn't do that to his master. Two, he couldn't sin against God. Other people might think about the possibility of jail, a ruined reputation, pregnancy, or a disease. Joseph thought about his friend and his God. Cultivate a close relationship and care for God and others.

But what if you don't feel close to God? You are certainly on dangerous ground! One tremendous help to me is remembering that God is sovereign (always in control). He is never surprised. Was it an accident that Joseph was sold into slavery? No! Before he was born, Abraham learned from God that his descendants would be sent into slavery for 400 years in a foreign land. Joseph could not have imagined as he was walking to Egypt, bound tightly, that this was the first step of his whole family moving to Goshen where the Jewish people would eventually be harshly kept in forced labor. God knew He would deliver them, sparing them with the Passover lamb — the foreshadow of Jesus' ultimate love and sacrifice on the cross.

The God of the universe wants to be with you! Your joy in the love of God will be your strength to stand firm in the face of fiery trials, testing, or fierce opposition.[185] Be faithful to God's Word in love and never, never, never give in!

184   1 Corinthians 13
185   Nehemiah 8:10

THINGS TO THINK ABOUT AND TALK OVER:

- *When have you faced a hard fight against temptation? What did you do? Did you see God engaged in the fight? Did any Scriptures come to mind? What would you do differently today, if anything?*

- *Why is it that feeling cool or distant from God is imminently dangerous? Given that everyone has times when their passion for God is fading, what do you think would help them to get that passion back?*

- *If you do "give in" to a fight that you should have stood firm on, what do you think God would say to do next?*

- *"Never give in" or "Don't compromise" are negative imperatives. How can we say it in a positive way? Is that more helpful?*

# HEALING FROM HURT

*"He will wipe away every tear from their eyes, and death shall be no more, neither shall there be mourning, nor crying, nor pain anymore, for the former things have passed away."*[186]

When you were little, you all took many spills, scraping your knees and cutting your hands. I wanted to take the hurt away that very instant. Thankfully, God in His wisdom and love knew that you needed to experience gradual healing to learn an important lesson, like how to be more careful!

Often a hurt in your heart can be much more painful than a skinned knee. Before I left for the mission field, I had heard that the number one reason most missionaries come home is conflict with fellow missionaries! I can tell you from firsthand experience that an unexpected attack from a friend is far more hurtful and may take longer to heal than a serious wound in the flesh.

What do you do when a dream slips beyond all possibility of becoming a reality? Maybe someone you wanted to marry is going to marry someone else. Perhaps you were rejected from a dream job or a school that said you were not good enough. How do you recover if you fail a test or get a terrible grade in school? No one wants to experience any of these things. But the reality is that if you live long enough, you will pass through many fires. How you react determines if you will become bitter or better.

#### #1. OWN YOUR PART.

Did you communicate the way you should have? Did you study the way you should have? Were there moments you were too lazy? Without saying who is mostly to blame, often we played some part. Be open and confess it to God and those affected by your failure, then ask for forgiveness whenever you can.[187]

---

186   Revelation 21:4
187   James 5:16, 1 John 1:8-9

## #2. DO NOT BE OVERCOME BY EVIL," BUT OVERCOME EVIL WITH GOOD.[188]

If anyone had earned the right to say those words, it was the apostle Paul. He had been beaten, stoned, and falsely accused, even by people inside the church. Jesus said to bless, not curse, those who mistreat you.[189] Give an evil person your other cheek when they strike you.[190] Why? Paul says if you feed your enemy and treat them with kindness, it's like putting a burning coal on their heads.[191] That is to say, your kindness in the face of their evil makes them feel guilty. Hopefully they will repent!

## #3. IF A PERSON, ESPECIALLY A CHRISTIAN HAS HURT YOU, GO TO THEM.

Many, many hurts I've experienced and seen in others over the years have been largely because of misunderstandings. Loving, open communication has healed many wounds. Follow Jesus' words in Matthew 18:15-20 and resist the powerful urge to "share" with other friends how this person has hurt you.[192]

## #3. KNOW THAT GOD SYMPATHIZES WHEN WE FEEL WEAK.[193]

Jesus knew what it was like to be betrayed. He knew what it was like to be misunderstood (like almost all the time!) He knew what it was like to suffer at the hands of evil men. When you have time, read or re-read the story of Lazarus' death and resurrection. Carefully consider why Jesus delayed for two days on hearing the news His friend was deathly ill. The hurt of his sisters, Martha and Mary, is gut-wrenching. But Martha's faith and hope is remarkable. Then Jesus asks to see the tomb. Do you remember His reaction? It's the shortest verse in the Bible: "Jesus wept."[194] Although theologians might debate why He wept, the context is that He was in the presence of many mourners who were hurt deeply. Does Jesus care? Does He know what it's like to feel horrible pain with you? Absolutely. He is with you.

---

188 Romans 12:21
189 Luke 6:28
190 Matthew 5:39
191 Romans 12:20
192 This is one of only two passages we have where Jesus mentions "the church." The potential injury from some conflict is so important to deal with that if the conflict is not resolved, the church should be called in to help
193 Hebrews 4:14-15
194 John 11:35

## #4. KNOW THAT PAIN IS A GIFT.

One of the most profound speakers I heard as a young Christian was an elderly surgeon and author, Paul Brand.[195] He was a missionary doctor in India and was one of the first to understand that leprosy didn't directly cause patients' toes, fingers, feet, or hands to fall off. Rather, it was the lack of pain. The disease attacks the nervous system. Dr. Brand said he accidentally dropped an instrument in a fire. As Brand lamented the loss, a leper said, "Don't worry!" He reached into the fire, picked up the item and gave it back to the doctor, all the time with a smile and not an ounce of pain. Dr. Brand looked at the leper's hand, saw the damage and realized the problem. Pain is a gift from God to protect ourselves and help us learn. Dr. Brand knew pain himself. He lost his dad, also a missionary in India,

Photo: A 24-year-old man from Norway, infected with leprosy, 1886. Public domain.

to a disease when Paul was just fifteen years old. Pain teaches us not only how to avoid it, but how to sympathize with others and help them. A very powerful verse, and one worthy of giving careful thought to, is Hebrews 5:8: *"Even though Jesus was God's Son, he learned obedience from the things he suffered."*[196] If Jesus learned obedience through suffering, should we be exempt?

## #5. GIVE IT TO GOD.

He knows how you feel. Let Him be your defender and avenger.[197] There will be many more sunny days and opportunities in your life. Brooding over mistakes and missed chances will only hurt your ability to recognize and receive the good ones yet to come. I had a good friend who thought he had missed his chance to marry his "soul mate" because he was too busy with his studies. Although

195 Paul Brand's book Fearfully and Wonderfully Made is an excellent book to read. He operated on over 1000 hands in his life, correcting the damage of leprosy that contracts patient's fingers and toes. His observations about how we are made by God are powerful and unique. Pain is, indeed, a gift from God.
196 If Jesus had to "learn" obedience, does that mean He was not sinless? No. Jesus, although God become flesh, was born just like all other babies. He had to learn His parents' language like all other babies. The root of sin is a lack of faith, not perfect knowledge. Jesus always trusted His Father, even when suffering. Do you?
197 Romans 12:19

the woman he loved married someone else, he remained nearly paralyzed with regret and couldn't consider an interest in anyone else. He is a terrific guy and there's no doubt God has the ability to bless him with an amazing, kingdom-minded young lady . . . but not if he is stuck in the past! A friend of mine loved to quote, "God never closes a door when He does not open another." Trust God when He says He will use this hurt for your good and no one can ultimately stand against you if God is with you. "He who did not spare His own son but gave Him up for us all, how will He not also, with Him, graciously give us all things?"[198]

All wounds, especially those on the inside, take time to heal. Give yourself time. God will bring healing. Keep looking expectantly to Jesus, who promises to bring you good and dry your tears. He promises to never leave or forsake you. Rest in Him who will bring healing to your hurt.

THINGS TO THINK ABOUT AND TALK OVER:

- *What has been your greatest disappointment in life? Do you think God knew it was going to happen before it happened? What is His plan, do you think?*

- *Who has hurt you badly? Do you think you should go talk to them? Can you bless them in prayer? How do you see God is using them in your life for good? Or how might He do that?*

- *Do you agree or disagree that pain is a gift? What do you tell someone who gives you a gift? If you see pain as a gift rather than a curse, how might that help you heal, learn, and grow in your pain?*

198  Romans 8:32

# HONORING PARENTS

*"Children, obey your parents in the Lord, for this is right. 'Honor your father and mother' (this is the first commandment with a promise), "that it may go well with you and that you may live long in the land."*[199]

Isn't that amazing? Would you like to live a long time? Honor your dad. Honor you mom. It's a good deal for us and a good deal for you![200]

Okay, you may be like many kids and suspect that's a good lure to get kids to be obedient written by some dad or mom. Parental Honor = Long Life. Of course, if we believe the Bible is God's Word, that refutes the idea that some selfish parent made up the connection. But think about this: Both Paul and Jesus had no kids. They had no ulterior motive and no one to manipulate into obedience. But each of them affirmed the command to honor parents.

Consider another reason. Everyone, even toddlers, think their way is best. "That's my toy. Give it to me. Give me candy. I don't want to nap now!" They don't yet know what you and I do. Not only are there more toys in the box, but sharing and the resulting friendship bring far more joy than getting the toy they want. Candy isn't good for you. Naps are. Those lessons and many others only come with time. Your mom and dad have lived many, many years and have experienced a lot in life. Doesn't it make sense when we say, "Put on some sunscreen. Put on your bike helmet. Don't sit alone in the car with someone of the opposite sex. Be home by 10 o'clock," even if you'd rather do something different? Do you think that we may be aware of some real dangers that you may not?

There's another part to the equation in honoring parents: God. He's completely in charge of the "long life" department. God not only observes us, but is intimately involved in our relationships. Isn't it reasonable that if children honor their parents because they are trusting in God's Word, that He is pleased and going to bless them?

---

199  Ephesians 6:1-3
200  Are there exceptions? Of course. Very parent-honoring young men have gone off to war to defend their nation and not come home. The Scriptures are teaching us a general principle about the connection between long life and honor of parents.

Of course! I'm just your earthly dad and a sinner to boot. But when I see you treating your mother with love and respect, I am thrilled! I will definitely find a way to reward you, whether with a movie night, a special shopping trip, or an extra privilege. Hopefully you didn't treat your mother nicely just to get something (parents can tell, you know), but just because you knew it was the right thing and you love her. How much more will God reward us?[201]

By the way, obedience $\neq$ honor. That is to say, you can obey but not honor. Mom says to wash dishes. Dad asks you to take out the trash. You are watching your favorite movie but you were supposed to do those chores hours ago and you know it. Let's say you obey but roll your eyes. Or you bark back, "What? Do I have to do everything around here? You always make me do the dishes." You get the idea. You obeyed but without honor.

Honor is valuing. If someone greatly values their bike, they will take care of it. It won't be left in the rain. Sprockets and chains will be oiled, maybe more than is needed. A dirty bike will get cleaned right away. Only very trusted friends will get to ride it.

Similarly, an honored parent is far more valuable than any teacher or friend. If Mom or Dad want some time with you, the answer is an enthusiastic, "Sure! That would be awesome!" If they help you do a tough homework assignment, fix dinner, pay for music lessons, or buy you some new clothes, you are effusive with thanks. If they ask you to do something hard, like choosing family time over an evening with your best friend, you may acknowledge the struggle, but with a genuine smile say, "But if you think it's important, of course I'll be there." (Believe me, we see that kind of sacrifice and you will be rewarded much more than if you find a way to go be with your friend.)

An even deeper honor follows an internal sense of what should be done, even when no one is looking, whether chores, kindness to siblings, or fixing something only you know is broken. Good initiative is rare and priceless.

How long should we honor our parents? Does that end when we move out or get married? You probably know the answer to that question, and I hope that your mother and I have modeled honor

201  Matthew 7:11, Luke 11:12

for your grandparents. But what does that look like? While parents no longer have daily authority to direct the  activities of their adult children, their words, time, and resources should still demonstrate that their parents have high value to them. They may be feeble or have poor eyesight. Do we see their needs and volunteer to help without being asked? Do you have a new challenge in life like a career choice or a stubborn two-year-old child and seek their advice? God will show you ways to honor your parents well after you leave home, if you ask. I can tell you from experience there is great joy in remaining well connected with them.

Of course, honoring parents, grandparents, teachers, or church leaders can be difficult at times. We may not understand their reasoning. They certainly sin at times. Of course, it would not be honoring to God or to them to follow them in that situation. However, when you simply differ in opinion or desire, choose to joyfully honor them, and you will be expressing love and trust in God. He ultimately controls the outcome of any circumstance for your good, even if it seems unpleasant at the time.[202]

Likewise, you will face many choices in your life, as simple as choosing not to give a second glance at an inappropriate photo or as serious as contemplating a temptation to forsake your future spouse. God's way may not be as appealing in that slice of time as what your flesh or desire clamors for. But if you develop the habit of honoring fallible humans like the parents God has put in authority over your life, then you will have the spiritual muscle and habits that will help you to pass through other fires of temptation without being burned. Even after the death of grandparents and parents, your honor or value of their lives will continue to serve you well. Remember the good lessons and memories. Choose to release the bad ones, knowing that even they were tools in God's hands to shape your life and character for good. Joy and a long life will be yours.

THINGS TO THINK ABOUT AND TALK OVER:

- *How would you advise a friend who was struggling with honoring their abusive mom or dad?*

202  Romans 8:28

- *When are the hardest moments for you to honor your mom? Your dad? How might God help you in those situations? Consider Jesus' hardest moment in the Bible to honor His Father. How did Jesus handle His desire to not go through crucifixion? (Look at Luke 22:39-42 if you don't remember the story.)*

- *The Bible says parents should not exasperate their children. Parents are sinners and have blind spots, too. Are their specific areas or times that your mom or dad exasperate or frustrate you? That is when honor can be very difficult. Have you tried to talk to them about it? (Try to find a neutral time to approach them, not in the heat of frustration!)*

# LOVING SIBLINGS

*"Behold, how good and pleasant it is when brothers dwell in unity!"*[203]

Charles and John were close brothers from a very large family. They went to college together and traveled abroad together. They even came to genuine faith in Jesus within three days of each other while in their twenties, even though they were both already ordained as priests. Charles loved music and wrote over 6,000 songs about God. John was a powerful preacher. Often ministering together, they reached over 135,000 people with God's message of love. Although the Wesley brothers didn't agree on everything, it was amazing what they were able to accomplish by encouraging each other and working together over a lifetime.

Everyone wants to "dwell," or live together, in peace and unity. But sadly, it is actually a rare exception when brothers and sisters genuinely love each other in that way. Friction is a natural result for all people living close together. What is the secret of living together in peace and unity? Learning to walk in the Spirit, not just hearing God's voice, but obeying Him when He tells us to love when it's hard. Paul told his readers in Rome, *"To set the mind on the Spirit is life and peace."*[204] Your relationship with your siblings may be the best training ground you will ever have to set your mind on the Spirit.

Brothers and sisters can be the best lifelong friends or heart-rending enemies. Cain and Abel are a sad example of second kind. Leah and Rachel were two sisters who were in bitter competition for one man.[205]

On the other hand, close brothers in the Bible served as disciples: James and John, Andrew and Peter. Siblings are so important that Jesus is called "Brother" to anyone who believes in Him.[206]

---

203  Psalms 133:1
204  Romans 8
205  Genesis 29
206  Romans 8:29

I've often told you that however you treat your brother or sister is how you'll treat your future husband or wife. If you are dating someone, ask about their siblings and how they get along with them. You'll find a good clue about how they'll talk about you someday to others.

When you are young, what is one of the worst things to spoil your friendship with your brother or sister? All younger brothers and sisters know this answer right away. Teasing! Almost all older brothers and sisters love their younger siblings, and find it hard not to tease even though they know it's wrong. They might even hate themselves for doing it. To this day, I am so sorry there were times we were cruel to our younger brother, your Uncle Charlie. It seemed so funny at the time. Maybe it was because we watched silly cartoons — everyone laughs whenever Elmer Fudd or Wile E. Coyote gets hurt. Of course, in a few minutes cartoon characters act like nothing ever happened. In real life, however, people almost never "bounce back" so fast. Mean words and teasing can cut deep. Wounds can last a lifetime. So what can we do to change? The answer is not so much what but with Whom.

For that, let's go back to a guy named Saul. Many years ago, he wrote that he didn't want to do certain things (like tease), but found that he did them anyway. Then, when he wanted to do others things like be nice, he found that he rarely did them. He was really sad and frustrated, crying out, "Who will set me free?" [207]

One unexpected day, he discovered Jesus set him free! How? By helping Saul give the "Spirit of life" full control. Not only can you be "born from above" and filled with God's Spirit of love, but you will have a new strength to do what is right.[208] Our old spirit likes to laugh and doesn't care much if it is at someone else's expense. Saul got renamed Paul when the Spirit of Jesus came to give him a new heart. Paul understood that he finally had the power to say "yes" to loving a brother or "no" to anger in response to a sister's teasing.

Your hungry sister might look longingly at the ham sandwich you

207   Romans 7:24, Some people believe Paul was writing about his experience of wrestling with sin as a Christian. Others believe he was referring to his life before Christ. I'm inclined to believe the second, because he is moving in his letter from talking about sinful life without Christ (Romans 1 and 2) to the great crescendo of Romans 8. But on this topic of resisting the temptation to fight with siblings, the main point would stand in any case: only Jesus can set me free of my anger!
208   See chapter on "Walking with God" for more on this.

are eating and really enjoying. Deep inside there's a little voice saying, "You know, she would be really glad if you shared. You'll enjoy a half sandwich, too, more than if you ate the whole thing!" If you choose to listen, you're learning to walk in the Spirit. I remember one day looking out from our college library window. It was a super cold day in Colorado and some cadets had pulled a prank by turning on the fire hydrants the night before. The whole marching area became a skating rink and the wind was howling. I winced but laughed as someone slipped on the ice and their books went flying in the wind. But the Spirit of God inside of us should make us sad when others are hurt, instead of making us want to laugh or point out what happened to someone else. If I were a believer then, I should have listened to God and run out and helped. Sure, I might be busy. But the Holy Spirit will quietly say, "Stop. Take a minute and help." The joy of helping is far greater than laughter (and the regret later).

*How good and pleasant it is when brothers (and sisters) dwell in unity.* That kind of relationship is not only a joy to siblings themselves, but also to everyone around them. Eventually, spouses, friends, and colleagues will benefit from your childhood because you have learned to set your mind on the Spirit of God and love siblings with whom friction was a natural part of life. When your flesh insists on its own way, let go of your demands and let the Spirit of love guide you.

THINGS TO THINK ABOUT AND TALK OVER:

- *Paul wrote in Romans 8: "For to set the mind on the flesh is death, but to set the mind on the Spirit is life and peace." Insisting on our own way comes from setting our mind on "the flesh," Paul's phrase for selfish desires. We may not die physically right away when we set our mind on the flesh, but what kinds of things can quickly die if we live that way? To enjoy "life and peace," we must live by "the Spirit," which means we die to ourselves and live for God. How does that happen? Are you living that way with your siblings? What could help make your relationship better?*

- *When brothers and sisters don't get along, who loses? When we have good relationships with siblings, who wins?*

- *What are some frequent areas of conflict with your siblings? How can you prepare yourself for next time, so that when conflict begins to arise, you can deal with it in a way that honors God? What might you do to prevent it from starting?*

# MONEY!

*"But godliness with contentment is great gain. For we brought nothing into the world, and we can take nothing out of it. But if we have food and clothing, we will be content with that."*[209]

"Money makes the world go round!" Really? People dream of it. They work long hours to get more of it. Some will even kill for it. Why? We learn early in life what money can do. We want a candy bar. We want to see a movie. We want a toy. You just need money. Here are some perspectives on money that have served me well and I believe will help you during your lifetime, if you follow them.

### MONEY HAS NO ETERNAL VALUE. YOU ARE RICH IF YOU LOVE WHAT GOD LOVES AND ARE CONTENT WITH WHAT YOU HAVE

The strange truth is that money is only paper! (Shhh! Don't let the secret out.)

I remember visiting several countries like Peru in the 1990s. I still have several 1,000,000 peso notes. You could buy a sandwich or a drink with it when I was there. I'm sure it has no value now. My host family with six kids from the Republic of Georgia told me that after the fall of the Soviet Union, the value of the ruble dropped so fast that they would stand in line all night for three loaves of bread. By the time they got to the front of the line, their money would only buy two loaves. If you google "hyperinflation," you'll find pictures of a wheel barrel full of German marks from the 1920s that would buy just one loaf of bread. This is what happens when governments print money with no real value backing the currency and no confidence from the consumers. It's just paper.

Paul wrote the verse I quoted just below the chapter title, what is truly great gain: godliness and contentment. He went a step further to talk about what God thinks about money and material wealth: *"Those who want to get rich fall into temptation and a trap and into many foolish and harmful desires that plunge people into ruin and destruction. For the love of money is a root of all kinds of evil."* He tells us, *"Some people, eager for money, have wandered from the faith and pierced themselves with many griefs."*[210]

Notice, he didn't say "money" is evil, but the "love of money." It's hard to tell when we've crossed the line into "love of money," but a good test is to look at your bank or credit card statement. What could I tell someone about your heart if I saw where you spend your money? A second test: how do you react when you lose a large sum of money? Do you get angry or upset? Or do you trust God to bring good from it? Third: when you see a real physical need, like hunger, sickness, or cold, what do you do? Do you tense up and begin to rationalize how to avoid helping? "That guy put himself in that situation. Somebody else will help. The government has programs for that." Or do you reach in your pocket or find a wise way to materially and physically help?

Please, whatever you do, don't make it your goal to be rich materially. By most of the world's standards, you are already rich. If you have a toilet that flushes and doesn't poison your neighbors, you are richer than 60% of the world.[211] Are you grateful to have a bathroom with a toilet, not to mention lights along with soap, hot and cold water at your fingertips?

Your Russian grandmother, who lived in a sparse Soviet apartment with an extremely difficult husband, said, "A rich person is not someone who has a lot of money, but a person who is content with what he has." She would close her eyes on her cot in her long narrow kitchen, lit by a single, bare fluorescent tube, and see herself with God. Baba Mira found a wealth that most materially wealthy people can barely dream of.

## MONEY CAN BE TRADED FOR ETERNAL VALUE

Jesus said, *"Make friends for yourselves by means of unrighteous wealth, so that when it fails they may receive you into the eternal dwellings."*[212] That sounds so contradictory to the saying, "Money can't buy friends." Of course, a true friend doesn't care if you

---

210   1 Timothy 6:9-10
211   Six in 10 people worldwide lack access to flush toilets or other adequate sanitation. ACS News Service Weekly PressPac: March 20, 2013 www.acs.org/content/acs/en/pressroom/presspacs/2013/acs-presspac-march-20-2013
212   Luke 16:9, To understand what Jesus meant by "unrighteous wealth" and His perspective on money (popularly called mammon in their day like we say dough or bucks and Russians say cabbage), read the context: Luke 16:1-13.

have money or not. Conversely, fake friends often flock around a generous person. But is the best alternative to be stingy? Of course not!

Jesus knows that a generous person will not only attract insincere but also sincere friends. If you have the means to alleviate suffering and help the poor, but do nothing, who will be glad to see you in heaven? Actually, I doubt anyone who lives indifferent to true suffering has genuine faith or will be in heaven.[213] Imagine sacrificing fast food and coffee for a year in order to send money to orphans in Syria or Bible translators in India.[214] You might not meet those who are blessed by your generosity on earth, but I have a feeling that God will arrange a joyful meeting in heaven.

Notice that Jesus does not say *if* wealth fails but *when* it fails. The richest person in the world who becomes old and is breathing on a ventilator will have no comfort in their wealth that cannot buy them another day.

Another way to picture what Jesus is saying is to imagine you can go grab all the play money in the house from Monopoly and Life and use it as real money for just one day in any store. The only catch is that you have to spend 90% of the money helping other people. Would you be excited? Would you keep some play money for tomorrow? No way! You'd spend every dime and relish giving every gift. That's how we *should* live now.

One of my favorite pastors, Fulton Buntain, used to say often, "Live simply so others may simply live." We have so many opportunities to make a difference in lives around us, often impacting them for eternity. Why would we be satisfied with accumulating more Monopoly money and trinkets?

Remember: in the end, it's not *your* money. Everything you have belongs to God. If you honor Him and use it wisely, you'll be glad for eternity.

---

213   I'm not saying you can be saved by good works but that your good works, including generosity, will show if your faith is genuine or fake. See James 2:14-17
214   Most statistics show Americans spend over $1000 a year on coffee bars and nearly $3000, eating out. Not only can you eat healthier at home but for 1/4 the cost. Imagine sending the savings over 30 years would equal $90,000! You could fund the construction of an orphanage or support national Bible translators for three different languages.

JOYFULLY GIVING TITHES, SACRIFICES, AND OFFER-
INGS FOR THE WORK OF THE CHURCH

I remember my old friend, Tom Cotton, who gave 10% (or a
tithe) from his work on a dairy farm. I thought he was crazy! At
the same time, I admired him for it. Still, I would rarely part with
my hard-earned cash as a teenager for anything, let alone for the
church. When I got saved ten years later, my perspective was
about to radically change. Our church challenged us to tithe and,
occasionally, to give sacrificially above the tithe. I can say that
I never lacked for anything after doing that. In fact, I saw how I
prospered *more* after that. Once, I felt led by the Holy Spirit and
promised $1000 for a missionary effort. That afternoon, I got an
unexpected check for that exact amount. Of course, God makes no
promise that He will bless us visibly every time we give. He may
bless us spiritually and not materially. He may only bless us in
heaven for some of our giving on earth. However, there is a general
principle that when we obedient to God's command to give, He will
abundantly meet our material needs.

*"Bring the full tithe into the storehouse, that there may be food in
my house. And thereby put me to the test, says the LORD of hosts,
if I will not open the windows of heaven for you and pour down for
you a blessing until there is no more need."*[215]

Tithing as a principle is found several places in the Old Testament.
Some estimate that the total giving by Israeli citizens to support the
temple and Levites was over 20% when totaling tithes, sacrifices and
offerings. The New Testament does not prescribe a specific amount
believers should give to support ministry work apart from weekly
giving.[216] But many have made a logical conclusion that parallel
to the Old Testament, 10% is a reasonable, minimum amount to
give. If we want to fund a central place to meet regularly as a larger
group, support missionaries and a teaching elder or pastor, and pay
for utilities, cleaning, and Bibles, this is a small sum in light of
the benefits. Certainly, there may be times for a greater offering or
sacrifice when the church roof leaks, a father with young children
unexpectedly dies, or an earthquake hits Haiti. Hopefully some of
the tithe will have been set aside for those needs, too, a reflection of
the "storehouse" in the verse above.

215  Malachi 3:10
216  1 Corinthians 16:2

By the way, God doesn't want us to give if we don't want to. Paul wrote, "Each one must give as he has decided in his heart, not reluctantly or under compulsion, for God loves a cheerful giver." [217] For me, it is a joy and a privilege. I'm so glad God changed me from being a selfish man into someone who loves to give. Remember my friend Tom? He is one of the happiest people I know. Overwhelming joy almost always fills a giver.

One of my favorite stories about tithing I learned in Panama. Pastor Bill Johnson told me that when he married Marla, they decided to give 10% of their income to God's work. Each year after that, they added another percent. If I remember right, they were married twenty-three years at the time he told me this, which meant their giving was at 33%! He told me the incremental increase was so gradual over the years that they have never missed it. Now they live in Boston and have been married for over forty years! I have no doubt God rejoices and blesses the Johnsons for their generosity and faith.

### STAY OUT OF DEBT

*"Owe no one anything, except to love each other,
for the one who loves another has fulfilled the law."* [218]

This command from Paul also radically transformed my financial world. Whether buying a car or even a house, debt makes no sense. Why? You are presuming on God's future provision to give you what He has not given you today. To get that "new" car, TV or sofa, you need another master, the bank loan officer. You will need to pay your new master every month in the form of interest. If you don't pay? Ask anyone who has had a car repossessed if they liked their "new" master.

Not only will God become secondary to your need to continue earning a paycheck for your money master, but you will pay more for the things you buy using God's money. Pastor Gino Grunberg shared how he and his wife discovered this to our college group thirty years ago. Over the lifetime of a $100,000 home loan, they would pay $270,000 for the purchase. If Gino or his wife got sick or lost their job during those thirty years, they could lose the house and all they had invested

---

217   2 Corinthians 9:6
218   Romans 13:8

in it. Instead, they decided to rent a cheap apartment and save the difference of a high house payment over the course of ten years.[219] At the end of ten or twelve years, they would have enough money to buy a house with cash. In the meantime, they didn't have to worry about ever "losing" their house to the bank and they were free to move to another city, state, or even country if God called them to go.

My dad always said, "The day you drive a new car off the lot, you just lost several thousand dollars." You'll pay more in taxes and insurance. Remember, like Pastor Buntain said, live simply. Cars mainly function to get you from here to there. I'm not suggesting to get a junker that will break down. But let someone else pay the dealer, the bank loan officer, the tax man, and the insurance company first, then pick up a reliable vehicle to do God's work: getting you to school and work, getting the kids to Sunday school, or going to help at the homeless shelter.

My friend and pastor, Tim Cox, often joked, "I never saw a hearse pulling a U-Haul!" All your things and money stay behind on planet Earth. Treat money for what it is — just paper! It is just paper that can help others see materially that God loves them. The only thing you can take to heaven is a legacy of life lived in faith and souls that likewise trusted Jesus as their treasure.

THINGS TO THINK ABOUT AND TALK OVER:

- *Are there any material things on your "wishlist" right now? If God says "No" or "Not now," will you be at peace with that answer? Are you content? If not, how can you become content no matter what? By the way, I have a garage full of old "wishlist" stuff like old computer parts, broken remote control cars and unused sports equipment. You probably have some toy boxes like that. Does that help you understand what is really valuable? How can we convert those unused treasures into real wealth?*

219  Some excellent Bible teachers disagree with my view of mortgages and I realize that in some cases a house payment can be less than rent. However, carefully seek the Lord for His guidance before entering into a house loan, knowing that you will certainly be obligated to another earthly master. You will probably enter into other contracts like employment (e.g. military for education), so it is conceivable to have a house or business debt in rare circumstances. Make sure your goal is well thought-out, done with God's leading and for His purposes, entered very cautiously, paid off expeditiously, and not done simply for personal indulgence. Sadly, many couples buy homes that stretch their finances to the breaking point just to have a better view, a remodeled kitchen or bigger garage.

- *Read from Paul, a shipwrecked, beaten, jailed Christ follower in Philippians 4:11-13: "I have learned in whatever situation I am to be content. I know how to be brought low, and I know how to abound. In any and every circumstance, I have learned the secret of facing plenty and hunger, abundance and need. I can do all things through him who strengthens me." What do you think was the "secret" that Paul learned? How can you let that sink beyond your head to your heart?*

# TEMPTATION

*"No temptation has overtaken you that is not common to man
[everybody]. God is faithful, and he will not let you be tempted
beyond your ability, but with the temptation he will also provide the
way of escape, that you may be able to endure it."*[220]

Temptation, a thought to do wrong, is a battle every human has
faced since Adam and Eve. Some people say when they are caught,
"The devil made me do it." There may be some limited truth in that,
but we have to own the final act and consequences!

The greatest strategy I have learned for fighting temptation is a
simple one: Love God with all your heart, soul, and mind and then
all temptations will appear as the rubbish they are next to the beauty,
majesty, and holiness of God. Think of it this way: a newly married
young man, passionately in love with his young, beautiful wife
will not cast a glance of desire at a woman working the streets with
bright red lipstick and excess rouge. Another man, however, who
has not cultivated love at home with his wife of many years may be
easily pulled aside in the same situation.

Borrowing from Ross Campbell, you can think of a relationship as
having a "love tank" which needs filling to be healthy.[221] We start
off every day with a finite number of minutes, thoughts, words, and
deeds until we lay down our heads to sleep at night.

If it helps, think of a sack full of marbles God gives you at the
start of the day representing each minute (about 1,000) that you
will have. You can begin to put marbles one at a time into different
buckets, a love-bucket for God like taking time to talk or sing to
Him, a chores-bucket like brushing your teeth or making breakfast,
or a relationship-bucket talking to your family and friends. If you're
smart, you can double your marbles putting one your love-bucket for
God and one in your chores-bucket if you can brush your teeth while
humming a song to Him or praying. You can drop bonus marbles in
your brother's love-bucket and your love-bucket at the same time by

220  1 Corinthians 10:13
221  Gary Smalley also did a fine job of extending Dr. Campbell's love tank idea from kids to
marriage

saying something like, "Samuel, I'm so glad God gave me a brother like you. I see Jesus through you every day!" Sadly, on the other hand, you can take several marbles out of your love-bucket and a friend's by giving in to the temptation to pass some juicy bit of gossip you heard about the new kid on the block. *God still loves you, but your relationship with Him suffers.* Your passion for His beauty withers every time you sin or simply waste time doing something meaningless (for example, think of most video games and TV shows). When temptation comes again and your love-bucket for God is rattling with air and three marbles, you're likely going to give in, and that can pull you into a downward spiral. You need to reverse that quickly with repentance and start filling your love-bucket for God again.

The best message I've ever heard on love for God as the only real defense against temptation is called "Sex and the Supremacy of Christ Part 2" by John Piper.[222] It may be the best message I've ever heard on anything. You could stop reading now, listen to that message, and have all you need to know about fighting temptation.

You probably know some temptations are harder for certain people to resist than others. You may have no problem with the temptation to drink too much. You don't even like the taste of any alcohol. But when it comes to eating too many sweets . . . well, that's a real problem! The temptation might be completely reversed for another person.

In other chapters, I've written about sexual temptation (one of the most powerful), but other temptations are almost limitless in number and can be just as alluring as sex. Power, fame, money, drugs, or anything that is not controlled by God's love will hurt or destroy others around us and ultimately, if left unchecked, ruin our relationship with God.

The battle for everything that comes out of our mouths or the works that come through our hands will be won or lost in our hearts and minds.[223] Our very lifeline to God depends on keeping our thoughts and desires in check. Jesus even said the offenses of lust and hate are no different than adultery and murder.[224] My old friend, Tim Cox, pastored

222   http://www.desiringgod.org/messages/sex-and-the-supremacy-of-christ-part-2
223   Matthew 15:18-19 "But what comes out of the mouth proceeds from the heart, and this defiles a person. For out of the heart come evil thoughts, murder, adultery, sexual immorality, theft, false witness, slander."
224   Matthew 5:21-22, 27

a large group of often struggling singles often quoted Martin Luther,

> "I cannot stop a bird from flying over my head.
> But I can stop it from building a nest in my hair."

Translation? I may not be able to stop a sexy popup on my computer screen, but I don't have to click on it or keep thinking about it all day long. Here's another helpful picture from Paul. (I've underlined words that you can memorize and use in a moment of temptation): *"Now in a great house there are not only vessels of gold and silver but also of wood and clay, some for honorable use, some for dishonorable. Therefore, <u>if anyone cleanses himself from what is dishonorable he will be a vessel for honorable use,</u> set apart as holy, useful to the master of the house, ready for every good work. <u>So flee youthful passions and pursue righteousness, faith, love, and peace, along with those who call on the Lord from a pure heart.</u>"*[225]

I can "flee" from temptation by turning off my computer or taking a different road home if my usual route takes me close to an area of weakness. I also need to substitute what I "fled from" with something wholesome.[226] I can pick up my Bible, spend time with my wife and kids, listen to encouraging music, etc. You will learn that the battle may be tougher than you think. Consider the temptation to stay angry about someone who offended you—your desire and plans for revenge. Maybe you broke something, and instead of telling the truth, you are thinking all day long about how to show it wasn't your fault.

Sometimes it may feel almost impossible to beat temptation. Without God, it would be impossible. But with Him, you can have victory! Here is a summary I believe will really help you:

### LOVE

Love God by sowing and cultivating seeds of worship, service, and intimacy in your relationship with Him. Fill your bucket of love for Him by giving Him the very best of every minute.

---

225  2 Timothy 2:20-22 (my underlining)
226  "Nature abhors a vacuum" . . . at least on planet earth. If you "remove" a bad passion or habit, you'll need to substitute it with a good one. See the chapter "Breaking Bad Habits".

## FLEE FROM TEMPTATION

Don't let the bird begin to build a nest in your hair. Be like Joseph who ran away from Potiphar's wife even though he landed in prison for it.

### PRAY

God will lead you away from temptation (before and when it happens) and into pure thoughts set on Him and right action.

### FIND

Accountability — a friend you trust— who will help and not condemn you.

### MEMORIZE AND UNDERSTAND

Powerful verses that will help, like 1st Corinthians 10:13. If Scripture is how Jesus fought off the devil's temptations in the desert three times, do you think you have a better plan?[227]

### KNOW

That in your struggle to not sin in a certain area, you are not alone! If you fail, you just joined a long line of struggling saints (like every real Christian who has ever lived.) They fell, got up, and many overcame. So can you. Get up, confess, start at point #1 if you need to, and keep going!

### KNOW

That God will never allow you to be in a situation where you are tempted beyond your ability to say "Yes" to God and "No" to sin.

### KNOW

That anytime you are tempted, God will always provide a way out

---

227  Matthew 4:1-11, Three times Jesus rebuked satan, saying "It is written . . ." One time, satan had the nerve to quote two Bible verses to Jesus saying, "If you are the Son of God, throw yourself down, for it is written, 'He will command his angels concerning you, and on their hands they will bear you up, lest you strike your foot against a stone.'" The Devil knows how to twist Scripture, which is why it is so important for us to not only memorize God's Word, but deeply understand and believe what we have memorized.

for you. Again, be like Joseph and run out the door, even if you are only in your underwear!

What happens if you don't stoke the fire of your love for God and pray and you don't memorize helpful parts of God's Word? What happens if you doubt God will help you, give you the power to say "No!" and take the exit? Well, join countless *other* sheep who get on the wide path to the slaughter house. Just remember that the pleasure of sin is only for a season and the pain can be for a lifetime. You don't have to live long to see examples: drug dealers in prison, alcoholics sleeping on a park bench, lovers dying of AIDS, cheaters longing to have their families back. For those who are apparent exceptions — people who give in to temptation and become rich and famous, and who seem to have no consequences — you can be sure their day of reckoning will come.

Is there hope for them or someone living in the mire of regret? Absolutely! As long as they have breath, the story of the prodigal son can be their story. Keep reading into the coming chapters, "When You Fail" and "Set Free," to learn more about that great hope.

Temptations are some of the hardest battles you will face during life. But be encouraged to know you are not alone. God is with you. Others have been tested, some have failed, but many have overcome. Use the many tools that God has given you and victory will come, especially as you sow and cultivate seeds of love for Him.

THINGS TO THINK ABOUT AND TALK OVER:

- *Do you know some areas of temptation that you are weak in? Looking at the summary above, what areas do you think you can improve?*

- *What are some practical things you can do in your day to fill your love-bucket for God more?*

- *What friend or relative do you have that you can trust to tell your temptations to and pray together with?*

- *What does "The chickens will come home to roost" mean? How can that principle help when you see people apparently getting away with a particular sin you are tempted by?*

# BREAKING BAD HABITS

*"I will make my dwelling among them and walk among them,*
*and I will be their God, and they shall be my people.*
*Therefore go out from their midst, and be separate from them,*
*says the Lord,*
*and touch no unclean thing; then I will welcome you,*
*and I will be a father to you, and you shall be sons and daughters*
*to me"*[228]

If you are reading this chapter, you are probably struggling with a habit you'd like to quit but haven't yet been able to. Here's the good news from my experience: you can be victorious! Don't let failure hold you back. God promises to give you all the power you need to win.[229]

Would you like the most powerful weapon ever known to man to help you conquer your bad habit? It's so simple, some people might say that it's too simple. If you remember the chapter on temptation, the key is the same (after all, a bad habit is a temptation that we've yielded to over and over). The ultimate weapon against every bad habit is love! First, God's love and then yours.

When I dated your mother and was hoping to marry her, I was always on my best behavior. (Later, I learned that she was doing the same thing.) Not a single bad habit came out. Why? Love! No one had to tell us to be on time, be faithful to attend our home fellowship, exercise or brush our teeth!

I won't repeat everything here from the chapters "Temptation" and "The Greatest Joy," but stoke the fire of your love for God. When your love for God cools, do the things that you did when you were "hot" for Him.[230]

228  2 Corinthians 6:16-18
229  1 Corinthians 10:13
230  Revelation 2:4-5

REMEMBER THAT GOD'S LOVE FOR YOU IS WHITE HOT.

He is for you, not against you.[231] He is working on you to change you into His image and He will complete that work one day no matter what it takes.[232] We cannot imagine the power of His mighty, sometimes terrifying, love at work in us, rooting out cancerous habits and replacing them with healthy ones. In pale contrast to His great love are our anemic hearts.

WE MUST SEE THE WICKEDNESS OF OUR TRAITOROUS DEEDS AND BE BROKEN IN SPIRIT FOR TREATING OUR SAVIOR SO POORLY, OR WE WILL NEVER BE HEALED.

The person who excuses himself by saying, "I'm only human," will lead a miserable, double life, swept on the waves of sin and doubt. Hate your bad habits and *keep hating them* because they betray your loving Father. Only then you will stay on the road to a victorious, joyful life as you *look to the grace of Christ and the power of the cross over canceled sin.*[233]

IF YOU WANT VICTORY SOONER THAN LATER, GET GOING ON THE BATTLE TACTICS AND TOOLS GOD HAS GIVEN YOU:

Scripture memory and meditation, prayer, worship, service to others.

KNOW THAT SATAN WILL CALL YOU OUT EVERY TIME YOU FAIL.

Throw back at him, "There is no condemnation for those in Christ,"[234] and the inexorable truth that your victory is coming. God is for you, not against you. If you fall, get up by His grace and keep going! See and celebrate the victory God is giving you, even if you have not yet completely seen your bad habit eradicated. Compared to a few months ago or a year ago, are you doing better? Rather than focus on your failures, rejoice and praise God in your victories!

Your ultimate victory will come from your love for God which is

---

231  Romans 8:31, God's promises are for His sons and daughters, those who belong to Christ.
232  Philippians 1:6 "And I am sure of this, that he who began a good work in you will bring it to completion at the day of Jesus Christ."
233  Your sins were "canceled" by the cross judicially (meaning at the final judgment of the world, your sins will be struck from the record and you will be innocent). The power now is that the Holy Spirit lives inside of you to defeat sin while you live in this sin-wrecked world.
234  Romans 8:1

fueled by God's love for you. Read that sentence again and think about it.

In His love, God has given you basic tools and weapons (remember, the Bible is called a "sword" for a good reason) in the battle to help you control your mind, flesh, and spirit.[235] The most foundational ones I've listed above. However, here are some more helpful strategies:

### FIND A FRIEND WHO CAN HELP

God calls us to bear one another's burdens, specifically in the area of sin.[236] He tells us to gently restore brothers and sisters. You weren't meant to fight alone. Has any war ever been won by an army of one? (Okay, Jesus is the exception.) Let someone help you and you will certainly return the favor to others someday.

### THINK LONG TERM, EVEN BEFORE BAD HABITS START

It may not seem like a big deal to give in to a temptation today, but just one bad decision can set off a chain reaction that will take you where you don't want to go. Almost no one ever set off in marriage to have an affair. But it's so easy to take that "second look." No one plans to destroy their life with drugs or alcohol. But millions give in to peer pressure to "just try it." Consider the following advice as you think about the destiny, character and habits you would like to have and the ones you would like to leave behind.

Sow a thought, reap an action.
Sow an action, reap a habit.
Sow a habit, reap a character.
Sow a a character, reap a destiny.[237]

### KNOW THAT YOUR MIND IS A BATTLEGROUND AND MAKE WAR ON TEMPTATION!

Your enemy, the Devil, prowls like a lion.[238] He literally wants *to kill you*. He knows all too well that if he can deceive your mind, even

---

235  Ephesians 6:17
236  Galatians 6:1-2
237  This is variously attributed to many different authors, from Chinese philosopher Lao Tzu (500 B.C.) to atheist Ralph Waldo Emerson and Gandhi in modern times. But the idea of reaping what we sow (good or bad) is found in the Scriptures at least 3000 years ago, Proverbs 11:18, 22:8, Job 4:8-9 through Luke 6:38, Galatians 6:7-9, 2 Corinthians 9:6
238  1 Peter 5:8

just incrementally, he can destroy your destiny and — ultimately — you. God will give you victory on the outside as you fight and win by His power on the *inside*.

## THE BEST DEFENSE IS A GOOD OFFENSE

Jesus told us we need to go on the offense against temptation. That means *before* temptation comes, you need a plan. Don't just react to the bird flying in the sky. Did you ever notice that in the middle of prayer Jesus taught His disciples to pray, "Lead us not into temptation, but deliver us from evil"? Do you ever pray that in your prayers? That would certainly be a request God wants to hear and will answer. Go on the offense against temptations by praying *before* they come your way, asking God to lead you instead on the right path.[239]

Jesus modeled this again on the last night of His life on earth in the garden of Gethsemane. The Lord and His disciples were pushed to the limits of exhaustion and stress. Do you think Jesus thought this was important? He admonished, *"Watch and pray so that you will not enter into temptation. For the spirit is willing, but the body is weak."*[240]

I've been fighting sin and bad habits for decades. Some victories came immediately, some came only after years of fighting. Other bad habits came back like ugly weeds that I thought were defeated, but their roots were still stubbornly in my heart. What could I do? After being discouraged and then disgusted, I could only return to the fight, fueled by the love of Christ. You will have victory, too, my dear children, as you look to Him with sorrow for sin but expectant hope, and with at least a sparkle of the joy that is coming.

## THINGS TO THINK ABOUT AND TALK OVER:

- *Think about this sentence again: Your ultimate victory will come from your love for God which is fueled by God's love for you. What do you think it means and how can it work to help you in your struggle over a specific bad habit?*

- *Read over the "armor" of God that Paul lists in Ephesians*

239  Psalm 23:3
240  Matthew 26:41

*6. I have a friend in his 80s who every morning puts on each piece one at a time during prayer, physically going through the motions with his hands while saying the words. Think about each one. Are there some you are missing? Faith? Truth? Readiness of the gospel?*

- *Everyone has excuses for not getting victory over bad habits. As you think about a specific habit that bothers you, is there an excuse that weakens your resolve? How can you defeat that excuse before the next temptation comes? If you are not sure, what is written in scripture? You might also check with your pastor or a mature friend.*

- *What are some good habits you believe God is directing you to take up to replace the bad ones? What or who might specifically help you in that effort? Can you set up a weekly time to meet for prayer and accountability, anywhere from one to six months, to help you stick with it?*

YOUR HEART - THE FOUNTAIN OF LIFE

# GETTING BACK UP

*"Brothers, I do not consider that I have made it my own. But one thing I do: forgetting what lies behind and straining forward to what lies ahead."*[241]

How do babies learn to walk? One of the most exciting moments for your mother and me was the day you began to learn to walk. But learning to walk takes time. You fell many times. But each time a you fell, you had to get up again! We can't conceive of a healthy baby on the 100th fall lying on the ground for the rest of their life, crying, "Well, I tried that walking stuff and it's not for me!" In your life, there will be many voices — outside and inside your head — telling you to give up. You need to listen to God's voice to get up and keep going.

There are three basic failures in life — physical, mental and moral. They often feed each other. Some people get around failures by changing the standards or pretending they are not failures, which makes matters worse. Here's an example: suppose you drove your dad's car after the oil light came on and the engine seized. You didn't pull over because you left home late for work. Now you've failed in all three areas. The engine is physically ruined, and the car is now scrap metal for your dad. Your judgment to leave home late and drive with a red oil light were both mental failures. Morally, you let down your dad, who was trusting you to be prudent, as well as your boss, who has a right to expect you to be at work on time. I think you understand how different failures can begin to compile and make matters worse.

Fortunately, most of our failures in life won't be that costly or embarrassing as my example. You may press your training too hard, tear a tendon, and miss an important race. You may fail an exam in school. You may fail to practice enough to get on a sports team or get through a musical tryout. Almost certainly, you will someday fail to get a job you are hoping for. Many failures include both circumstances beyond our control, and the poor choices we may make within our control. The good news is that any failure can become very

241  Philippians 3:13

helpful to you and others if you handle it in the right way.

Without a doubt, you will have moments when you will let down those who are close to you, yourself, or God . . . or all three. What will you do then? Will you benefit or flounder? Maybe you are struggling with a deep failure right now. If not, keep reading.

I experienced an accident many years ago. A sage and sympathetic, senior pilot told me, "There are those that have, and those that will."[242] Although that set a difficult chain of events in motion, I learned to trust in God through it. I missed an Air Force mission because of the accident and was threatened with harsh repercussions. My commander strongly encouraged me to seek a fresh start elsewhere. Reluctantly, I accepted a remote tour in Korea, far from my favorite place in the world. My new commander kindly sent me to instructor school in my "fresh start" airplane, a King Air. After a year in Korea, the assignment officer wanted to know if I would take a job in Panama as the theater check pilot for all the embassy King Air planes. What an improbable outcome to a distressing failure! Someday you will experience a seemingly catastrophic failure. How successfully you deal with it (or make it worse) may depend on what you decide beforehand.

242  Our accident was officially designated an "incident" since, thankfully, no one was hurt. I could not have imagined on that frustrating day the chain of events set in motion that enabled me to become an embassy theater check pilot. Now well qualified in a new plane, I was later accepted to a flying job in the Republic of Georgia where I learned Russian, and then moved on as chief pilot for Air Serv, opening doors to fly relief in Africa, Indonesia, Honduras, and Afghanistan. God turned my failure into blessing and help for others. Many times that "accident" caused me to think of 1 Corinthians 2:9, no eye has seen, nor ear heard, nor the heart of man imagined, what God has prepared for those who love him.

## PHYSICAL AND MENTAL FAILURE

Some of our "failures" are simply limitations. We all have them. Some people are better at math than others. Some, at music. Still others, at sports, writing, or leading. Frustration comes when we don't measure up to some expectation, either ours or someone else's. Several Bible verses tell us that comparing our God-given abilities or our plans isn't wise.[243](However, comparing moral inspiration, like generosity, is a different issue.[244])

My first pastor, Fulton Buntain, gave a helpful formula to his congregation:

### FRUSTRATIONS = UNMET EXPECTATIONS

What can we change in that equation when we are frustrated? We can only change our expectations. Our plans will be upset. Our dreams may be cut short. Peace will come when we trust God with our expectations.[245] We will pass a great milestone when we can join Paul and say:

> *"I have learned in whatever situation I am to be content. I know how to be brought low, and I know how to abound. In any and every circumstance, I have learned the secret of facing plenty and hunger, abundance and need. I can do all things through him who strengthens me."*[246]

### PROBLEMS CAN BE OPPORTUNITIES

Many writers and speakers have pointed out that "problems can be opportunities" if we rightly approach our challenges and failures. When we recognize God's love, power, and desire to bless us in Christ, we can embrace Paul's contentment, not just in the "serenity of accepting circumstances" beyond our control, but as tools intended to shape our character and future for good! Paul had a physical pain that he called a "thorn in the flesh." After asking God to take it away, he learned that there was a purpose in his problem: to keep him humble. Most of our limitations or "failures" bless us with greater humility and dependence on God.

243   John 21:23, 2 Corinthians 10:12, James 3:16, Proverbs 14:30
244   1 Corinthians 8:1-9
245   Philippians 4:7
246   Philippians 4:11-13

But the other lesson God may be wanting to teach us in our failure is perseverance. But not so we can just have what we want or so we can boast in ourselves.[247] Instead, God is looking for perseverance in doing good, walking by faith, and giving Him the credit. I love Paul's advice to the Philippians, *"Let us not lose heart in doing good, for in due time we will reap if we do not grow weary."*[248] He also says that everything we do, like math, music, our jobs, or sports, we should do as unto the Lord.[249] So if we fail at a task for Him, let's keep at it! James encourages us to keep our minds fixed on the future goal of God's reward if we are faithful. *"Blessed is a man who perseveres under trial; for once he has been approved, he will receive the crown of life which the Lord has promised to those who love Him."*[250] So when you experience a physical or mental failure, don't let your frustration keep you down, or you'll never learn to walk or run. Be like that baby learning to walk, and get up! *The only person who really fails is the one doesn't get up again.*

THINGS TO THINK ABOUT AND TALK OVER:

- *Is there a task you have failed at and feel like God is telling you, "Get up! Try again. I am with you!"? Should you tell a friend or family member who can encourage and help you?*

- *What is the biggest failure so far in your life? Was there a better way to respond to it than the one you chose? What did you learn or believe God wanted you to learn? Is there a task God gave you in the past and you gave up after failure? Is He telling you to get up, fix what you can, and try again?*

- *Paul wrote, "But one thing I do: forgetting what lies behind and straining forward to what lies ahead." What was he pressing on towards? (You may need to go to Philippians 3 to find the answer.) As you think about past failures or contemplate future ones, what do you think God wants you to press forward to? Does this mean we shouldn't ever remember failures or wisely share them to help others move ahead? What does it mean to "forget what lies behind"?*

---

247 James 4:3-4
248 Galatians 6:9
249 Colossians 3:23-24
250 James 1:12

- *Sara Blakely is a young billionaire who started her own business. When she was a girl, her dad would ask her and her sister at dinner how they had failed that day. He would give them a high five and then talk about what they learned through the experience. Can you talk about failures with someone close to you and learn from them? Although wisdom says you probably should not discuss certain failures with just anyone, should anything prevent you from talking with someone who loves you and can help you?*

# I REALLY MESSED UP!

*"Have mercy on me, O God,*
*according to your steadfast love;*
*according to your abundant mercy."* [251]

"I did something really dumb!" The young man's face was a distraught mixture of fear and hate for his poor judgment.

My friend Matt and I were praying outside of Planned Parenthood after business hours when he pulled up. We felt for the guy as we offered to help. "I messed up really bad and did something dumb in a moment of passion." With genuine concern, we suggested where he might find real assistance.

## MORAL FAILURES

Moral failures can be much harder than physical or mental ones. We still need to get up and try again, but the process is more complex. Moral failure often starts in, and injures, the deepest part of our being. How can you experience healing and freedom moving forward? Ignoring or redefining failure will only lead to further damage. Raw honesty, brokenness, and trust in the victory Christ gave us at the cross can heal, restore, and bring amazing joy to anyone — even the vilest offender. You are never beyond restoration as long as your heart is not hard and you continue to hate your sin.

Every victorious warrior needs to know who his enemy is and where he likes to attack from. In theology class at CIU, we were taught that temptation comes from "the world, the flesh, and the devil." All three may be at work at once. I don't like to give the devil credit for anything, which is why I don't spell his name with a capital letter. But one thing satan is good at is accusing. He even knows how to use the truth when it's helpful to his cause. Have you ever heard these words in your head: "You call yourself a *Christian*? Look at what you did! You are a disgrace. Just give up."? Ouch. But don't stop reading. Like all of satan's tricks, that's only half the truth. Two guys come to mind when I think of moral failure — Judas and Peter. Of course, the Bible is filled with characters who failed,

251  Psalm 51:1

which helps me realize I'm not alone. This isn't to provide us with a guilt-free, lame excuse, "Well, I'm only human." Instead, we can genuinely repent again, understanding there are no perfect saints, encouraged that there's hope, love, and forgiveness available for me, too. We can also learn from how others recovered . . . or sadly failed to recover . . . from their sin retold in scripture.

Judas and Peter were both Jesus followers. Both failed God in many instances, but most starkly on the day of Jesus' death. If there ever was a time that betrayal and denial would hurt the most, it would be as you were about to be captured, humiliated, and brutally murdered. Although I don't think Judas realized his betrayal would end in Jesus' death, since Judas tried to right his wrong by first giving back his bribe.[252] When that failed to help assuage his guilt, he took the drastic and horrible measure of killing himself. That, of course, is no real solution and removes any possibility of enjoying God's love, mercy, and gracious restoration. It also leaves family and friends without the benefit of watching from the sidelines as God displays His greatest work of glory — bestowing grace on the broken.[253] Instead, they are left with a dark emptiness and an example that excludes the ongoing work of God's hand of love.

Peter, on the other hand, betrayed Christ not just once, but three times. When he realized what he'd done, he wept bitterly. Perhaps you've wept like that over your sin. I hope so.

But Peter didn't try to "right his wrong." He just hung on. Something Jesus said to Peter probably helped him, and I hope it will help you, too: *"Simon, Simon, behold, satan demanded to have you, that he might sift you like wheat, but I have prayed for you that your faith may not fail. And when you have turned again, strengthen your brothers."*[254]

Hold on to these three things. One, Peter's denial didn't catch Jesus by surprise. Two, Jesus already had prayed for Peter. Three, God can and will use your sin to help others if you repent and allow Him to restore you.

Do you know that nothing you do surprises God? Not once did you sin and God said, "Woah! I didn't see that one coming. Well, I'm

252  Matthew 27:3
253  Ephesians 1:6
254  Luke 22:31-32

through with him!" Sounds silly, doesn't it? But that is often how we think.

Did you know Jesus is praying for you right now, just as He was praying for Peter? *"Christ Jesus is the one who died—more than that, who was raised—who is at the right hand of God, who indeed is interceding for us."*[255] Interceding is just a fancy word to say that He is praying, defending, and taking the heat for us so that we don't get incinerated.

So what did Peter do? By faith, he hung on. When the tomb was reported empty, he was there. When the others gathered together and were waiting in Jerusalem, he was there.[256] When he was told to go to Galilee, he went.[257] When John figured out it was the resurrected Jesus who was standing on a distant shore and told them how to make a record catch after a night of getting skunked, it was Peter who first jumped into the water to get to Jesus. It was Peter — by just hanging on and trusting the Lord — who was able to rejoice in his restoration by Christ Himself and was given his mission in ministry.[258]

So what should you do when you sin? Admit the fullness of your rebellion against God. Don't minimize it or make excuses. Don't complain about the consequences. Make restitution if needed. Know that God can fully forgive you.

One last important topic on moral failure: what about sexual failure? Paul had some strong words for the Christians who lived in Corinth (a city known for sexual immorality) where some of the believers were clearly failing:

*"Flee from sexual immorality. Every other sin a person commits is outside the body, but the sexually immoral person sins against his own body. Or do you not know that your body is a temple of the Holy Spirit within you, whom you have from God? You are not your own, for you were bought with a price. So glorify God in your body."*[259]

Sexual immorality is in a category by itself as a sin.[260] Why? Because

255  Romans 8:34
256  John 20, Luke 25
257  Matthew 28:16
258  John 21:15-19
259  1 Corinthians 6:18-20
260  The Bible defines this simply as sexual activity outside of marriage — mental or actual. Even sex inside of marriage can be sinful (the Bible calls it the marriage bed being "defiled";

it unites the deepest part of our being, our spirit, with something horrific. For the Christian, we are pushing our Lord into contact with that filth, because He resides in our heart and has purchased our freedom with His own life. How could we treat Him with such disdain? Yes, of course, sexual sin is usually pleasurable, but only for a moment. Imagine someone is making a cake and offers you a taste of the batter. Your mouth is watering as you dip your finger in the bowl. Only just before you put it in your mouth, you figure out it contains raw sewage. That is what illicit sex is like. It may be tantalizing and look sweet. But in just a little while, you'll find out it can put gangrene in your soul. Can other sins do that? Some. But few have the perverse ability to draw people back and into even worse levels of deprivation.

Failure of any kind is hard — physical, mental or moral. But how we allow God to deal with our failure will make us either bitter or better. Decide now that you will allow Him to refine your expectations. Know that none of your failures ever catch Him by surprise. Know that His mercy and grace are always enough for anyone who embraces the cross of Christ.

### THINGS TO THINK ABOUT AND TALK OVER:

- *One of the most grievous sexual and moral failures of the Bible was David's sin with Bathsheba, followed by his murder of her husband, Uriah. Incredibly, our righteous God forgave David. How could He forgive such a monstrous crime? Consider that Jesus took on His back the stripes for David's sins. The nails went in Jesus' hands and feet for the adultery and the heinous murder of a righteous husband. How can God forgive you of your worst sin? You might want to read Psalm 51 to get a better picture of an undeserving, contrite heart that can receive God's amazing offer of forgiveness and grace. Does guilt still give you pain? Stand with Paul and declare, "There is therefore now no condemnation for those who are in Christ Jesus." (Romans 8:1)*

- *Near the end of Romans 1, Paul notes that people who trade the living God for false gods can actually have their hearts hardened, making them desire more and more perverse sexual*

---

see Hebrews 13:4) if a husband or wife are thinking about someone else or engaging in dishonoring or unloving behavior in the marriage bed. Clean, pure, and loving sex inside of marriage can be one of the greatest experiences of life. Remember the chapter "Marriage as God Made It."

*sin. If you find yourself far from God and desiring any kind of perverse sin, what should you do? Even though it may seem impossible to you now, did you know that your disordered desires can become joyfully reordered by God?*

- *What can you do when your desires are different than God's? I find a good key here: Psalm 27:3-7, especially verse 4. Remember the brightest differences between Peter and Judas in how they dealt with their sin? How do you deal with yours? Do you need to change?*

YOUR HEART - THE FOUNTAIN OF LIFE

# SET FREE

*If you abide in my word, you are truly my disciples,*
*and you will know the truth, and the truth will set you free.*[261]

John Newton, a deeply repentant slave trading captain wrote about the horrible plight of the African slaves he once transported across the Atlantic. "Their lodging-rooms below the deck . . . are sometimes more than five feet high, and sometimes less; and this height is divided towards the middle (bunks so low that no one can sit up), for the slaves lie in two rows, one above the other . . . like books upon a shelf. . . . the poor creatures, thus cramped for want of room, are likewise in irons, for the most part both hands and feet . . .makes it difficult for them to turn or move, to attempt either to rise or to lie down, without hurting themselves, or each other. . . . The heat and smell of these rooms would be almost insupportable (unbearably putrid) to a person not accustomed to them. If the slaves and their rooms can be constantly aired, and they are not detained too long on board, perhaps there are not many who die."[262] "Not many" meant just one in five succumbed to a terrible death in the dark holds of a foreign ship — beaten, shackled, starved and thirsty, surrounded by the groans of human suffering, deep depression, the stench of diseased waste, violent sea-induced vomit and death.[263]

PLAN OF LOWER DECK WITH THE STOWAGE OF 292 SLAVES
130 OF THESE BEING STOWED UNDER THE SHELVES AS SHEWN IN FIGURE D & FIGURE 5.

Can you imagine being one of those slaves? Imagine your ship is

261  John 8:32
262  Newton, John Thoughts upon the African Slave Trade (London: J. Buckland and J. Johnson, 1788), pp. 33-34.
263  Slave ship drawing shows how tightly and inhumanely people were packed, Wikimedia Commons on Middle Passage pamphlet, 1790

intercepted by the Royal British Navy because slave trading has been declared illegal in their empire. You, your friends, and your family are brought up into freedom, fresh air, and sunshine. The shackles come off and you're given clean water to drink and something to eat. Your joy, gratitude, and relief would be beyond imagination.

You and I should experience a freedom that is even more exciting. How? Jesus gives us the key of faith to be set free from sin that destroys everything good in life. All we have to do is use it.

*"If you abide in My word, you are truly My disciples. And you will know the truth, and the truth will set you free."*[264]

Fresh air. Sunshine. Fresh water. Jesus' words are plain, but a new Christian may not know what to do next.

First, Jesus says "if you abide in My word . . ." So step one is to learn to abide in His Word. What does that mean? A newly freed slave doesn't need to be told that he needs food and water. The easiest way to get daily nourishment is to learn as much as you can of the Bible. Especially learn what it plainly says about God, you, and others. Don't be overly obsessed with harder, fine theological points at the start. Apply the practical truths of Jesus' teaching. Love your siblings. Go to a good Bible study, youth group, or home group. Give from your possessions to help others, even to your enemies. When you read a verse, put it into action.

Second, to really abide or live with someone, you need to talk to them and hear what they say. Some people live together but don't talk. That's not really abiding. It's just coexisting. That won't set anyone free.

Third, remember it is Jesus who is the One setting you free. The words are His, with tremendous power — "if the Son sets you free, you will be free indeed."[265]

You might say, "I don't feel like I'm a slave!" You would be like many people if that's how you feel. But consider what Jesus said to people who felt that way: "Everyone who practices sin is a slave to sin." Paul said something similar, "You are slaves to the one you obey." Some people say, "I can quit smoking anytime, I just don't

264  John 8:31-32
265  John 8:36

want to." Do you think they really have the willpower to quit, or does that sound like an excuse because they can't stop a bad habit? Without admitting we're trapped, we can never be set free!

THINGS TO THINK ABOUT AND TALK OVER:

- *Have you experienced the joy of the moment when Jesus said to you, "You are mine! I love you. Be free!" If you haven't, why not close your eyes right now and ask Him to do that? Don't stay below deck in the stench, shackled by your sin.*

- *What would you say to a friend who says, "I'm not anybody's slave. I've always been free"? What do you think Jesus might say? (One place you might look is John 8:33-34.)*

- *If Jesus sets someone free from sin, but they struggle and fall back into their old way of life, what do you think they were missing? How would you describe "abiding" with God to a friend?*

# NO MORE CHAINS

*"I am sure of this, that he who began a good work in you will bring it to completion at the day of Jesus Christ."*[266]

Being set free happens both in a moment and over a lifetime. When slaves were set free after the American Civil War, certainly there was great joy. But then began the long process of rebuilding life as a free people, an intense internal and external struggle.

As a Christian, you have all the power you need to be free of sin. Many, however, don't experience that freedom and joy because they are deceived. When your mom and I visited Thailand, we saw a baby elephant. He was tied firmly with a chain he could not break. We learned that forlorn baby elephants separated from their mothers will cry and try to break the chain for a day. Once they learn they can't succeed, they give up. Adult elephants who had that  lesson when they were young can be restrained by a rope they could easily break and a human they could simply crush. But they remain under control and submissive their whole lives because of what they learned when they were young. A Christian can believe the same lies . . . until they learn the truth. Let's consider some poisonous lies that keep people trapped in sin and then the antidotes that can set them free.

LIE NUMBER ONE: I can't stop this bad habit (insert whatever has trapped you: gossiping, smoking, porn, anger, etc.).

ANTIDOTE: God says He has given me all the power I need: *"No temptation has overtaken you that is not common to man. God is faithful, and he will not let you be tempted beyond your ability, but*

266 Philippians 1:6

*with the temptation he will also provide the way of escape, that you may be able to endure it."*[267]

LIE NUMBER TWO: I'm so ugly. I'm so stupid.

ANTIDOTE: God says He made me in His image and said after He made people, it was very good (Genesis 1:31). God doesn't make junk. He chose me before the foundation of the world and prepared good works for me to do in advance. I may not be the sharpest tool ever made, but I'm perfect for what He wants me to do (Philippians 1-2).

LIE NUMBER THREE: No one loves me. God doesn't care.

ANTIDOTE: God says He loves me. He cares so much for me that He sent His own Son to die for me (John 3:16). No one can love or care for anyone more than that, especially since He knew what a big sinner I would be (Romans 5:8).

LIE NUMBER FOUR: I'm all alone.

ANTIDOTE: God says He sent Jesus as "Immanuel" to be "God with us" (Isaiah 7:14). Jesus said that He would be with us *always, and never, ever leave us or forsake us* (Matthew 28:20, Hebrews 13:5-6).

LIE NUMBER FIVE: There's no purpose to life.

ANTIDOTE: God says He has given me spiritual gifts so that I can care for and help others! God tells me that I am a unique and important part of His big family and that even if I'm small, my role is essential (1 Corinthians 12).

How about two "positive" but lethal lies?

LIE NUMBER SIX: I'm a pretty good person. God will probably let me into heaven.

ANTIDOTE: God says *"all have sinned and fall short of the glory of God,"* and *"The heart is deceitful above all things, and*

---

267  1 Corinthians 10:13

*desperately wicked: who can know it?"*[268] Paul became an apostle but still said he was the "chief of all sinners."[269] In front of God, Isaiah the prophet said he was a man of unclean lips and Job put his hand over his mouth when God confronted him. We can cry out with joy, "Thank you, Lord Jesus, that if you could save the thief on the cross, you could even save me! There is now no condemnation for me as I stand made right in Christ."[270]

LIE NUMBER SEVEN: God knows I'm only human. Nobody's perfect. I've had this bad habit for so long. I'm sure He understands.

ANTIDOTE: God says, *"But nothing unclean will ever enter it, nor anyone who does what is detestable or false, but only those who are written in the Lamb's book of life."*[271] Or *"do you not know that the unrighteous will not inherit the kingdom of God?"*[272] And again He says: *"Humble yourselves before the Lord, and he will exalt you."*[273]

Are you seeing how the truth of God's Word sets us free?

I'm sure there are hundreds, if not thousands, of poisonous lies out there that the world, the devil and we ourselves use, which keeps imprisoned and suffering. Remember that just like the spreading poison from a snake bite, the clock is running. The longer we wait to find the antidote, the longer we will suffer and the sooner death may come.

One more important question — If you were bitten by a snake, would you tough it out or call a friend to help? You'd better call a friend quick! A brother or sister in Christ can be a great help. But there is no greater helper or friend than Jesus Himself.

Enormous joy comes when you are set free from the enslavement and poison of deception and sin. Keep that precious freedom and walking close to Jesus, remembering how His love sets you free from horrific oppression. Not long before my first pastor retired, I was going through a difficult time in life. Ministry was hard and I was lacking joy. Pastor Buntain brightly stood out to me as someone

268 Romans 3:23 ESV Jeremiah 17:9 KJV
269 1 Timothy 1:15
270 Romans 8:1
271 Revelation 21:27
272 1 Corinthians 6:9
273 James 4:10

who ministered faithfully and never lost his joy. On a short visit home, I caught him after a service in Tacoma and asked him, "Pastor Buntain, how do you keep your joy?" His answer surprised me, but deeply resonated with me: "It would be hard for me to say just one thing, but if I had to say one, it would be that I never forget what a sinner I am." Without elaboration, I understood what he meant. It was the same fuel that allowed John Newton, a horrible, slave-trading captain, to rejoice in a merciful God and write the hymn Amazing Grace.

THINGS TO THINK ABOUT AND TALK OVER:

- *Do you feel like you have been set free from your old passions and sins? Do you feel as joyful as a slave who has just been set free? If not, how might you get that feeling?*

- *Are there any poisonous lies that might be in your life? What do you think the antidote might be? If you aren't sure, do you know someone who would probably know the Bible well enough to help you? Is there any good reason why you shouldn't call or visit them right now?*

- *Can you effectively help someone else who is enslaved if you are still a slave? If you are set free from sin by God (not by your own hand), how can you help others?*

# WHEN TO FIGHT AND WHEN TO RUN

*"Defend the weak and the fatherless;*
*uphold the cause of the poor and the oppressed."*[274]

When I was a kid, Kenny Rogers sang a song about playing cards and living life, "You gotta know when to hold 'em, know when to fold them, know when to walk away and know when to run!"[275] While I probably wouldn't take Kenny Rogers' personal advice on life too far, there is some good insight in his hit song.

## WOULD A BRAVE CHRISTIAN EVER RUN?

I remember our first lesson of "unarmed combat" at the Air Force Academy. The instructor asked, "What is your best defense when you are faced with certain conflict and you have no weapon?" His answer came after we thought for awhile, "Your legs! A smart individual avoids conflict when possible." Paul wrote, *"If possible, so far as it depends on you, live peaceably with all."*[276]

At least partly with that in mind, Paul decided to run several times, often at the advice of friends. First, as a brand new Christian threatened with death in Damascus, he escaped by being lowered in a basket out a back window. Later, as an apostle, he miraculously escaped death in the town of Lystra during his first missionary journey. He ran from threats in Thessalonica and Berea on his second journey and avoided a murderous crowd in Ephesus on his third missions trip.[277]

Jesus slipped away from a crowd after quietly healing a crippled man on a Sabbath day.[278] Later, Jesus had to stay up north or visit Jerusalem unnoticed, because the Jewish leaders in the south wanted to kill Him.[279] Even up north in the town where Jesus grew up, He had to escape angry neighbors who wanted to throw Him off a cliff.[280]

---

274  Psalm 82:3 (NIV)
275  Schlitz, Don 1978.f
276  Romans 12:18
277  Acts 9:22-25
278  John 5:13
279  John 7:1-13
280  Luke 4:29-30

Over and over, John tells us that they couldn't kill Jesus because "His time had not yet come."

## WHEN DOES A SMART CHRISTIAN STAND HIS OR HER GROUND?

Of course, Jesus, Paul, and many others chose to stand at other times, even when death was a strong possibility or certainty. In fact, in the example above when Jesus' neighbors wanted to kill Him, it was precisely because He chose to stand up to them with truth. He confronted their pride and condescension so powerfully that they were ready to murder Him. In the end, when Jesus' time to give up His life finally came, He rode straight into Jerusalem on a donkey, fulfilling the prophecy foretold 500 years earlier by Zechariah about the King coming with salvation.[281] His provocation of the priests and leaders was powerful. The time was right and the Passover was at hand. The Lamb of God had come to give His life.

Years later, in spite of tears and appeals from friends warning Paul not to go to Jerusalem, he went anyway, where he was nearly killed and ended up imprisoned for years. Many prophets, apostles, and servants like Stephen paid the ultimate price because of their stand for truth. A smart Christian will stand his ground when He knows the the honor of God, love or lives are at stake. The Holy Spirit will tell you, "Stand! Speak!

## WHAT DO YOU STAND FOR? WHAT SHOULD YOU STAND FOR?

Jesus said, "Greater love has no one than this, that someone lay down his life for his friends."[282] A few hours after saying that, Jesus did exactly that. Most of us, if we are honest, would struggle with the idea of dying in order to save someone. That's normal. That's also why we honor firemen, police officers, and soldiers who do. Do you love God that much, that you would die for His honor? Do you love others so much that you would give up a well-paying job, study Bible translation, and take the gospel to cannibals or hostile people? If not, pray that God would give you that kind of passion for Him and for others.

There are foolish principles people stand on, the worst of which is

281  Zechariah 9:9
282  John 15:13

personal pride. Alexander Hamilton, a famous American founding father, died in a dual while still in his forties. The reason? He didn't like Vice President Aaron Burr, who was running for Governor of New York and insulted him publicly. Burr challenged Hamilton to a duel, who accepted in spite of knowing it was illegal, not God's will, and that his first son died at the age of nineteen also in a duel. Jesus told us to "turn the other cheek"[283] when someone strikes us or "go the extra mile," even when an enemy asks for the first one. Never stand or fight for the sake of pride.

However, *for the sake of love, we should always be willing to risk our safety.* A husband should always be willing to lay down his life for his wife. A father, for his children. A Christ follower, for those who are lost. Of course, the risks are not always so evident before we make a decision to stand. But even the ultimate sacrifice for the Christian means they pass from life to life, into the amazing presence of God Himself. That doesn't mean we look for an opportunity to be a martyr, but we should be willing to lay down our lives when God calls on us for the sake of love.

### WHAT ABOUT WHEN JESUS, PAUL, AND OTHERS CHOSE NOT TO STAY IN HARM'S WAY?

One, they were willing to die, and ultimately did die for others. The leading verse for this chapter is *"Defend the weak and the fatherless; uphold the cause of the poor and the oppressed."* You should always stand your ground to defend the weak, defenseless. Two, they knew how to hear the voice of the Holy Spirit and move as He directed.

### BUT WHAT IF I AM AFRAID?

I would be surprised if you were not! Even Jesus asked the Father to take away His cup of suffering. But do you trust God? Do you believe He has the power and desire to protect you, but also in His wisdom may allow you to suffer for the sake of others? If you struggle, ask God for faith and boldness. Ask others to pray for you in that way like Paul and others did.[284] There's no shame in being honest with God and others about your fears. God will certainly help you.

283
284  Acts 4:23-31, Ephesians 6:19

So when do you stand, fight, walk away or run? If you are supposed to walk away or run, the Holy Spirit will tell you and there is no shame in that. He will also help you deal with wrong pride or fear, if you are listening. Ultimately, always be willing to stand for crucial truth, God's honor, other's lives and for love. Our lives are in God's hands. Before missionary Jim Elliot was murdered in 1956, he said it well, "He is no fool who gives up what he cannot keep to gain what he cannot lose."

THINGS TO THINK ABOUT AND TALK OVER:

- *Have you ever had to make a choice to either stand or run?*

- *What did you do? What do you think would help you in future confrontations to do the right thing?*

- *David was another character in the Bible who stood his ground in the face of danger (1 Samuel 17) but ran at other times (1 Samuel 19-20, 23, 2 Samuel 15). How could he stand up to Goliath but run from Saul? Do you think God was directing David's direction? Was God protecting him in all those situations?*

- *How do you think you can hear the Holy Spirit in a tense moment? Have you tried to cultivate an ear for His direction when everything is going well? Do you know any Bible verses that help you know how to hear God and know His will? (Romans 12 is a good passage.) Do you know any Scriptures that can help you be bold or trust in Him? (Matthew 28:20 and Joshua 1:9 help me.)*

# WHEN LIFE DOESN'T GO THE WAY YOU PLANNED

*"Many are the plans in a person's heart,
but it is the Lord's purpose that prevails."* [285]

"It's a girl, it's a girl!" The women outside burst into jubilant cheers. Jairus and his wife had been childless for years. They prayed and visited the doctors, but nothing seemed to help. Jairus was from a prominent family and was himself well respected. He was climbing all the social and professional ladders. But emptiness gnawed at his heart without little ones to come home to after a long day. That feeling of hopelessness was all replaced when his dear wife missed her monthly cycle almost nine months earlier. Now they had a precious daughter to call their own. Jairus kissed his tired but smiling wife on the forehead, and together they thanked the Lord for this tiny bundle of joy He had given them.

Meanwhile, just a few houses away, a young woman grew distraught. More than a week had gone by and her monthly cycle was not ending. In fact, it seemed to be getting worse. She felt sick, clammy, and dizzy. Her mother sent for the doctor, but he was puzzled. He gave her some advice and a few herbs, but they made no difference. The blood continued to flow. She couldn't go to the house of worship like this. That wasn't allowed for unclean people. If she actually touched someone else, they would also be unclean for a day. She hardly dared to put her head outside her home, but in the evenings just before dark, she'd sneak down to the lake to wash her blood-stained rags. Even though she tried to keep it a secret, soon the whispers began. Surely she had "sinned" to be so punished by God. But she held onto the hope that in the end Job was declared righteous by God. She knew that no man would ever want her hand in marriage, although she longed for love and a family. She spent all she had looking for a cure and endured painful treatments that didn't work. Her closest friends stopped coming around, and she felt dirty, hopeless, and unloved. Her life became one lived in the shadows as the months stretched into years. She hated to count, but twelve years had passed, and she hoped this might be the year that her suffering

285  Proverbs 19:21

would end. She wondered if God saw her miserable existence or even cared.

Back in Jairus' house, their daughter was all that they could have dreamed for — better than ten sons. She was the apple of her father's eye. Fathers are often close to their daughters, and this was especially true in their family. Jairus loved to see his daughter smile, and it felt like heaven when he came home from work. She could hear his footsteps far down the street, and would run to the door and throw her arms around his neck, saying, "Daddy! I love you so much!" She played the flute to everyone's delight and loved to recite the Holy Scriptures. Truly, Jairus felt like a blessed man. His daughter began to grow tall and look like a young woman. Jairus knew he'd soon have to keep a wary eye on the young men and was looking around at prospects that he might recommend to his daughter in a few short years. His heart skipped a beat to think that he might have granddaughters that were like her. Maybe even grandsons! He would delight in either.

All that changed in a blinding moment. Whether it was her becoming a young woman that triggered some illness in his precious girl, or some unclean, diseased person had gotten too close to her at the market, he didn't know. Maybe he had sinned in some way. The doctors were of no help. His princess, the light of his life who reminded him so much of his dear wife, was slipping from life and there was nothing he could do. She was ashen grey and began to make a raspy noise as she labored to breathe. The doctors said it wouldn't be long. With tears streaming down his face, Jairus cried out to God, "Please, God! Don't! Don't take my little girl! I don't think I could live! Tell me what to do. I'll do anything you say." Instantly, he thought of Jesus, a visiting Rabbi who had healed so many others.

Although I've added some color to paint a picture, these were real people. Real circumstances. Life was good and then changed in a moment. The threads of their lives intersected, but barely. They had probably even fellowshipped together in the town synagogue before the young lady had gotten sick. They may have even lived a stone's throw apart from each other. For twelve years, their worlds were light-years apart — or so they thought. That was about to radically change. What do you do when life is going great, but then suddenly takes a sharp turn to despair? What is God doing? It may be your first romance that vaporizes overnight. It may be the college or job you dreamed of, but your advisor or supervisor says, "You don't fit here anymore." Or like Jairus' family, an illness or an accident puts your best friend on life support.

First, you'll probably do what everyone naturally does and cry out, "God! I don't know what's going on here, but I really need Your help! Maybe I did something wrong. If I did, please forgive me. Show me what I can do. I feel so helpless. Please, only You can do something!" Resist any urge to accuse God of wrongdoing. He is working even this situation for good.

Trust in God's Word. If you can't remember any verses by heart, go to the Bible and open the Psalms, Romans 8 or First Corinthians 13. There you will find rock solid promises that God loves you and is working all things together for good, if you love and trust Him even if you can't yet see the big picture.

Have you ever seen a tapestry?[286] On the back side, it looks like a mess. But the artist knows exactly what he or she wants the picture on the front to look like. As God weaves the different colors of your life, He is creating a masterpiece of beauty that will be completed on the day Jesus comes back for us. You will be breathless someday when you see the front. But for now, you see the back. God takes a smooth golden thread and weaves it close to a rough gray one. Then a black one by a yellow. So it goes for countless ages. You may

286  Photo from Lisa Blatchford, Rug Secrets, 2005.

occasionally get a glimpse in this life. But what joy and peace you can have when you tell the Master, "I may not understand, but I trust Your hands and Your heart."

Your hard season will not likely last for twelve years. It could. It could even last longer. But be assured that it will end in a glorious way if you trust the Lord to have His way.

To finish reading the story of what happened to Jairus, his family, and the suffering woman, turn to Luke 8. God heard their cries and Jesus intersected their lives for eternity. I can't help but believe they became friends in the days that followed. God is always laboring to bring His estranged family together, even at great cost. The question is, how will you respond?

THINGS TO THINK ABOUT AND TALK OVER:

- *What do you fear may or may not happen in life? Do you believe it helps to think about hard times before they happen and how you might respond? Can anyone insulate themselves from every hurt? Is it healthy to make that a priority? What will help you respond in a healthy way that honors God?*

- *What is the hardest disappointment you've experienced? Do you think God knew beforehand what would happen and even planned for it? If He loves you so much that He planned Jesus' death for your salvation, do you think He can and designed good to come out of your pain? Can you think of anyone in history for whom that clearly took place? Was their response a part of the blessing that came?*

# BEING THANKFUL

*"Give thanks in all circumstances;*
*for this is the will of God in Christ Jesus for you."*[287]

There are some languages in the world where there is no word for "thanks." Still others may have the word but don't use it. I remember my first trip to Kazakhstan. My dear Russian host family, who was so kind to me, thought it strange that I said spacibo or "thank you" so much. One day their son even asked me about it, "Why do you say spacibo so often?" I told him it was because I was so grateful for all they did, knowing that they didn't have much, but they were still wonderfully generous and kind to me. That was the truth and my answer seemed to satisfy him.

Do you want to know a secret? Genuinely thankful people are happy people! They see things that most people pass right by and don't notice. Gratitude is also a key part of love — a way to say to someone, "I saw what you did for me and really appreciate it!" Most people do things all day long that others rarely notice. Your mom cleans clothes, makes meals, shops, drives you everywhere, and helps you with school work. How often do you say "thank you" for those things? Do you think you would brighten her day if you let her know you specifically appreciate what she does for you rather than grumble about having to eat the same breakfast or that she makes you do sports and homework or just makes you get out of bed?

What about your teachers who work so hard but don't expect their students to say "thank you"? Imagine their surprise if you and your friends at different times either said, "Mrs. Hiett, I don't know how much you work at home to make Latin lessons, but I'm sure it's a lot. Thank you, so much. We love your class." Or what if you made Mrs. Christensen a card, telling her thanks. What about the people who work at Walmart for little pay? Do you think it would cheer their day to hear someone say, "You know, we are so grateful for your work here. You keep things on the shelves, pick up messes, and smile all day for customers. Thank you!" Many people have

287  1 Thessalonians 5:18

hard problems at home or tough bosses at work. A kind word of thanks can bring them real joy and peace.

An interesting thing happens when we start noticing what people around us do for us. We begin to connect more, which helps us to love more. When we give thanks and encourage others, that gives us more joy!

But what about God? Sure, we thank Him before we eat or when something really big happens, like somebody gets healed or we find an unexpected twenty-dollar bill in our pocket. But when is the last time you thanked God for water? Ice? Air? How about the sunrise? Your skin? Eyelids that blink by themselves? (You can actually go blind if your eyes don't do that.) Have you thanked God for flies that take care of rotten garbage for us? What about mosquitoes that feed fish so we enjoy fishing and eating seafood. How about dinosaurs and billions of tons of plants that lived a long time ago so we could get oil from the ground and drive our car to soccer, school, and the store? Are you beginning to get the picture? We could start in the morning and not stop thanking God for all kinds of things until we went to bed. How cool would that be? Glue. Light. Birds. Wasps that eat caterpillars instead of letting them eat our garden. Plastic. Wood. Bonfires. Marshmallows. Photosynthesis. Apples and cinnamon. Gravity. Imagination. Noses and ears. Salt.

Have you ever wondered what God's will for your life is? Re-read the verse on the last page from First Thessalonians 5:18. What is God's will for you in Christ Jesus? That you give thanks! He also put a tough qualifier on it. Give thanks in all circumstances. It's easy to give thanks when we get what we passionately wanted or when someone does something unusually kind for us. But what about circumstances when we are sick or we are disappointed with a friend? Why should anyone give thanks then? Simple. We are telling God, "I love You and trust You right now. I know You will bring good even out of hurt and disappointment."

One of the brightest examples of this I have heard is from Corrie Ten Boom. She was in a miserable Nazi concentration camp because her family had harbored Jewish people in their home. Her sister, Betsie, had a deeper faith than Corrie had back then. When Corrie was complaining about the deplorable conditions there, Betsie reminded her of the verse they had read that morning, the one above from First Thessalonians: "Give thanks in all circumstances!" So they gave thanks for the fact that they were still together, that they had smuggled in a small Bible, and even that the prison was so overcrowded. This would allow more people to hear the good news. Betsie even gave thanks for the biting fleas. For Corrie, that was a step too far! Biting fleas? Some time later, Betsie found out that the guards stayed out of their barracks, allowing them freedom to share God's Word, because they wanted to avoid the fleas![288]

You know what? Giving thanks by faith can actually make you begin to *feel* thankful. When you feel thankful, joy will follow. Experience joy by saturating your life with gratefulness.

THINGS TO THINK ABOUT AND TALK OVER:

- *When you are feeling sad or discouraged, make a list of ten people or things you are grateful for. Tell God directly, "Thank you, God, for _____." For me, that's one of the fastest ways to disperse any fog of depression. Have you ever thought you could give God thanks for giving us words to say thanks?*

- *Who have been some influential people for good in your life? Take some time to send them a note or text, or make time to call or visit, and tell them thanks.*

288  Ten Boom, Corrie The Hiding Place

# BEING CREATIVE

*"[The Lord] has filled him with the Spirit of God, with skill, with intelligence, with knowledge, and with all craftsmanship . . ."*[289]

Who is the most creative Being in the universe? Here is my candidate: He made nebulae, galaxies, stars, and planets in a stunning array of different sizes, colors, temperatures, and elements. He designed dragonflies, horse flies, and house flies. He shaped hummingbirds, emus, woodpeckers, and harpy eagles. He made goldfish, flying fish, lionfish, stingrays, and electric eels. He hewed adventurous boys and warm-hearted girls. He made gerbils, koala bears, hippos, and zebras. We could make more lists of crystals, precious metals, flowers, and insects. Then we could take endless pictures of rainbows, sunsets, and changing clouds. I think you have the idea. God loves beauty and creativity!

You know what else? Out of everything God made, only you and the angels can be creative, too. It makes sense that our creative, beauty-loving Father put that passion into His children. He loves it when you take the special gifts you have and turn them into an act of love for Him in a new and different way. Of course, poetry, music, and visual arts (sculpting, painting, and stained glass) are traditional and wonderful expressions of love for God. But there can be so many more.

I remember a wonderfully creative and popular musician, Michael Card, came every two years to CIU to teach a class on being creative. He asked what the class did for their profession. What hobbies did they enjoy? For their final exam, they had to express creative worship to God in one of their passions or gifts. One architect designed a beautiful building that gave glory to God. Another student prepared a five-course meal for the class that had meaning behind each dish and tasted fantastic.

How else might we use our unique gifts and insights to delight and glorify God? How about a cabinet maker who picks the finest grained woods for his customers and engraves in the corner of each: TGBTG (To God Be The Glory)? A boy might build a tree fort where his

---

289  Exodus 31:3

friends can come on a sunny Christmas morning. He could have a specially drilled hole through which he could cast a spotlight on a manger scene carved on the wooden wall inside just when the sun is at the right angle on that day. On July 4th, he might drill another hole that points to a verse carved on the wall: "He whom the Son sets free is free indeed." An accountant might be awoken early in the morning yearning for a way to worship God with her gifts. Then she realizes how to help her church free up 10% of their expenses to support a Bible translation for people who have never had the chance to worship God in their own language. The possibilities are endless.

As many stars as there are in the sky multiplied by the number of people on earth is the number of possibilities for how we might creatively express our love to God. The Bible tells us to sing a new song to the Lord.[290] Maybe you can dance a new dance. Maybe you can write a new book. What are your ideas?

### THINGS TO THINK ABOUT AND TALK OVER:

- *What gifts and skills do you have? Ask a few people close to you what you are good at or might become good at if you tried. Think of a project that might take a few days (or maybe even months or years) to complete that would express your love to God.*

- *Not all gifts and skills are easily perfected. In fact, most take a great deal of time and effort to develop. What would you like to work on? What do you think God would like you to work on? Who or what might help?*

- *Read Colossians 3:23: "Whatever you do, work at it with all your heart, as working for the Lord, not for human masters." What do you think? Would a fitting creative expression of love to God be anything less than your very best?*

290  Psalm 96:1

# READY FOR SURPRISES

*"In your hearts honor Christ the Lord as holy, always being prepared to make a defense to anyone who asks you for a reason for the hope that is in you; yet do it with gentleness and respect"*[291]

"Dad, would you like a surprise?" Miracle's young eyes always sparkle when she holds out a closed fist with some treasure inside.

"Sure! It's not a new belly button is it?" That was our inside joke from the "train robber" at Silver Dollar City. Bad Bart was caught by the sheriff who asked if he liked surprises. After Bart's goofy enthusiasm at the thought of a surprise, the sheriff offered him a new belly button surprise while pointing a pistol at him.

Of course, Miracle's surprises are always sweet — a cookie, a paper heart, or a drawing that says, "I luv u, dad!" Samuel also loves to surprise his mom and sisters, ideally with a frog or a lizard. But in the end, I think the message is still the same: "I love you."

Did you notice that things happen unexpectedly every day from the time you wake up until you go to bed? Some people get nervous about the "unexpected" and try to create a world to protect themselves. Sure, almost everyone likes to be offered a cookie, but who wants a frog? Well, I do. Why? Because I know Samuel loves me. I also know God loves me way more. He has surprises in store for me every day. Some are pleasant. Some unpleasant. But they are all in love and for greater purposes than I can usually imagine.

Peter tells us in the verse above to be ready to give an answer for the hope inside us. Hardly ever has anyone come out and asked me how I have hope that gives me joy. They can sometimes see something unusual and might feel God's love for them through me. But I often help them ask the question so I can answer it. How does that work?

First, I pray in the morning something like this, "God, forgive me of my sins. I want to be a clean instrument in Your hands to bless other people and love them in Jesus' Name. Thank you for forgiving and

---

291   1 Peter 3:15

cleansing me! Help me to see unexpected opportunities and to have words to say that will open people's hearts to You." I also read God's Word so He might speak something fresh to me and encourage me by His love, correction, and guiding hand.

Second, I try to have some helpful Bible verses or stories memorized that will interest someone and help them to think about God, life, and eternity. I might even review a good question or two before heading out the door: "When you leave this life, do you know where you are going? May I tell you an interesting, short story? Is there anything I can pray for you about? Is there anything keeping you from giving your life to Christ today?"

Next, as I'm going about my day — buying groceries, going to the doctor's office, or talking to kids at school — I'm always asking God what I can say to help someone be encouraged, smile, or see His love. If I'm on a run and see someone who looks gloomy sitting on a park bench, I'll pray and see if God wants me to pause and ask how they are doing. Whenever I ask anyone how they are doing, I always listen carefully for their tone or a shift in their eye or body that may indicate a "fine" answer is covering something else.

If I ever get the chance (and I wait on the Lord's leading), I always try to share two things. One is my testimony, either about my salvation or healing or something else God has done in my life. Second, I really want to give them a Bible verse that I think God wants them to have. Those are two of the most powerful, potentially life-changing things we can offer anyone — if they are done in love.

Finally, I try to write their name down so I can pray for them.

Most people will respond well to a "surprise" encounter when they sense you are caring and sincere. The only way to do that daily is to ask God to sand off your rough edges and fill you with His love.

Still, some won't respond well to your efforts or ideas. Peter says that's okay, too. In fact, he even says that God may want you to suffer for doing good.[292] For some people, your kind response to an ugly threat may be the best way they will see the reality of God's love.

292  "For it is better to suffer for doing good, if that should be God's will, than for doing evil." (1 Peter 3:17)

There are many other unpleasant surprises you may experience in a day. Your eggs for breakfast were burnt and then cold by the time you ate them. You were late for school. You forgot there was a math test today. A good friend "unfriended" you on social media. You got cornered by a bully. Very often, people are looking at our response, either for entertainment or to be surprised as they catch a glimpse of God's love and power at work when hard things happen.

"Forewarned is forearmed!" my eighty-year-old friend, Jerry Capel, likes to say. That means since you know something difficult is probably going to happen, you'll be ready. That takes a little of the edge off. But we don't know exactly what it will be. Who does? God does! He will not allow you to be challenged harder than you can respond in faith.[293] If the Holy Spirit is inside of you, you have all the power and knowledge you need to react with wisdom and love. This gives me tremendous peace and confidence before walking out the door in the morning into an unknown world. My heavenly Father has already gone before me and no matter how hard my day may get, He will enable me to handle any surprise well.

What is our main problem when we don't handle a situation well? We are all "clogged up." We don't take time to ask for God's forgiveness, washing and filling. We don't talk to Him during the day, asking for guidance. When we do ask, we often refuse to obey. "What?! Tell her I'm sorry? She started it."

Are you seeing that you can be forearmed in the morning because God has forewarned us, "I'm going to bring some challenges into your life today. But I will tell you what to do if you are open." That means I have to get my big, sensitive ego off the throne and let Jesus rule. What a great way to live and love in an unpredictable, surprise-filled world.

THINGS TO THINK ABOUT AND TALK OVER:

- *Have you ever watched Bruce Lee or some other tough movie character walk into impossible odds? Although there may be a moment of concern before the fight begins, there is a fun, sure confidence we enjoy as we know that he knows he can handle*

293   "God is faithful, and he will not let you be tempted beyond your ability, but with the temptation he will also provide the way of escape, that you may be able to endure it." (1 Corinthians 10:13b)

the bad guys. Is there a picture here that helps you trust in God in crisis?[294] He is a thousand Bruce Lee's in you and around you, ready to deal with the situation with a smile. (No that doesn't mean you do martial arts on your brother or math teacher!)

- Can you think of a recent, unpleasant surprise you didn't handle well? What would have helped you be ready to deal with it better?

- We all like nice surprises. What kinds of fun things can you think of to do or give tomorrow to bring joy into someone's life? Is there anyone you know who is going through an especially hard time right now? What is something can you do for them as a nice surprise? What will you do if they didn't receive your effort well?

- Why do you think God brings hard surprises into our lives? Wouldn't it be a lot easier if we all could see everything in advance and be ready? Even better, why not just remove the unpleasantries in life completely? If you struggle finding an answer, talk to an older, wise person and see how they answer. Or consider this John Piper quote: Nobody ever says, "I made my greatest advances in holiness on the happiest days of my life." Nobody says that. Everybody says, "I made my greatest advances in holiness on the hardest days of my life."[295] You might read again my chapter "When Life Doesn't Go the Way You Planned."

294  Image from Pixabay Common Domain
295  Piper, 2005 Desiring God Conference, https://www.desiringgod.org/interviews/interview-with-john-piper

# WHEN YOU ARE AFRAID

*"There is no fear in love, but perfect love casts out fear. For fear has to do with punishment, and whoever fears has not been perfected in love."*[296]

When I was little, I had this repeated, terrifying dream about bears that were trying to get me. I don't know why I was so afraid. They weren't growling or drooling and didn't have especially big teeth. But some nights, I hated to go to sleep for fear that my nightmare would come back.

Don't ever think that fear comes only to kids. After a youth camp in Panama, I got a phone call from a young man. "Are you Rob Stone?" "Yes, I am." "I'm Greg's brother and I'm going to kill you." Greg had been in my cabin the past week and had come to faith in Christ. He had been a satanist and the change was dramatic. I didn't know Greg's brother, but his threat sounded deadly serious. I could only guess that he had a gun and that if he knew my number, he probably knew where I lived, too. I wasn't overly afraid, but the situation was definitely disconcerting.

What should we do when we are afraid? Of course, the first thing we should do is talk to God. He has total control. He loves us and knows exactly what to do. We should do what He says, even if we are trembling. That is when we are most likely to see Him turn a fearful crisis into a marvelous triumph.

### CRAZY LOVE

My friend, Kevin, went with a team to distribute aid to refugees in Iraqi camps. But the fighting became so desperate that refugees weren't allowed to go to camps anymore. Instead, the team took the aid directly into Mosul. They took sniper fire from a roof but every bullet missed them. Their relief truck got hit by an RPG that didn't explode. They even rescued a squad of Iraqi soldiers who had been ambushed by radicals. The team heard about a Sunni village that lost a family due to a Western coalition airstrike and decided to go and offer help. As the team drew near, they realized they had

296   1 John 4:18

actually arrived during the funeral. An older man came running up, full of rage, yelling in Arabic, "You killed my family!" Kevin said they were afraid of what the man might do in his anger. The team leader knelt on the dirt and then put his face to the ground in front of the man, "We are so sorry! We didn't have anything to do with the attack and came to offer help. But if it will make you feel better, kill me right now!" What do you think the Sunni man did? He actually fell on the ground in tears and hugged the team leader!

### A SWORD WOULD HELP

Learn some verses that will help you. The Bible calls God's Word a "sword." Fear is a normal first reaction to a threat. But what we do next depends a good deal on what we know to be true. One of the greatest truths to help you is: *God is with us.* "Never will I leave you! Never will I forsake you!" [297] And, "Lo, I am with you, even to the end of the ages." [298] And the apostle Paul writes, "Nothing can separate us from the love of God that is in Christ Jesus." [299]

### UMM, IS THAT YOUR LION?

When I was in high school, I knew a girl whose family owned a wild game park. She had several tame, large cats (think tigers, lions.) She could walk in the most dangerous park at midnight with zero fear. No one dared touch her. How much greater is the God Who is with us! We are the apple of His eye. I feel sorry for anyone who would threaten us or do us harm. King David, who faced many scary moments, said, "I will fear no evil for *you are with me!*" [300] If you pay close attention to this famous Psalm by a shepherd boy who faced the teeth of wild beasts, you might notice that he shifted from talking about God ("*The Lord is my shepherd ...*") to talking to God ("*you are with me!*") at the very moment of danger in the middle of his song.

### LOOKING BACK TO LOOK FORWARD

Truthfully, most fears never become a reality. They fade or change with time. My dreams about bears gradually stopped. I used to be afraid of having no place to live or nothing to eat if my parents died.

297  Hebrews 13:5b
298  Matthew 28:20
299  Romans 8:28-29
300  Psalms 23:4 (The underline style is mine, which is the center point of David's famous Shepherd's Psalm, when he shifts from talking about God to talking directly to God.)

But God has always taken care of me. Look back. Has God not taken care of you? You've had some tough moments and He has seen you through, even when you may not have noticed. Those hard times should make us stronger and cause our faith to grow. Journaling is a great way to help both look back and remember how God has helped us and look ahead to the future without fear. I can't tell you how helpful it has been during my low moments to look back in my journal and remind myself how many times God has delivered me. I really encourage you to journal about your life — and especially answers to prayer! Don't make the mistake of thinking, "I'll *never* forget this amazing moment!" You will! Write it down. Even if you just keep one page of "Answered Prayers, Miracles, and Stories of God's Hand in My Life," you will have a rich collection to help you keep trusting in Him on dark days.

### POWER, LOVE, AND SELF-CONTROL

Some fears may be irrational or exaggerated, and yet can still be inexplicably terrifying. There are different fears like fear of heights, small places, dirt, or spiders. Some fears are very real, like the threat of death to first century Christians. Whether fear of spiders, soldiers, or bankruptcy, Paul's wisdom to his young friend, Timothy, still helps me today:

> *"God gave us a spirit not of fear but of power and love and self-control."* [301]

When you feel fear gripping you for any reason, God will strengthen you more and more as you:

- Ask for help and wisdom. He will be there for you.
- Remember the almighty Lion of the universe is with you and will not fail you; remember He has always delivered you before.
- Quote the truths of Scripture that will strengthen you. The flashing sword of God's Word is enough to scatter every fear, old and new.

Remember Greg's brother who threatened to kill me when Greg became a Christian at camp? I prayed and knew that the thought of a surprise attack by an unknown young man was not something God wanted to terrify me. I told some friends I was going to visit the

---

301  2 Timothy 1:7, Paul wrote these words from a terrible prison — probably his last preserved letter before he was executed.

family and asked them to pray. After meeting face-to-face, Greg's brother realized I was just a regular person who only wished his family well. He even apologized for his phone call. Apparently, Greg had arrived home so hot for God that he was preaching to his mom and brother, who weren't very interested yet to hear about heaven or hell. I reminded Greg that he had lived many years before coming to Christ, so he should extend grace and patience to his family, showing God's love to them without being overly pushy.

I learned that even though persecution will come as we try to live for God, our faith grows and fears diminish as we turn to God for help. I've faced a dire aircraft emergency, lived in hostile countries, and received other death threats with no feelings of fear. May God's presence and Spirit of love course in your veins to overcome all fear of evil.

THINGS TO THINK ABOUT AND TALK OVER:

- *Is there a fear that comes to you over and over again? Is there something in this chapter that could help you now? Can you share it with someone you trust? Have you overcome another fear that could encourage you today?*

- *What verses do you know from memory that help you with fear? Are there some more (perhaps from this chapter) that you need to know by heart?*

- *Corrie ten Boom and her sister, Betsie, witnessed Jews being abused by others many times. More than once, Betsie cried out, "Oh, Lord! Have mercy on them!" Corrie found out later that Betsie was praying for the abusers. "They have touched the apple of God's eye." Facing the wrath of God for hurting those whom He dearly loves will be a terrible thing. How does that help you if you fear abuse?*

- *Is all fear bad? Fear of falling? Fear of God? Remember that the fear of God is the beginning of wisdom and knowledge (Proverbs 9:10). What would the fear of evil be? Or an evil fear? When are the last two wrong?*

# I'M SO MAD I COULD JUST KILL HIM! DEALING WITH ANGER

*"Be angry and do not sin;*
*do not let the sun go down on your anger"*[302]

Everyone has experienced anger. Maybe someone teased you or gossipped about your best friend. Maybe you lost a really close game. Sometimes anger is justified and sometimes it isn't. You need to learn the difference between the two and how to deal with anger in a way that honors God.

## BE ANGRY . . .

Anger can be justified when we see unrighteousness — in ourselves or in others. I should be angry at my lack of self-control. We should be angry when we see children or the elderly being abused. Jesus was angry when He saw His Father's temple being turned from a house of prayer into a place of business, that He turned over tables and made a mess of the market.[303]

Before you think someone's sin is a license for you to blow up, consider how merciful God is with you. You and I wouldn't make it through the day if His righteous anger blasted us each time we sinned. We would all be incinerated. Instead, God expects you to extend His grace to others. In fact, Jesus says that if you forgive someone, your heavenly Father will forgive you. If you do not forgive? Your Father will not forgive you.

But what if someone steals from you? What if they hit you? What if they cheat in a game? Remember what Jesus said: if someone strikes you on the cheek, turn the other cheek. Right after that, He said that if they want your shirt, offer them your coat also![304] Consider Jesus' example. He went to the cross for you when He could have called an army of angels to save Him.[305] He returned mercy and love to overcome your evil. In the same way, He expects you to trust Him to

302  Ephesians 4:26
303  John 2, Matthew 21
304  Matthew 5:39
305  Matthew 26:53

overcome evil in others.[306]

## . . . AND DO NOT SIN

Okay, so you should be angry against evil. But how can you react in a way that is not sin? First, you need to understand what sin is. Sin is not believing God's Word. If God says He is your shield, do you believe Him? If He tells you not to seek revenge, do you still think you should get them back? So anger becomes sin when we are not trusting God in any situation. We respond as if only we can deal with the offense. An eye for an eye and a tooth for a tooth. Jesus tells us, however, that we should love our enemies and pray for those who persecute us.[307]

Usually, our first response is with our tongue, and before we know it, our cutting words have done more harm than good. Some people say when you are angry that you should count to ten before speaking or acting. While counting may be slightly useful, your first and best reaction is to hold your tongue and pray. Let the Holy Spirit direct your response. When you are attacked personally, Peter said, *"Do not repay evil for evil or reviling for reviling, but on the contrary, bless, for to this you were called, that you may obtain a blessing."*[308] Even Jesus, while suffering on the cross, responded with love to the people abusing Him: *"Father, forgive them for they do not know what they are doing."*[309]

Second, you will far more prepared if you have verses committed to memory before you face a frustrating or unjust situation. Paul wrote in Romans 12, *"Do not be overcome by evil, but overcome evil with good."* Certainly he had justification to be angry with the Jews who had attacked Paul and wanted him dead. Truthfully, if you are in the habit of dying to yourself daily (preferring God and others over your personal comfort), it will be much easier to let Scripture direct your words and actions when you feel you've been wronged.

Third, note that silence in the face of sin is not always the right response. Jesus did go to His death quietly, meek as a lamb, not answering Pilate's questions or the mocking soldiers. But in previous confrontations, He abruptly met sin head-on. Jesus' words

306  Romans 12:21
307  Matthew 5:38-48
308  1 Peter 3:9
309  Luke 23:34

were sharp to Peter when Jesus prophesied of His death. He minced no words about the cheating market by the temple. Most of Paul's letters confronted sin in the church. Jesus told us to take the log out of our own eye before helping our brother take the log out of his. When you do this — examining your own heart for sin and repenting of it — you can then go in a gentle, uncritical manner to help your brother or sister repent.[310] Obviously, the Holy Spirit needs to give you wisdom if, when and how to confront someone. A person continuing to hurt others or give false teaching needs correction. In Matthew 18:15-20, Jesus gives us wise instruction on how to confront a brother or sister who has sinned against us in a serious way.

. . . DO NOT LET THE SUN GO DOWN ON YOUR ANGER

Hatred is anger left to fester. Imagine a deep, painful splinter that is left under the skin so the wound becomes pussy and rotten. That's what happens when we remain angry about an offense. We need to remove the offense from our heart and cleanse our wound with God's love.

One of the best bits of wisdom I heard in premarital counseling was to never go to bed at night angry. That may not mean you will never go to bed with tears, but it does mean you've forgiven your spouse and asked forgiveness for any of your part in a conflict that day. (Yes, you can always find something you did wrong.) The great danger, Paul tells us, is that harboring anger after the day is over can actually give the devil a place to work in your life.[311]

Jesus shocked His listeners when He said, "*You have heard that it was said to those of old, 'You shall not murder; and whoever murders will be liable to judgment.' But I say to you that everyone who is angry with his brother will be liable to judgment; whoever insults his brother will be liable to the council; and whoever says, 'You fool!' will be liable to the hell of fire.*" [312] So be careful when you say (or think), "I'm so angry, I could just kill him!" You may not mean it literally, but God is very concerned with our hearts. Anger rises in all of us at times. But if you want to become more like Jesus, you will need to let your heart and response be ultimately ruled by love. Search the Scriptures and memorize verses that will

310  Galatians 6:1
311  Ephesians 4:29
312  Matthew 5:21-22

help you before conflict comes. Ask the Holy Spirit to help you know when to remain silent and when (and how) to confront — but always to love.

THINGS TO THINK ABOUT AND TALK OVER:

- *How can you practice "dying daily" to yourself, so that when you face evil and feelings of anger, you can respond without sin?*

- *Is there a person in your life that has angered you by what they did (to you or someone else) whom you have not forgiven? If so, what are you going to do about it? What does God want you to do?*

- *What verses do you need to memorize that will help you in a moment of anger to respond the way God wants you to?*

YOUR HEART - THE FOUNTAIN OF LIFE

# DEPRESSION AND SUICIDE

*". . . neither death nor life, nor angels nor rulers, nor things present nor things to come, nor powers, nor height nor depth, nor anything else in all creation, will be able to separate us from the love of God in Christ Jesus our Lord."*[313]

If you've ever been deeply discouraged, depressed, or thought about ending your life, you are not alone. More than half of college students have had suicidal thoughts at some point in their life.[314] Even if you never experienced those thoughts and feelings, you certainly have friends and acquaintances who have. What could you say to them? No matter what has happened, you are extremely precious and loved beyond words. We love you. God loves you even more. He promises to always be with you if put your faith in Christ.[315] If you are far from God, why not come to Him now? If anyone thinks they are too awful and God won't take them, ask: "Who are we to tell God whom He will accept?" He took murderers like Moses and David. On the day Jesus was crucified, He took the criminal on the cross next to Him to paradise. Jesus said, *"Come to me, all who labor and are heavy laden, and I will give you rest."*[316] When Jesus said all, He meant all. You can find countless promises and stories in the Bible that will lift your heart. If you don't have a list of passages in mind, just google *Promises in the Bible*.

There are two more important facts to keep in mind. First, God has put people into your life that care about you and want to help you. You may be down because someone you trusted hurt you. But don't let that betrayal prevent you from reaching out to others who really can help — and want to! Text a pastor telling him you need help. Call your mom or brother or sister. Send a private message to a trustworthy teacher or a truly mature friend. Second, know that whatever discouragement you are going through right now will pass. God has designed us so that time brings healing. We gain perspective. We discover other joys waiting for us that we could

---

313  Romans 8:38-39
314  Sharon Jayson, USA Today, Aug. 18, 2008, "More Than 50% of College Students Felt Suicidal" http://abcnews.go.com/Health/DepressionNews/50-college-students-felt-suicidal/story?id=5603837
315  Matthew 28:20, Hebrews 13:5
316  Matthew 11:28

have never imagined. Give yourself grace and let time pass as you look to God for help.

Here's a summary of helpful points to keep in mind when you are down:
- You are not alone in your thoughts. Many others have been there, too . . . and life became good again.
- You are loved! We love you. God is always with you and promises to love you in Jesus, no matter what has happened.
- God has put others into your life to help you. Reach out to them.
- Give yourself time. Feelings come and go. The future holds joy for you in the Lord Jesus. He wants to bless you and others through you. Hold on and trust that rich times will come.

Here are a few more ideas — if you can do them — that will help you get through a difficult time and return to joy:

- **Read God stories**. The Bible and good, true Christian biographies can tremendously help you take your eyes off yourself, focus on God, and give you His perspective.[317] If you don't like to read, you can find audio or video of the Bible and Christian biographies online.
- **Praise.** Thank God for ten things He has given you. Find music on the radio or internet that glorifies Jesus for Who He is.
- **Give.** Help others with their physical, emotional, or spiritual needs.
- **Eat right**. You might look to some unhealthy foods to make you feel better. They probably will. But just for a moment. Your brain and body need good fuel, plus you'll feel better about good choices.
- **Get exercise, fresh air, and sunshine**. It's no secret that people who enjoy these three things feel better and live longer. Even if you can only start with five or ten minutes, get out the door! Slowly work up to thirty minutes or more of exercise outside. Find an encouraging friend to go with.
- **Sleep**. Especially when you're struggling, you need eight hours. If you can't get to sleep, cut caffeine or late-night eating. If worries keep you from falling asleep, read your Bible before bed, or rehearse verses that talk about God's love and care for you.

317   Jim Elliot, Nate Saint (especially as told by his son, Steve Saint), Amy Carmichael, and Richard and Sabina Wurmbrand are just a few Christians with great biographies. John Piper has several excellent messages online (https://www.desiringgod.org/) of other biographical sketches.

One of the many things I like about the Bible is that the stories are terribly honest and practical. There are many characters, some of them heroes of the faith, that despaired of life. A few actually took their own lives, like King Saul, who didn't want to be captured and tortured by his enemies, and Samson, who brought down a pagan temple on his enemies who had blinded him.[318] Of course, these are extreme examples, but they help us to see the Bible is not a book af milk-toast advice. These stories show us God understands the harsh and painful situations humans sometimes face in life.

Jesus was so distraught as He faced the cross and the weight of sin of humanity, that He sweat drops of blood. Some translations say He was in great agony or anguish. How did He keep going? Hebrews tells us the answer: *"Jesus, the founder and perfecter of our faith, who for the joy that was set before him endured the cross . . ."*[319] Jesus chose to trust His heavenly Father (*"not my will, but yours be done"*[320]), and He knew that the future held great joy because He was about to redeem His captive bride in love for all eternity. Don't give up. Keep pressing on so that you will enjoy the blessing God has planned for you.

What about the great apostle Paul who wrote to the Philippians to "rejoice always"? To the Corinthians he also wrote, *"For we do not want you to be unaware, brothers, of the affliction we experienced in Asia. For we were so utterly burdened beyond our strength that we despaired of life itself."*[321] We don't know for sure what happened to them in Asia, but something discouraged them so much that Paul and his friends were ready to give up — even on life. But God was at work! I think we are more open to His caring touch and teaching when we are at a low point. Knowing that God has a loving, very important goal in my suffering helps me to keep going, to look up, and to try to figure out what God wants to teach me. Of course, the answer may take a long time, so be prepared to be patient.

What did Paul learn? First, he knew that when we have walked through great suffering and then God delivers us, we can help

---

318   I've included these two examples, not because the Bible endorses suicide as an escape (it doesn't), but because Biblical history is brutally honest. Sadly, Saul and Samson lived by the sword and died by the sword, lacking earlier wisdom and faith that would have given them an alternative to the path they took. Trust God that He will give you wisdom if you ask. Then follow Him!

319   Hebrews 12:2

320   Luke 22:42

321   2 Corinthians 1:8

others in their difficulties. Second, we learn to look to God, not to ourselves, to fix our problems. *"But that was to make us rely not on ourselves but on God who raises the dead."*[322] Next, when God delivers us, we gain confidence that He will surely deliver us the next time we face a brick wall. As you get older, you gain rich experiences of God's faithfulness that become a great reservoir of strength to take you through deeper challenges in the future. Several years after Paul's despair, he could write while wearing chains, "Rejoice in the Lord always" to Philippian friends who were involved in a hard personal conflict.[323] Through your discouraging challenges and subsequent stories of victory, *you will be able to give wisdom to others* going through trials. But to see that day, you must trust in God and not give in now.

## I'M TRYING ALL THAT, BUT I STILL FEEL GLOOMY

When I was going through a year of chemotherapy, I was feeling depressed and gloomy for a long period. I might have excused myself since I had been told I wasn't going to live much longer. However, I knew I wasn't afraid to die. I was feeling very weak, dizzy, and nauseous most of the time. But I'd had a debilitating flu before. Although the flu is no fun, I was never so gloomy. When the doctor asked me if I was depressed, I didn't want to say "yes," but I did confide that I felt blue, especially for the days following each weekly shot of Interferon. He told me that this drug can cause several side effects, including depression, and asked if he could prescribe an antidepressant. I accepted, and although it didn't solve the entire problem, it took the edge off my heavy heart.

Although I'm not a big fan of many prescription drugs and this was no magic happy pill, I learned something. The brain is an organ just like any other organ.[324] If you are exercising, eating right, and looking to God for your joy, your brain can still malfunction if there is a chemical or hormonal imbalance or if you have a physical injury. There may be a time in your life after you've done all of the above, confessed any known sin, and been prayed for by the elders of your church, when you need to visit a doctor who specializes in brain and hormone health.[325]

322  2 Corinthians 1:9
323  Philippians 4:4
324  Brain image, Pixabay, Public Domain, https://pixabay.com/en/brain-lobes-neurology-human-body-1007686/
325  James 5:14

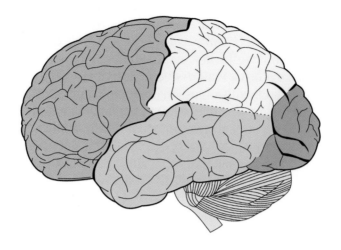

In every case, an essential key to getting better faster is being open with people who love you and can help. Satan loves secrets. Don't keep your thoughts inside. God's light and love shine brightly through a caring brother or sister in Christ.

Remember, God is always with you. He will take you through the other side and joy will return. In time, you will have many opportunities to help others be free from darkness and live in joy again.

*"Come to me, all who labor and are heavy laden, and I will give you rest."* - Jesus in Matthew 11:38

THINGS TO THINK ABOUT AND TALK OVER:

- *Everyone makes bad choices that can impact their lives in a negative way. Maybe you didn't study before a test. Maybe a close friend caught you in a lie. Maybe you crossed appropriate lines with the opposite sex. The results of poor decisions can cause us to be depressed. How can you get your joy back in a healthy, God-honoring way? Is there someone you trust and is mature that you can talk to about bad choices?*

- *Everyone gets hurt by others, a cruel date, or an uncaring relative. How can holding a grudge against them continue to* hurt you? How can you let those bad feelings go? If you need some help with ideas or a specific situation, go find a mature friend or pastor to talk to.

- If a friend came to you and said they felt sad all the time, what would you tell them? Do you think the four summary bullet points in this chapter would be helpful? They are talking to you because they trust you and are probably crying out for help. It's always a good idea to ask if they have ever had thoughts about killing themselves. If your friend said "yes," what would you say or do? (Beside encouraging them with your love and God's love, you need to point them to someone with experience to talk to. How can you follow up to make sure they found a good counselor or to alert someone close to them about your conversation? Is it worth risking your friendship to make sure they get help?)

- Can God forgive suicide? There is no definitive verse in the Bible to tell us the answer. But we do know that murder requires the blood of the murderer because they have destroyed a human created in God's image (Genesis 9:6). Certainly self-murder does the same. Of course, we know any murderer (for example, David or Moses) can be forgiven when they repent, because their debt was paid by Jesus' blood. But are we sure we can repent before appearing at God's judgment if our last earthly act was self murder? We may not have a clear answer, but who wants to go to God under that circumstance? Who wants to leave family and friends with such questions and grief?

- If Paul told the Philippians to "rejoice always" while he was held in chains, how do you think he would encourage you in your bonds of discouragement? How can you find something to rejoice about in the middle of your depressing circumstances? Right where you are, can you see or feel three things for which you can thank God? More than three? (I often start with "air" and then take a big breath.) What blessings do you think God might have in store for your future?

YOUR HEART - THE FOUNTAIN OF LIFE

# WITHOUT WAX - BEING SINCERE

*"As I remember your tears, I long to see you, that I may be filled with joy. I am reminded of your sincere faith, a faith that dwelt first in your grandmother. . ."*[326]

When potters fire their work, some pieces crack because of an unseen air pocket or imperfection. In ancient times, unscrupulous potters would fill cracks with wax and paint over the temporary repair in order to sell their wares. An unwary buyer would only find out after he got home and tried to cook dinner with his new pot. A more experienced buyer would hold the pot up and let the sun's rays reveal cracks. That's where the word sincere comes from. It's really two words: *sin* (without) and *cera* (wax).

Are you "without wax" in your relationship with God and others? Your sincerity and honesty should be a hallmark of your life. It can either set you and others free. The lack of it can injure you and those

you love when light and heat come. This is also called *integrity*.

I'm thankful God taught me a tough lesson about integrity in fifth grade. I got a terrible grade on an assignment and my teacher, Mrs.

326   1 Timothy 1:4-5

Burke, sent me home with an even harder assignment — I had to take that awful paper, have my mom or dad sign it, and bring it back to her. I faced a real dilemma. I was already in trouble at school. If I did what Mrs. Burke said, I'd be in trouble at home, too. I had seen my mom sign her name hundreds of times on notes and checks. How hard could it be to fake her signature? With a little fear, I did my best to forge my mother's signature and brought that horrible paper back to Mrs. Burke. Mission accomplished. Or so I thought.

Mrs. Burke smelled something fishy. So she made a phone call to my house while I was at school to see if my mom had actually seen the offending paper. I walked home that day, happy as usual, not knowing the firestorm waiting for me. "Your father wants to see you in the bedroom." That's code for: "You are in big trouble!"

"Son, Mrs. Burke called us today." Uh-oh. The jig was up. My father continued, "You know, a man is only as good as his word." The dismayed look on Dad's face was enough to break my heart. Of all the men I knew in the world, I loved and respected him the most. He was always a man of integrity and honesty. I know I got spanked that day, but that didn't hurt nearly as much as seeing my dad's disappointment.

Some time later, I learned about Mom's great-grandfather, Fritz Jahncke, who had built a tremendous brick and concrete company in New Orleans after immigrating as a young man from Germany with just $20 in his pocket. He also built ships, helping the local economy recover from Civil War doldrums. Fritz was renowned as an honest man. In fact, when he shook hands on a business deal, no contract was needed. He would honor the agreement even if he lost money, and everyone knew it. The ship company motto was:

WE SHALL BUILD GOOD SHIPS HERE
AT A PROFIT IF WE CAN
AT A LOSS IF WE MUST
BUT ALWAYS GOOD SHIPS[327]

Do you see character here without wax? Fritz wanted his employees to have integrity, too. Lives depended on it. Even if it hurt Fritz Jahncke's pocketbook, he would produce safe, good ships.

---

327  Hill, Megan. Inside Northside The Jahncke Shipyard: Building a Place in History. Sept-Oct 2011. Internet.

How about you? Will you cheat or help friends cheat on their schoolwork? "Everyone else is doing it," right? Will you compromise on reporting all of your taxable income to the IRS because "they'll never find out"? But Who does know? Whose opinion really matters?

Jesus teaches us to be the same person behind closed doors as we are in public. You might object, "But I've never met anyone like that!" Or while reading this chapter, you may have had a troubling and haunting crack in your character suddenly come moaning out of your secret closet. Without repeating the chapter "When you Fail," I want to say I believe this is exactly why Paul wrote:

*Not that I have already obtained all this, or have already arrived at my goal, but I press on to take hold of that for which Christ Jesus took hold of me. Brothers and sisters, I do not consider myself yet to have taken hold of it. But one thing I do: Forgetting what is behind and straining toward what is ahead.*[328]

God's grace is the fuel that enables us to press on when we (or others) discover cracks in our character that shouldn't be there. His love enables us to trust Him to bring good from the mess we've made, and then to know He is transforming us into His flawless image through this trial. We are not yet what He will make us into. No cracks. No wax. No paint. Our job is not to hide our cracks, but to let Him fill them by trusting the unbreakable power of His Word and grace. Make integrity a hallmark of your life shaped by God's hands.

### THINGS TO THINK ABOUT AND TALK OVER:

- *When have you faced a trial of your character? What did you do? Is there a secret "crack" you are hoping no one will find? Can you tell a trustworthy friend or mentor?*

- *How do we avoid becoming self-righteous as we grow in sincerity and integrity?*

- *Can a lie ever be the right choice? Imagine you just took a bite of a meal at your aunt's house and it tastes terrible to you. It's her favorite dish and she spent hours to make it just for you. She says, "Well? What do you think?" Are you being insincere*

---

328   Philippians 3:12-13. Also read Isaiah 43 to be encouraged and set back on the "path" again

*if you protect her feelings? Is there room for tact in integrity? In a different scenario, would you lie to stop someone from hurting themselves or someone else? How do we balance truth-telling in unusual circumstances that may genuinely call for something more loving than brutal honesty? Or is this possible?*

- *Do you know any verses that would help you or a friend during a temptation to compromise character? Do you have one to help you "clean house"? Here are a few of mine: Galatians 2:20, Second Timothy 2:20-26, and First Corinthians 10:13.*

*Galatians 2:20 "I have been crucified with Christ and I no longer live, but Christ lives in me. The life I now live in the body, I live by faith in the Son of God, who loved me and gave himself for me."*

*2 Timothy 2:20-26 "Now in a great house there are not only vessels of gold and silver but also of wood and clay, some for honorable use, some for dishonorable. Therefore, if anyone cleanses himself from what is dishonorable, he will be a vessel for honorable use, set apart as holy, useful to the master of the house, ready for every good work. So flee youthful passions and pursue righteousness, faith, love, and peace, along with those who call on the Lord from a pure heart. Have nothing to do with foolish, ignorant controversies; you know that they breed quarrels. And the Lord's servant must not be quarrelsome but kind to everyone, able to teach, patiently enduring evil, correcting his opponents with gentleness. God may perhaps grant them repentance leading to a knowledge of the truth, and they may come to their senses and escape from the snare of the devil, after being captured by him to do his will."*

# PLEASURE AND DISCIPLINE

*And whatever you do, in word or deed, do everything in the name of the Lord Jesus, giving thanks to God the Father through him.*[329]

Everyone loves pleasure and comfort. We are wired for it. Imagine a big, soft bed with a crackling fireplace and snow falling softly outside. Add a nice steaming cup of rich hot chocolate with whipped cream on top or a fragrant spiced apple cider. Maybe include your favorite movie on a huge, crystal clear TV screen with surround sound. Sound nice? Perhaps your ideal spot would be a lush, tropical island with your own super-sized yacht, floating on a beautiful lagoon teeming with brightly colored fish. If only life were that comfortable and easy.

We all know that behind each beautiful dream is discipline and hard work. Someone had to build that beautiful house with the fireplace when the sun was blazing hot outside. Someone had to stack the firewood in the fall. Someone had to bring in the wood when it was freezing outside, light the kindling, and eventually take the ashes outside — plus carry the sticky, empty hot chocolate mugs to the kitchen. Someone had to get a really well-paying job to afford that amazing TV and sound system.

We all quickly learn that there's a system of work and reward. Some enjoy the work itself. You should find joy in your work, especially if you are doing it as an act of love for God. Still, many others trudge for eleven months a year or more to get that vacation to Disney, Vail, or their favorite fishing spot. Often, however, there can be a bitter side to our "reward." A snarly waiter. Tourist price gouging. Bickering kids in the car. The first flu of the season. Even if you suddenly won the lottery and could vacation every day of the year, sitting on a big cushy bed surrounded by soft pillows, you'd soon turn into a bored, disgusting and disgusted marshmallow. You might say, "Oh not me! I'd be doing sports every day and enjoying the sunshine." Help me visualize the end of that road in twelve months! Perhaps you'd be a beach bum, looking in every reflective storefront window to catch a glimpse of your bod. Of course, your friends

329  Colossians 3:17

would be the same. Shallow. Bored again. Looking for the next "fun fix." Bigger waves are forecasted tomorrow.

Yes, we were made for work and for wonder. If these two are kept in balance, God provides us with a steady joy that is unshakable and rooted in Him. Whatever you do, whether work or play, do everything as unto Him.[330] What does that look like?

Many years ago, there was a story about a flight attendant that was extraordinary. In fact, she was so kind, helpful, and happy that virtually every passenger took notice and other crews enjoyed having her on their team. One day, a business owner on a flight was impressed. He complimented her and told her he would like to write to her company president and tell him what a fine flight attendant she was. "Thank you very much, sir," she replied, "but I'm afraid that is not possible."

Surprised by her refusal, he insisted. "Your level of hard work, attention to detail, and customer care is unparalleled. I own a large business, and as the owner, I really want to know who my star employees are when either my supervisors or I are not looking. Now, please, give me your boss's contact information so I can write a letter."

"You are very kind, sir, but I'm afraid that's simply not possible."

Not used to being refused, the man became a bit frustrated. "And exactly why is that 'not possible'?" he asked.

"Because my Boss is the Lord Jesus Christ."

Do you see where her joy came from? Do you see why it didn't matter if no one was looking? She wanted to do her best for her beloved King.

If you love God and want to glorify Him through your work, what will you need? Excellence in work demands *self-discipline*. Discipline keeps us focused on God's purposes. Here are some foundations for discipline I would include, but you can probably add others:

330  So, whether you eat or drink, or whatever you do, do all to the glory of God. 1 Corinthians 10:31

- GOOD DIET AND REGULAR EXERCISE. I will write more about this in the chapter on sports. Many people do these things so that they will look good, feel better, and be healthy. Those reasons are fine if we are not obsessed with them. Even the best diet and exercise plans never guarantee our goals, nor do we always stay faithful to them. Many newlyweds, especially men, gain twenty pounds in their first year of marriage. They already got what they were looking for! What's a better reason to discipline our bodies to say "no" to junk food and "yes" to regular exercise? We want to serve God to the best of our ability. A flabby, caffeine-injected body that is supposed to be the temple of God will simply not respond like a fine-tuned machine that can habitually say "no" to the comforts of life. Your brain is an organ. It needs a good supply of oxygen, clean water, and healthy food to be at its best

- TRAIN YOUR MIND AND SPIRIT. Read the Bible everyday. Don't close your eyes at night before reading something in the scriptures and being moved or challenged by what you've read. Make it your goal to read through the Bible every year or two. This is the best way to gain the "full counsel" of God. One good method is to read an Old Testament chapter in the morning and a New Testament chapter in the evening. Start the New Testament over again when you finish because it is shorter. Memorize verses, whole chapters, or even entire books that you need.

- SET GOALS. Ask God what He wants you to do with your life. Draw up a road map of what you need to do to be the best in your field or with your gifts. Who can you learn from? What skills will you need? Would certain languages, certificates, or diplomas help? What kind of life experiences would be helpful? Where can you get them? Set a timeline and find someone to be accountable to.

- MAKE A LIST OF PRIORITIES AND STICK TO THEM. Do the essential (and often difficult) tasks first. Don't let the easier, pleasant, or less important tasks come first. You'll either not get to the important ones or you'll do them in a sloppy way because you'll be short on time. Prayerfully update your list of priorities every day or two.

- GET SLEEP, BUT DON'T OVERDO IT. Almost every adult needs about 7 ½ to 8 hours of sleep a night. Kids need a little more. We can get by on less, but only for a time before we begin to get grouchy and lose our focus and the physical ability to perform our best. Sleeping more is usually a waste of time. Set your alarm. When it goes off, never hit the snooze!

- BE ON TIME OR BE EARLY. If you can be five or ten minutes late, you can be five or ten minutes early. Even in cultures that tend to run late, they don't start movies or school classes late. Trains and planes usually leave on time. Your arrival on time can communicate a lot about your concern and honor for the other person you're meeting with. Stop doing extra tasks that will make you late. Suffer being hungry or thirsty, if you must, to be on time.

- ORGANIZE YOUR THINGS. When you come home, put things in their places! Right away! Looking for shoes, keys, your wallet, or a textbook is a terrible waste of limited time God has entrusted to you — not to mention that frantically searching for these things when you're in a hurry is frustrating. Put your clothes away. Right away. Do your dishes. Right away. You might think it's silly for me to write this in a book, but you'd be surprised by how many people in their 20s, 30s, and beyond never learned this simple discipline. Keeping a house in order that is already organized is much easier than delay and organizing a disaster. Having organization in your home or bedroom will allow you the ability to be spontaneous and hospitable when a friend wants to come over. If you struggle with organization, find a friend, book or video to give you pointers.

- DON'T LET THE DESIRE FOR COMFORT OVERRUN YOUR SELF-DISCIPLINE. You might enjoy a muffin once in a while, but buying a dozen and putting them on your desk is sheer lunacy. Enjoying something pleasant can be a gift from God, but don't let it become a consuming force in your life. Our primary joy should always be to bring glory to God.

- LET THE HOLY SPIRIT GUIDE YOUR STEPS. This may not seem like discipline at first, but it may, in fact, be the highest form. The Holy Spirit will guide you and help you know when to take time to relax and be refreshed and when to deny yourself and press into a fast, stay up all night with a discouraged friend, or risk everything to save someone in the face of a tsunami. Learning to listen and obey God when you would like to do something else is an extreme level of discipline that expresses both faith and love.

If you have to, put this list on your bathroom mirror until discipline becomes a habit. Did you know self-disciplined people are generally happier people? How much more if their self-discipline allows them to love other people, watching them fall in love with God and start enjoying eternal life. There is simply no greater pleasure than loving God Himself, impossible without good Spirit-driven discipline.

### THINGS TO THINK ABOUT AND TALK OVER:

- *When I was a young Christian, I went on a missions trip to Acapulco, Mexico. My team called it "a vacation with a purpose." The first part of the trip, we worked with a poor church, painted walls, did a mimed skit in the streets, played with kids, and enjoyed great worship, teaching, and fellowship. During the second part, we took a few days to sit on the beach, swim, be tourists, and try paragliding. You know what? Virtually everyone agreed that the first part of the trip was way better than the second. We all wanted to go back and help at the church. When lots of people dream of a vacation in Acapulco, how could it actually be so dissatisfying? How might you change your vacation plans or life goals to maximize your joy by serving God?*

- *What are some areas in your life that need more discipline? Circle or underline some in the list above. What practical changes in your life can you make to improve in those areas? Share your ideas or plans with someone.*

- *What does the following proverb warn us about?*

  *How long will you lie there, O sluggard?*
  *When will you arise from your sleep?*
  *A little sleep, a little slumber,*
  *a little folding of the hands to rest,*
  *and poverty will come upon you like a robber,*
  *and want like an armed man.*[331]

331  Proverb 6:9-11

# THE WORLD'S BEST SELLER
# THE BIBLE - A PRICELESS GIFT

*I have stored up your word in my heart, that I might not sin against you.* [332]

Anybody who's ever tried to play tennis knows what it's like to hit the ball on the corner of the racquet. After ten attempts to hit the ball, solid contact happens by chance with the "sweet spot" on the racquet. The ball suddenly rockets down the court to everyone's astonishment. "Wow! Do that again!" Unfortunately, hitting a tennis ball precisely on the sweet spot with perfect aim takes a lot of practice. So does planting God's Word deep in our hearts for great effect. There is a powerful reason that year after year, the Bible is read and bought by more people on our planet than any other book.[333]

If you want to be an ultimate champion in life, grab your Bible, wrestle with it, prove its authenticity, and devour it day after day, year after year.

When I coach kids in running, I remind the ones who are struggling that you never know when you might need to be able to run well. What if there's a fire and you need to run for help? What if you meet a bad character in a dark alley? You can't suddenly "get into shape." Adrenaline helps only a little in running. The same is true of God's Word. If you have developed strength when you need it, you'll do well. In an earlier chapter, we talked about resisting temptation. Is there a better way to do this than the way Jesus did it? He had important parts of the Bible in His memory, ready for instant recall in the exact moment He needed to resist the devil. What about when a friend is feeling discouraged? Or even rarer: when you meet someone considering suicide? (If you live long enough, you will face that situation.) What will you do then? Offer come nice, homespun advice that everything will be alright? Or will you give

---

332   Psalm 119:11

333   Did you know that the Bible is the best-selling book of all time? Not just over time in history, but this year and every year? Throughout history, a total of 5-6 billion Bibles have been printed, easily eclipsing any other book. One hundred million copies are printed annually. You won't find Bibles on any "Bestseller List" from Amazon or the NY Times, however. Comparing 20 million Bibles sold annually in America to the next leading book at 600,000 would certainly draw attention and maybe cause a few more people to pick up a copy and find out what the enthusiasm is all about.

them the most powerful words ever written, designed to bring hope, truth, and light to every situation?

There's something even better than having the power of God's Word at your fingertips to help others or yourself in times of critical need. Memorizing and meditating on the Bible will give you immeasurable opportunities to enjoy knowing and walking closer with your Father in heaven! I could give you countless examples, but here's one from today, as Grace has been memorizing Ephesians:

*Now unto him that is able to do exceeding abundantly above all that we ask or think, according to the power that is at work in us.*[334]

You may have heard a pastor speak this benediction at the end of a service and thought it sounded nice. Later, you may have read the book of Ephesians, which has many good and memorable verses. This one may or may not have jumped out at you. Then, you memorize it. You begin to think about it. You go to sleep thinking about it. In the middle of the night, when you can't sleep, you recite the verse in the dark and think more about it. Then, suddenly, the words sink deeper and you feel God is speaking to you. *I love you. I am able to do far more than you ask or even imagine. The mighty power with which I raised Jesus from the dead is working in you and around you for good.* Then one day, after a very difficult and long period of struggle, you see a sudden change like Joseph did on the day he was freed from jail and made vice president of Egypt. Paul's words from Ephesians come into your soul like a symphony, *"exceeding abundantly above all I ask or think"*! Your walk and relationship with God will never be the same. Your trust in His Word will be deeper and more unshakeable than ever.

Here is a good visual way to think of putting God's Word into our hearts which I have seen presented in various ways: hold up your five fingers outstretched. Imagine trying to pick up a Bible with just your pinky. That's what it's like when you simply sit in a church on Sunday or hear the Bible on the radio. It may be helpful, but it's unlikely to stick with you very long. Distractions like meal preparation, finances, or an unpleasant phone call quickly cause us to forget. If someone came up Monday morning and asked, "Do you remember any Bible verses that were read yesterday at church?" most of us would have a hard time recalling even one.

334  Ephesians 3:20

If you go home and read your Bible from the same section, it's likely you'd remember the verses for a day or two, maybe even a week. It's like picking up a Bible with two fingers. Your grip is better but still not very strong. But then, perhaps your smart atheist friend at work or school has a good challenge to an apparent contradiction in the Bible and you have no answer. Your confidence in the words you read Sunday afternoon fly out the window.

Then you decide to memorize a key verse that will help you. Your grip strengthens. You begin to meditate on those words early in the morning before anyone has woken up yet. You ask God what one of the words means and then look it up on the internet in a couple of commentaries. Now colors and shades of meaning are coming into sharper vision.

Finally, take the verse to your Sunday School and teach it to them, using a story from your own life or from the Bible. Your grip is now unshakeable.

1. Hear God's Word
2. Read it
3. Memorize it
4. Meditate on it
5. Teach it[335]

"But I'm not very good at memorizing!"
Lots of people feel that way, but the Bible doesn't give us an option. We might learn in different ways or different quantities. Find the method that works best for you. Ask God to help. Probably using more than one method is how most of us can better memorize. Here are a few suggestions:

• USE FLIP CARDS. Write the verses on one side and the verse addresses on the other. When waiting in line, review them. Tape your cards to your bathroom mirror and review them when brushing your teeth or combing your hair.

---

335  Not everyone is called to be a formal teacher. In fact, the Bible warns us not to presume to be a teacher, because we will be held more accountable before God for how we teach and how we live (also a form of teaching.) But, if you are a Christian, you are always called to make disciples. To do that, teaching in some way is always necessary. There is no more powerful information to give to another person than Scripture. Memorization and prayerful meditation will help ensure you give it to others in the right way.

- IF YOU ARE ARTISTIC, WRITE YOUR VERSES IN CALLIGRAPHY. Draw a painting with a verse. Do needlepoint with one and make it a gift.

- LEARN VERSES TO MUSIC. You can borrow someone else's song or make your own. When you were little, we had great success teaching you verses with tunes we made up.

- ONE METHOD FOR LEARNING LONG PASSAGES (OR EVEN WHOLE BOOKS) takes only five to ten minutes a day and has helped me tremendously:
  - ⇨ Read one verse ten times (anybody can do that.)
  - ⇨ Close your Bible and try to recite it ten times. You might be surprised at how easily it will come to you. Check it to be sure you are right.
  - ⇨ Tomorrow, say it again ten times and add another verse.
  - ⇨ On day three, say the first verse just once, but add a another verse, reading and reciting only the newest two verses ten times.
  - ⇨ Keep going for six days and then take a day off.
  - ⇨ Start with a new section the next week, but on your next day off, review the first week's verses.
  - ⇨ Recite your new verses to a friend and have them check you. Sometimes we think we have memorized a verse but still have a few mistakes.

Memorizing, meditating on, and teaching God's Word can sound intimidating. But it's no different than getting in shape with exercise. Start with just a few minutes a day. Pretty soon, you will look forward to those times and feel cheated when you skip.

Finally, make it your goal to read through the Bible as a whole every year or so. This will help you to know the whole of God's wisdom for us. Some people "cherry pick" the verses they like but ignore other passages. Paul tells us that all scripture is God-inspired and useful for us (2nd Timothy 3:16). That would include ones that we may think are boring! Pray for God's help as you read. Reading the whole Bible over and over will also help you make valuable connections between testaments or understand difficult concepts between books. You can find many systems to read through the Bible in a year online like the Bible App. Or you can make your own like I sometimes do, reading a chapter or two of the Old Testament in the morning and a chapter in the New Testament in the evening. Find a system that works for you.

Time spent every day in God's Word will give you results that will amaze you and give you great joy. Put God's best seller deep into your soul; obey and share it. You'll be a champion of life that will inspire others with a passion for God and eternity.

THINGS TO THINK ABOUT AND TALK OVER:

- *Do you have any fears or hesitation about learning Bible verses? Share those with a mature Christian friend and ask their advice.*

- *What would you say to a friend who didn't think memorizing scripture was important?*

- *What kinds of verses or topics would you like to memorize? If you don't know where to start, when you are reading your Bible, underline or highlight verses that stand out to you. Or here are some classic and very helpful verses to start with: John 3:16, Romans 8:28, Psalm 23, 1 Corinthians 13, and Ephesians 2:8-9.*

- *When is a good time to meditate on a verse you've recently memorized? What would you suggest to a friend who is struggling with debts and wakes up at three in the morning in a cold sweat worrying about losing everything?*

- *I've known some people who know parts of God's Word well and use like a weapon (like telling others they should submit to the speaker). How can you avoid using well memorized verses to hurt others?*

- *Do you have a plan to read through the Bible this year? Go online and see what's available. After you finish, don't put your Bible away! Start again. How long would it take to read the Bible out loud in one sitting? (hint: you can't do it, but it's a lot less than a year!) I knew of a many who read through the Bible at least 60 times in his lifetime. Imagine how well he knew God and was able to help others!*

# SEX AS GOD MADE IT

*Daughters of Jerusalem, I charge you*
*by the gazelles and by the does of the field:*
*Do not arouse or awaken love*
*until it so desires.*[336]

WARNING: You need to be mature to read this chapter!
Heed Solomon's advice above if you are not ready,
and skip this one for now.

God made marriage and intimacy so awesome that it is one of His best pictures of *His* love for us and the culmination of history, when Jesus returns to gather His people.[337] With total devotion and unashamed openness, a man should love his wife and vice versa. Some religious people believe all sex is bad. Some irreligious people believe all sex is good. The truth is that only sex between a loving husband and wife is what God designed. And it's great! Only that kind of sex is safe, satisfying, and beautiful for a lifetime.

Hollywood and advertisers terribly overrate muscles, clothing, body shape and even perfume as a source of great physical pleasure. If true, we should see actors and sports stars in the pinnacle of perpetual joy. But do you know the most powerful influence over your sex life? Your mind—by far—is the most influential organ in your body that will give you either great joy or great pain. If you guard your mind and care for it, only stoking the fire of passion when the person and time of life is right, your pleasure will be immeasurable. Sadly, those who don't carefully guard their minds often discover the truth that sexual thoughts can pull them into degrading experiences and

---

336   Probably the most erotic book in the Bible, Song of Solomon, says three times, "*Do not arouse or awaken love until it so desires*" (2:7, 3:5, 8:4). That's not a license that says, "If it feels good, do it!" Rather, it is a warning *in* God's wisdom and love: don't stir up physical, sexual passion before the right context (deep relationship and the commitment of marriage). Prematurely awakened desire is like a freight train we've got to stop or risk facing a terrible wreck. On the other hand, the Bible beautifully illustrates intimate God-given love — Solomon's Gazelles in nature and humans in marriage —      is powerful and wonderful.

337   See the marriage feast of the Lamb (Jesus) in Revelation 19:6-9 and read Ephesians 5:22-32. For many people, this is an awkward comparison, probably because of how we have degraded sex to be simply a physical act of passion. But think of the *other* aspects of marital sex that it was *intended* to be: unification of life, a declaration of absolute and total devotion, and extreme and indescribable joy. Consider those attributes when thinking of the comparison of marriage to the joining of Jesus to His Church at the end of the age.

desires with scars that can last a lifetime.

In the chapter "Thrill and Danger," I mentioned that sex is a wonderful gift from God. It's an important way He bonds us together as husband and wife. Josh McDowell explains that when something extremely painful or pleasurable happens, hormones called endorphins (norepinephrine) are released that make a *permanent* memory implanted in our brains.[338] Most of our first childhood memories are pleasurable or painful. In one of my earliest memories, I was about three years old and barefoot on our driveway. As I was peeking in a crack into the garage, the door suddenly swung out and up and my big toenail ripped off before I could blink. I can't tell you how I was dressed that day, but I remember that old, wooden door! Likewise, God designed those endorphins so that most people can instantly remember the first time they had sex, either pleasurable or painful. Imagine what a wonderful memory it will be if the first time you have sex is on your wedding night with the person you tenderly love and have waited patiently for. You'll have that memory for the rest of your lives and it *will* bond you together.

Sex is similar to double-sided tape that can hold your favorite photo to the wall.[339] The first time you use it, the tape sticks well if both surfaces are clean. But if you peel the picture off the wall and put it somewhere else, the picture doesn't stick as well. If you peel and stick it about ten times, the picture will fall to the ground. Think of Josh McDowell's explanation of the permanent memory (good or bad) that is implanted during extreme pleasure or pain. Sex forms a great bond between a married man and woman, but that glue can be lost through physical intimacy with others. In the same way, the danger of pornography is very great, which I'll write more about in the next chapter. Healing from this is possible, but God's design for sex is the most powerful when you experience it for the first time on your wedding night, not on a video screen or printed paper.

Run from sexual temptation! God wants the marriage bed to be pure, so don't carry into your married life the memory of real or imagined sexual encounters.[340] Sadly, there are few greater joys than

---

338   Jesus Northwest 1988; McDowell, Josh. *The Bare Facts*, 2010, Josh McDowell Ministries, p. 22
339   Josh McDowell (both in the conference in 1988 and in his PDF above) tells about another chemical released in sex called *oxytocin*. It makes couples want to cuddle, affects their feelings towards one another, and causes them to "bond."
340   Hebrews 13:4

sex in marriage—purely devoted love to just your spouse. There are countless marriages where either the husband or wife is never truly "alone" with their spouse in the bedroom because of memories they cannot escape.

However, if you have blown it and lost your sexual purity, there is hope. Re-read the chapter "I've Really Messed Up!" to claim the forgiveness and beautiful cleansing God offers us (see 1 John 1:9 and Romans 8, as well.) There can be a strong measure of restoration and freedom, although it will never be the same as if you had waited. Thankfully, over time, past sin will become more and more of a distant memory as we embrace God's love and truth.

Rather than living with regret, decide early to protect yourself and your future spouse. Put plenty of hedges around your exposure to temptation, like not being alone with someone of the opposite sex that would allow compromise. Follow the guidelines in the chapter on courtship and include a fun, caring chaperone in your times together. Protect yourself from pornography when surfing the internet, using software, prayer and any strategy you can. Find a close friend to whom you can tell anything and know will hold your feet to the fire as you seek a pure life. If you fall into any sin, confess it to someone you trust and is wise in God, so you can be strengthened, enjoy forgiveness, and be restored.

Once you marry, remember that part of great intimacy embraces and rests on *God* to open or close the womb, knowing that children are a tremendous blessing to a caring family.[341] This runs counter to most of Western culture today. Of all the exciting and fulfilling things I've experienced in life, some of the most joyful ones include being a dad to you kids. So don't fear becoming a parent!

One last thought. Sex in marriage for a healthy couple gets better the older you get! You may remember that sentence and smile with time. But why wouldn't it be that way? As a beautiful picture of God's intimate love for His people, our joy with Him will only

---

341    Psalm 127:3-5 *Children are a heritage from the Lord, offspring a reward from him. Like arrows in the hands of a warrior are children born in one's youth.Blessed is the man whose quiver is full of them.* I am not suggesting that there may not be a time to delay having children due to illness or to complete schooling. Any kind of birth control, of course, should not involve danger to a conceived baby. There are natural methods that can work well. Research well. There is much misinformation on the internet. But even when delaying pregnancy after prayerfully seeking God for a specific reason and a season, rejoice if God still gives you a precious child in spite of your efforts!

increase as we move into eternity.

THINGS TO THINK ABOUT AND TALK OVER:

- *What are some of the things that our culture teach us about sex that are different than what the Scriptures teach? Do you think those cultural ideas are harmful? Why or why not? If you agree that scripture trumps culture when they conflict, how can you overcome the overwhelming mass of messages you get from the world?*

- *What do you think about the idea of God's design for sex in marriage, particularly endorphins that imprint memories, is like double-sided tape?*

- *Do you agree that premarital sex and the permanent memories it creates can keep the marriage bed from being "pure"? Do you think that "window-shopping" (but not buying) is harmful to marriage? What do you think your spouse or future spouse would say? Do you think that kind of "looking" would it have no impact on intimacy?*

- *One of the best aspects of "waiting" for marriage is telling your spouse you fought the battle for God's sake and for the love of your spouse before you even met! On the other side, if you have given in, it will be certainly difficult to tell someone you are interested in for marriage that you have not waited. Would it be right or wrong to hide past failure? If think the one you want to marry cannot forgive your past, what would that tell you about their maturity and understanding of God's grace? What if they do forgive you?*

# WHAT'S THE HARM IN LOOKING? THE PROBLEM WITH PORN ... AND SEX OUTSIDE OF GOD'S DESIGN

*But I say to you that everyone who looks at a woman with lustful intent has already committed adultery with her in his heart.*[342]

In the last chapter I compared sex with double-sided tape. Tape is great stuff when it works right. What do people do with tape that doesn't stick anymore? That's right. They throw it away.

If you are cringing right now because you wonder if people might throw you away like an old piece of worn out tape, good! Keep reading. If you look at porn and try sex with different people (you will if you do porn), someday those people will leave you like an unwanted, fuzzy piece of used tape. But God won't. He never leaves His beloved children.

If you think you'd like to take your tape and stick it for life to just your spouse — just the special person God gives you — **awesome!** If you think it's too late, however, because you blew it, remember that God is in the miracle-making business. He can make your tape clean and stick again if you get serious and radical. (That's a big if. Don't play games with God.) Are you ready?

**SPOILER: If you don't yet know what pornography is, I am really glad. You can skip this chapter and come back to it someday when you are older.**

The effects of porn are subtle. God wired us to be attracted to the opposite sex for very special reasons. Porn takes that good desire and removes all the other important parts of that connection, including friendship, commitment, support, care, love, and family, to name a few. Porn takes the beautiful exterior of a person and turns them into a simple object for satisfaction, not for a relationship.

342  Matthew 5:28

Besides ripping the real person from an exposed body (we don't even know what language they may speak, how they smell, what they laugh at, or what their dreams are), the viewer (you or me) are silently debased. We begin to think we know the other person or make up a pretend lover. We think we know what they physically feel like. How they would do what we want, anytime we want. You know what? That's not reality. Now the viewer marches into the real world and begins looking for sex with a real person that fits their fantasy world. No wonder relationships rarely survive, and even young men in their 20s are becoming impotent (meaning they can't have sex with a real person).[343]

I was twelve the first time I remember seeing pornography at a friend's fort (beware of and run from friends that have pictures of naked people in a secret place!) For a couple of years I had been attracted to some girls and wanted to see what they looked like and how they were different from me. Well, in porn I found young women who were ready to do just that, and my body responded just the way that God designed it to for my honeymoon. Only this wasn't my wife, but some airbrushed ink on a page that thousands of other guys were looking at and wishing they could be with, too.

After studying the pages carefully for many days (I can still remember what the young woman looked like . . . it is strange to think she is now probably a wrinkly grandmother), an odd thing happened. I discovered that she wasn't so interesting anymore. I wanted to see some other girls. (Are you thinking of my double-sided tape analogy right now?) Some girls were prettier to me than others. I began to hope the girls at school and in my neighborhood would do the same things in real life.

Looking back now, I had become so obsessed with thinking about sex that it was becoming harder for me to be real friends with girls, which had been much easier when I was younger. It's embarrassing to admit now, but I no longer told as many jokes or listened carefully to their thoughts, because my head was so full of thoughts that were no longer clean. It was horrible and even made me shyer.

---

343   There are so many studies available on the internet supporting this sad impact of porn on young men, like impotence, perversion, violence,lack of intimacy, insecurity or inability to commit and loneliness.I elected to not pick just one to focus on. The high numbers of injury and statistics are not as important as it is for you to know that you should run far from pornography and look for mature help to keep you free.

There's a reason that the final commandment of God's Ten Commandments has to do with our thoughts. He used the word "covet," which means wanting something that is not rightfully yours. What comes in through our eyes and soaks in our heart will someday come out of our hands and mouth. The tenth commandment says, *"Thou shalt not covet thy neighbour's house, thou shalt not covet thy neighbour's wife, nor his manservant, nor his maidservant . . ."*[344] The first nine commandments involve action. But if a person's thoughtlife is not under control, action will follow that will break God's design.

Our culture is so broken and most of us have become as shallow as a cell phone video or a piece of paper with an image on it. The price of sexual immorality is severe. Three thousand years ago, a wise man wrote, *"Can a man carry fire next to his chest and his clothes not be burned? Or can one walk on hot coals and his feet not be scorched? So is he who goes into his neighbor's wife; none who touches her will go unpunished."*[345] I would add the same, with Jesus' authority, for someone who looks at porn and doesn't turn away. Porn and lust will lead to action that will horribly burn you and others. You can probably list several potential, devastating outcomes right now. If you can't, just read a few news headlines. Sexual diseases can destroy your body and kill you. You can't protect yourself. STDs are everywhere now. Six million people contract HPV every year in America, and there are thirty kinds of STDs transmitted sexually. HPV is killing more people than AIDS or HIV. Gonorrhea and syphilis terrified my parents' generation. Now there are twenty-three more diseases and many are far more deadly.[346]

God doesn't want to spoil our fun, but increase it! Clean sex and passionate marriage are safe, exhilarating, and abundantly joyful. A lustful look, suggestive movies, and "soft" porn feel pleasant, but are stepping-stones to a horrible future. But there's something worse than potential, unwanted pregnancy, child support, divorce, abortion, disease, and death. What could that possibly be? An ever-hardening heart. Soft porn never satisfies. Counterfeit pleasure corrupts what is real. We look for something that will bring back the first illegitimate thrill.

344  Exodus 20:17 (KJV)
345  Proverbs 6:27
346  The increase in sexually transmitted diseases is overwhelming. We often either ignore these facts, or dismiss them as though nothing has changed. Please, download Josh McDowell's free PDF The Bare Facts, not just so you can look at the statistics that would shock even the most hardened sexually active person, but to look at the hard facts to help you stay far away from sexual sin and in the safe arms of your loving Father.

Unbroken pornography watchers find ever more degrading and disgusting images. God says He will actually take people who prefer to worship images of mortal men (or women) over worshipping Him and harden their hearts. The Scriptures tell us that sex with the opposite sex will not satisfy them. They will seek the same sex and be consumed with lust.[347] If the trajectory away from God and everything right remains unbroken, the soul will end up in the torment of hell, separated from Him and His love forever.

That was my *trajectory* until 1986. I shudder to think where I would be today if God had not resolutely and lovingly stepped into my path. Even if I was alive now, you would not be. I would never have met or married your mother. Most likely, I would have left a trail of destruction like many of my dear friends who are now divorced and are painfully distant from their children. Without a doubt, I would be hollow and would be a sliver of who God wanted me to be.

Was my delivery from pornography and lust instantaneous after my salvation? Sadly, no. Some sin did stop instantly. I knew right away that porn and lust were wrong, but it probably took me two years to be really set free from porn, and several years more before the images in my head began to disappear. By God's grace, I'm thrilled to say there is no longer any desire in me to seek out an illicit photo on the internet or pick up a pornographic magazine, even when I'm alone. But, I also don't linger somewhere where the old desires can pull me back in.

Do you remember what Joseph did when Potiphar's wife tried to seduce him? First, he reminded her of the confidence her husband had in him; it would be unthinkable to break his trust! But more importantly, Joseph protested that sexual immorality is extremely wicked — a sin against God. When she wouldn't listen and pressed him harder, Joseph ran! Even though he might have looked foolish running out without his coat on, Joseph still ran.[348] Be like Joseph. Don't try to stare down temptation. You'll lose.

Am I completely free of all lust and the poison of porn in my early life? Probably not. I may wrestle until my last breath. But I can tell

347  Romans 1:18-27
348  Genesis 39, I will always remember my friend Glenn from pilot training. He had a similar circumstance happen to him when he was on his way home from vacation. I wasn't a Christian then. When I heard he ran away from this beautiful girl who wanted him, I thought Glenn was crazy! Still, I secretly respected him. Years later at a reunion, I asked him if he was a Christian back then. He said that he was, but only a weak one. Wow. That was faith in action that I could barely comprehend at the time.

you that victory does come in long stretches of time that I couldn't have imagined as a younger man.

But I wish for you, my children, not to have any specters in your closet that will need to be beaten back. I pray for you that your double-sided tape for God and for your spouse will be as pure and strong as possible in this fallen world. There will be joy for God, you, and all those who are in your life.

### THINGS TO THINK ABOUT AND TALK OVER:

- *You probably have seen some sexual images, or perhaps even some porn. Those images can be "stuck" in long-term memory and easily recalled. But they can be dulled and eventually forgotten. What do you think would help? Do you know any Scriptures or have any images that are just, pure, lovely, excellent, or praiseworthy (Philippians 4:8) that can be substituted when the old thoughts come up? What were you doing when you saw those inappropriate images and how might you avoid that kind of setting in the future?*

- *What would you do if a friend invited you to their fort (or house) and began to show you sexual photos or videos? Knowing that there's a side of most of us that does want to look, how do the dangers of porn and sex before marriage help you to run away fast? Without being a "tattle tale," how do you think telling an adult would be helpful to you and your friend? Are you willing to risk your friendship for the sake of both of your souls?*

- *How might you enjoy forgiveness and a clean heart if you have fallen into any sexual sin? Do you think satan will come and accuse you? What would you tell a friend who is in the same situation and is broken over their sin?*

# SECTION 4

## THE PERSON IN THE MIRROR

# THE PERSON IN THE MIRROR

*But the LORD said to Samuel, "Do not look on his appearance or on the height of his stature, because I have rejected him. For the LORD sees not as man sees: man looks on the outward appearance, but the LORD looks on the heart."*[349]

Do you know how we are made in God's image? That question is difficult because God is spirit.[350] Spirits don't have images like we generally think of them. Jesus, as the Word of God, took on the outside form of man, not vice versa.[351]

A physical image is a reflection of an original. That's what mirrors, selfies, and portraits are for. But they are not the original. In what way are we to be a reflection of God to the universe? The first thing we need to reflect is that God is love.[352] God is also righteous, holy, compassionate, creative, beautiful, intelligent, truthful, and every imaginable good trait. Unlike animals, He designed us to reflect those qualities. When God looks at us, the heart is the image He is concerned about. He sees our hearts in the way He told Samuel above, "The LORD looks on the heart."

Our culture is terribly consumed with appearances — our outer shell. While it can be helpful to consider our appearance at times, we are in danger when we are overly concerned about or looks. What would you think of a friend who liked the gift wrapping more than he liked your gift? The giver, the gift, and the receiver are all degraded. Prize the inside like God does.

Sadly, we often give extra grace or credit to people who have nice packages and bows. In return, they spend inordinate time and money taping and re-taping the old, crinkling paper. Eventually, they are set aside for newer and prettier packages. Meanwhile, the boxes grow emptier and less reflective of the beauty and love they were originally intended for.

There's another important secret you will discover. The more your

349   1 Samuel 16:7
350   John 2:24
351   John 1:1-14
352   1 John 4:8

heart reflects the heart of God, the more attractive your outer shell will become. Some of the most beautiful women I have ever known were in their 70s, 80s, and even 90s. They were wrinkly and had thin hair and few teeth. But their eyes sparkled with the love of their Maker. Their smile, gentle touch, and wisdom made me joyfully linger in conversation with them.

Competition is another aspect of outward appearance that can be especially difficult and even destructive. Or, if done right, it can be a tremendous inspiration for good character. Fields of competition are endless: beauty, popularity, politics, sports, grades, money, promotions, titles, cars, houses, and clothes.. Probably any possession or quality you can think of has been turned into some kind of competition — or will be!

Rather than lamenting that we were born into this strange and crooked world, we can learn to appreciate outer and inner beauty, while discovering the integral and healthy links between the two. Let's celebrate the world God has made, while making our best effort to reflect God's character to anyone watching.

### THINGS TO THINK ABOUT AND TALK OVER:

- *Given that both our culture and our fallen nature put so much emphasis on our exterior, how can we fight that pressure as we look at others? Or as we look at ourselves?*

- *Who would prefer an oyster shell over a pearl? What did you think about this analogy? There are shops that sell shells all over the world. Shells can be very beautiful. Without depreciating the beauty of a shell, how might someone new to the world of pearls begin to appreciate the greater beauty of pearls? How can you appreciate exterior human beauty while discovering new facets of much more attractive interior beauty? Where would you go? Or to whom?*

THE PERSON IN THE MIRROR

# BEING BEAUTIFUL

*Charm is deceptive, and beauty is fleeting;*
*but a woman who fears the Lord is to be praised.*[353]

A helpful teacher told a story about a young teenage girl who came into his office at school for counseling. She was one of the most popular kids, a blonde cheerleader who had a clear complexion, while most of the other kids struggled with acne. Everyone thought she was beautiful. She sat down and began to tear up. "What's wrong?" he asked.

"What!" She was incredulous. "Can't you see?" Then she pointed at her nose and turned to show her profile. Sure enough, he could see a natural hook in her nose. "It's so ugly!" she despaired.

He wisely told her, "You know, God made you. God doesn't make junk. He knew exactly what you needed when He made you. You are a friendly girl that relates to a lot of the unpopular kids. If you had a perfect nose to go with the rest of the beauty He gave you, you'd probably be so stuck up that you'd be a snob like many of the other popular kids. He may have given you that nose to keep you humble so you could relate to and love other kids."[354]

The teacher then challenged those of us at the conference to consider our bodies. "Think about the one thing that you hate about how you look, and take a moment to thank God for it. God knew exactly what He was doing when He made you."

For me, it was easy to think about the things I didn't like about how I looked. And there wasn't just one thing! From the time I was a little kid in elementary school, other kids called me "Needle Nose," "Carrot Top," and "Freckle Face." I can spit those names out decades later. I was a beanpole.

Suddenly, I realized that if I had looked like Arnold Schwarzenegger, I would be unbearably proud. No doubt, I would have joined the cool jocks who threw things at the geeks like my friends and me. Instead,

353  Proverbs 31:30
354  Basic Youth Conflicts, Seattle, 1987

God gave me a deep sense of humility and the ability to relate to others who don't fit in. This was the case even after I became athletic and realized that the painful teasing of mean little kids doesn't hold water when you get into your twenties. After I got over being shy as a young man, I realized that most people don't actually care what we look like and that there is someone for everyone.[355]

Fortunately, the Bible has some very helpful things to say about beauty. Have you already seen that God isn't as concerned about our outside as our inside? We need to unlearn what movies and friends tell us about beauty, because then we can walk in great joy!

*Your beauty should not come from outward adornment, such as elaborate hairstyles and the wearing of gold jewelry or fine clothes. Rather, it should be that of your inner self, the unfading beauty of a gentle and quiet spirit, which is of great worth in God's sight.* [356]

One of the most beautiful people I ever knew was short and wrinkly. She was my grandma, and she loved God. I'm not saying you'd want to marry someone who looks like a grandma, but you need to learn to see where real beauty lies. You certainly don't want to make any compromises on inner character just because someone's outside looks nice! If you let God work in you a "gentle and quiet spirit," your natural beauty will be magnified. Conversely, if you are demanding and unkind, any natural beauty you might have will be greatly diminished.

Note that Peter didn't say above that a girl or woman of God cannot put on jewelry or nice clothes. He is just saying that your beauty should not be what is external.

Was I attracted to your mom physically when we met? Of course! She has a natural beauty and never even gave much thought to

---

355   My teacher for Human Sexuality at CIU in 1995, Al McKechnie, told a good story about the theory that "there's someone for everyone." A young lady had been asked by the young man she was dating to marry him. She was extremely self-conscious of her large legs and couldn't imagine he would really want her. When she finally told him the reason she was hesitating to say, "Yes, I'll marry you," he pulled a picture from his wallet of his deceased mother. "I never showed you a picture of my mother. She was unable to walk and sat in a wheelchair throughout my childhood. I loved my mother dearly and always wanted for her to have strong legs. So, you see, one of the things I like most about you physically is your big, strong legs!" After that explanation, she exploded with love for him and, of course, agreed to marry him. And there are people who would love to marry the right person even bound in a wheelchair — someone they could care for and help. There is someone for everyone!
356   1 Peter 3:3-4

makeup or jewelry. She wasn't lazy and loved sports and being outdoors. But what attracted me far more than her outer beauty was her quiet and gentle spirit. She genuinely cared for so many people, even for her very difficult father. She loved and cared for rough street kids. Without that reflection of God's love in her heart, I would never have been seriously interested, even if she was the most beautiful woman I'd ever know.

Read again the wise words of Proverbs above:

*Charm is deceitful, and beauty is vain, but a woman who fears the Lord is to be praised.*[357]

The beauty of youth is a very small window of life. If we live a normal lifespan, wrinkles, sagging skin, and graying, thinning hair will become a reality in our lives. As some people have observed, we come into this world bald, toothless, and drooling. If we live long enough, we go out the same way! Obsession with outer beauty will leave you an old, lonely, and toothless mess. Confidence in God's grace, love, and might will leave you with a legacy of joy and you will be surrounded by friends and family who will want to savor every minute of your days. Best of all, you can pass on that kind of beauty to others.

### THINGS TO THINK ABOUT AND TALK OVER:

- *Girls and women today are surrounded by non-stop messages of how to be "beautiful." No one can or should try to measure up or maintain that photoshopped image. What should you do? You could live like a hermit and remove all media and mirrors from your house, but that would make you wholly weird, not wonderful. How can you submerge yourself in the life-giving truth of God's vision for beauty while still living in this world?*

- *Does it honor God if you completely ignore outer beauty, for example, never taking a bath, never shaving, never combing your hair, never brushing your teeth, and never changing your clothes? How do you keep outer beauty and inner beauty in balance? (Imagine you are a 90-year-old answering this question.)*

357  Proverbs 31:30

- *In the verse from Peter, he tells women and girls that, "Your beauty should not come from outward adornment, such as elaborate hairstyles and the wearing of gold jewelry or fine clothes." Some Christians say women should never wear jewelry, braid their hair, or wear nice clothes. Others forbid makeup, pierced ears, or painted fingernails. Did Peter forbid those things? What was his main point? "Rather, [beauty] should be that of your inner self, the unfading beauty of a gentle and quiet spirit, which is of great worth in God's sight." If you agree with me that fixing your hair to look nice or wearing some simple jewelry is okay but not the source of your beauty, how do you prevent over attention to your appearance? If spending five minutes in front of the mirror to be presentable is okay, how much is too much? 10 minutes? 30 minutes? An hour? If you spent 10 minutes in front of a mirror today, how much should you spend reading your Bible? Serving others?*

- *Is there a downside to being exceptionally beautiful on the outside? Have you ever seen a slice of sweet watermelon on a summer picnic table? Flies and yellow jackets are all over it! How can a pretty girl sort out who's fake and who's real? Some quality guys may also pass by and think they don't have a chance because of the competition. Where could you go or do to lose the flies and find a sweet, quality lad? (Hint: Isaac's matchmaker went to a spring outside of town where he found Rebekah. Read more in Genesis 24.)*

THE PERSON IN THE MIRROR

# BEING HANDSOME

*Kish had a son named Saul, as handsome a young man as could be found anywhere in Israel, and he was a head taller than anyone else.*[358]

If there ever was a stunning guy, King Saul was the man. As a rising star, he was humble, merciful, and powerfully filled with God's Spirit.[359] But he had a critical character flaw. He believed in his good looks, popularity, position, and ability to minister were all about him. Saul was most important to Saul. He was exactly the king the Israelites demanded and deserved.

What makes a guy handsome today? Muscles? Clothes? Or do most women and girls care much about the outside?

I don't recommend it, but if you look up the question on the internet, you'll have to sludge through some pretty unsavory ads and backyard pundits to learn what women in our culture find attractive in guys. In the end, you'll discover that there's nothing conclusive, in spite of what Hollywood would like to tell us. One statistic says that 50% of women prefer a guy who is taller than they are. But that means that another 50% don't care if he's the same height or shorter!

My wife likes me with a mustache and beard stubble. But one of my daughters likes me with just a beard and no mustache. Another daughter can't stand me with any beard or stubble at all! How can we guys win? Another way to look at it is that we can't lose, either! There is a great match for everybody who will appreciate them for who they are and what they look like. You just have to be patient until you find her or she finds you.

Of course, if you want to increase the likelihood that a special girl will take notice of you, it's helpful to take a shower occasionally, brush your teeth, and comb your hair. Yes, there are exceptions — I know.

---

358  1 Samuel 9:2
359  1 Samuel 9:21 But am I not a Benjamite, from the smallest tribe of Israel, and is not my clan the least of all the clans of the tribe of Benjamin? Also 1 Samuel 11:6, 12-13

Many guys would be shocked to find out that most girls don't care that much about a guy having big muscles. She wants to feel safe and protected, but you don't have to be Mr. Universe to do that. Besides, if after you've spent years pumping iron, you find the rare girl who ranks big muscles high on her list of what she wants in a man, guess what? There's always some guy who has more muscles! Plus, if you marry her, what will happen when you get sick, pull a tendon, or just get that normal middle age bulge in your belly? In spite of what advertisements say to the contrary, keeping a six pack is impossible.

Having said that, most women (just like most guys) are not attracted to a spongy couch potato! Eat healthy and have a regular exercise program, not mainly to attract a girl, but to take care of the body God gave you. Your girl will appreciate it, too. But don't place your trust in your appearance.

Consider King Saul again. Everyone thought he was hot. No doubt Saul reveled in his looks and the attention they gave him. His smoking good looks were probably part of his downfall, which is something you should think about. Are good looks and popularity so wonderful at the end of your time on earth? Where should a wise young man's focus be?

There was another king God was preparing — one who had a heart after God. David wasn't very inspiring. He wasn't tall like Saul. He was the smallest boy in his family, not old enough to go to war like his brothers. Sheep-watching and running errands was all he was good for. Although he did have a healthy and handsome look to him, David's most important quality was that he trusted in God.[360] That's what enabled him to kill bears and lions that took his father's sheep. That's what enabled him to stand up to mocking older brothers. That's what enabled him to kill the God-cursing giant, Goliath. David's trust in God also stopped him from killing King Saul, who was hunting David down to kill him. God said, *"I have found in David the son of Jesse a man after my heart, who will do all my will."*[361]

Ultimately, Jesus was the One destined to sit on the throne and had one hundred times the heart of David. Have you ever wondered what Jesus looked like? Was He handsome or homely? Interestingly, we

360   1 Samuel 17:42
361   Acts 13:22

have little recorded to physically describe His earthly appearance. Only one verse in the Bible says something clearly:

*He had no beauty or majesty to attract us to him, nothing in his appearance that we should desire him.*[362]

Jesus was not good looking by the world's standards. But billions of people have fallen in love with His beauty. What is it about Jesus that makes Him so adored? What should men emulate in Jesus that would be attractive to women of character and make Jesus look great? You might have your own list of what draws you to Christ, but here is mine:

- He is patient, caring, and kind
- He is fiercely loyal and protective of His bride
- He is always available — willing to put others first — even though we don't deserve it
- His character is always trustworthy and pure
- His words are always helpful and wise

Our character is often shaped by the people we spend time with. If you spend a good deal of time with God — reading His word and letting Him direct your feet, hands, and mouth — His traits will become yours. Very few people will care if you are fat or thin, freckled or fair, bald or frizzy.

Can I tell you a secret that few of us guys figure out? One of the best ways to become patient, caring, and kind like Jesus is to become a good listener. I've seen some beautiful women with good character next to some pretty homely guys. But they were men who could listen well and give good feedback. As you are listening to your woman, listen to the Holy Spirit at the same time. If He gives you something to say, don't hold back. On the other hand, if you don't know what to say, just be sympathetic or empathetic. *Oh, really! Wow, what did you do then? How did that make you feel?* Resist giving empty advice. Pray while listening and God will often give you a fitting word when the time is right. Usually, a question is a gold setting to a gem of wisdom. *Do you have a verse that helped you in that situation? What do you think God was trying to teach you? I'm amazed how you let God lead. What would you tell someone going through a similar situation?*

362   Isaiah 52:2

Remember, though, being a good listener takes time to learn. You won't meet the girl of your dreams and suddenly become a world class listener! Some guys can fake it for a day or two. But a world class bore can't help talking about themselves or getting distracted by virtually anything. Practice being a good listener with people you find it difficult to be with. Not only will your future love appreciate your super ears and heart, but you'll gain an essential key to loving everyone you meet.

Having a good sense of humor — a close cousin of good character — can also open the heart of many girls. I'm not talking about becoming a clown. Learn to laugh at your mistakes. Everyone makes them. You don't need to memorize a list of jokes, but you can enjoy laughing at good, clean humor.

Don't worry about trying to become someone you are not. That will take *a lot* of stress out of your youth.

Guys, put God first in your lives and you will be one of the most handsome young men around. You may even have a hard time sorting through the godly (and attractive) young ladies who may be seeking your attention. If that happens unexpectedly, go back and read the chapter on courtship. Be humble and trust that God will give you wisdom and discernment as His character and appeal shine through you.

Don't make Saul's mistake. If by God's grace you attain a measure of good character and become handsome to others, it isn't all about you! Be a "man after God's own heart." Jesus always sought to love, obey God and bring Him honor. "But seek first his kingdom and his righteousness, and all these things will be given to you as well."[363]

THINGS TO THINK ABOUT AND TALK OVER:

- *Who were the most popular presidents in American history? Were they handsome by the world's standards? Especially homely was Abraham Lincoln. What do you think made those men attractive to the people?*

- *Since we are bombarded on every media outlet about the importance of appearance, how can guys fight the world's*

363  Matthew 6:33

*shallow definition and put God first? How do you keep balance, knowing that appearance is not completely irrelevant? (For example, Jesus didn't dress in shabby clothes nor did He resist Mary's anointing Him with fragrant, expensive oil.[364])*

364   John 12:3, 23

THE PERSON IN THE MIRROR

# BOY OR GIRL?

*So God created man in his own image, in the image of God he created him;*
*male and female he created them.*[365]

Years ago, only God saw the miraculous spark that began your life inside your mama. God instantly combined the DNA from your mother and me to decide your hair color, eye color, and blood type, and with just one X or Y chromosome decided if you would be a boy or girl. Before ultrasounds, people could only guess if their baby was going to be a boy or a girl. Everyone waited with excitement for months.  On the big day, proud fathers posted the news in the front yard with pink or blue balloons: "It's a girl!" or "It's a boy!" Both are a wonderful blessing from God. We should celebrate how He has made us unique and special — whether girl or boy.

Boys generally love adventure: climbing mountains or exploring forests. Many of them like to play Cowboys and Indians, wrestle, or play football. They might also like to play army or be the knight in shining armor. They love it when their mom makes their favorite dessert for their birthday, praises their good work at school, or tenderly cares for a skinned knee. God gave boys a nature to be tough and a desire to defend girls and their family. If they grow into godly men, they may become fathers and grandfathers who leave a legacy for generations, even as they work hard day-to-day, providing a joyful and safe home. Kids and grandkids love to sit on their laps and hear stories of wisdom and humor learned in their boyhood.

Most girls like to have tea and talk to each other, sharing compliments and encouragement. God gives many of them a tremendous appreciation for beauty, whether nature, art, or music. They enjoy a dress-up party, cherish a gift of flowers, and adore kittens. They love a special date with their dad or when he tucks them in at night. They also love to be a princess — and all the better when a handsome prince rescues them! Girls often grow into wonderful mothers and grandmothers, if God gives them the gift of children. They write books like this one in the hearts of little ones.

365  Genesis 1:27

Those "pages" are passed on to grandchildren with such beauty and love that generations later are blessed, even if the faithful girl's name is forgotten.

*Of course*, many boys and girls enjoy *similar* things. Most boys and girls love playing some kind of sport. They both laugh at funny movies. Some boys may enjoy things that "only girls" are supposed to do. Of course, some girls like doing "boy things." One of my favorite boys liked to sew. Another very special girl liked to help me work in the garage. That's not only okay, but we should be glad when anyone finds something wholesome and good to do that brings them joy and gives glory to God. Bringing glory to God starts with faith and character rather than a particular hobby, leisure activity, sport, or job.

Are there some activities, though, that are just for girls or just for boys? Of course! Today, there are people who criticize traditional values considered normal for boys or for girls. A local kindergarten we know suspended a boy for pointing a finger at another boy like a gun. Some local stores allow men into the girls' bathroom so that men dressed like women won't feel "awkward" by going into the boys' bathroom. There are girls who would like to engage teen boys in competitive wrestling. How can we know if and when we've crossed the lines of right and wrong?

While the Bible does talk about some sins like men dressing to look like women, women trying to look like men,[366] or men being wrongly intimate with men, [367] I don't think we need to take time to argue each point in detail. Rather, God put deep inside your being an understanding of what is right and wrong. Just like Monarch butterflies know how to return to the fields where their ancestors mated in Mexico — never having been there themselves — you know what is right. No one needs to tell you. You know what is right and good for boys to do and what is wrong. You know what is right and good for girls to do and what is wrong. Besides the conscience God put inside of you, His Holy Spirit is at work, teaching and guiding you, especially when you are willing to obey.[368] No one

366  Deuteronomy 22:5, 1 Corinthians 11:14-16
367  Romans 1:26-27
368  As you meet people who do not believe in God, they will challenge both the Scriptures as a guide to what is right for boys and girls to do, as well as our internal sense of right and wrong. Having been an atheist/agnostic for many years, I can tell you that this is a ploy to justify wrong behavior or immorality. If a denier of God does this long enough, he or she can even begin to "feel" like wrong is right, a frightening judgment from God (Romans 1:24, 26).

needs to tell you that boys may be called to go to war someday to defend their nation, so that pretending their finger is a gun is normal. No one needs to tell you that it's not normal for a man to dress like a woman or go into the girls' bathroom.

What does the Bible teach us positively about the wonder and beauty of how God uniquely created boys and girls, men and women?

You might be surprised to know that even before Adam was created, God wanted him to "work the ground."[369] So, guys, work is not a curse! In fact, if you boys work hard, it can be one of the most rewarding things you will do in life. Providing a safe home — a refuge for friends and an abundant table for family and others — can be very satisfying to a man. We can expand our homes into God-honoring communities and impact the nations. Working men have tamed killer, flood-prone rivers by building dams. In turn, they created energy to heat homes and run factories. Others have cut wild woods and turned them into carefully run farms to feed thousands.

Girls, God declared it wasn't good for man to be alone.[370] Men were not intended to be alone and many struggle without a woman's help, advice and love. Some people cringe at the idea of being a helper. I don't think I've met anyone who wouldn't want to be in charge (except possibly those who feel the onerous weight of serious leadership). At the Air Force Academy, we were taught that to be a good leader, however, you must first learn to be a good follower. A good leader knows that he is not better than his followers. A successful team rejoices when an amazing and beautiful project comes together, whether a new business, a growing ministry, or — especially — a mature, God-honoring family. Everyone understands that success came because leaders and followers worked together and they all share in the celebration.

By the way, girls, don't think you will need to be married and have children someday to best fulfill God's purpose for your life! Consider faith-filled women like Betsie and Corrie ten Boom, Amy Carmichael, Gladys Aylward, and sisters Martha and Mary in the scriptures. Their great joy in Christ could never be exceeded by the woman with the best husband or children.[371] One of the most

369  Genesis 2:5, 15
370  Genesis 2:18
371  1 Corinthians 7:32-35

impactful Christians in my early walk with God was Krista Ford, a funny, single redhead who was several years older than me. She taught me how to memorize Scripture and how to pray. She always encouraged me in the pursuit of ministry and missions. Krista was a terrific example of someone who gave to anyone in need. Although she has gone to heaven, I still count her as one of the most significant friends that influenced my spiritual life.

Should people look at a "serving" role with disdain? Jesus celebrated service to us. There was no servant greater than He. Why did He serve? He loves us. He wanted us to grow through His example. Do you remember when Jesus washed the disciples' feet? That was the job of the *lowest* slave in the house. No one wanted to wash stinky, dirty feet. But on the last night of His life on earth, the King of the universe put on a towel and washed the feet of twelve guys — guys who, in a few minutes, would argue about which of them would be the greatest! Jesus even washed Judas' feet, knowing that in a few hours he would betray the Lord. *"I, your Lord and Teacher, have washed your feet. So you also should wash one another's feet. I have given you an example. You should do as I have done for you." (John 13:14-15)*

Be compassionate with others as you grow in your understanding of what it means to become a boy or girl or man or woman of God. Many boys look in the mirror and don't see a muscular man's body. Did God make a mistake? Many girls also look in the mirror and don't see the curves like they see on magazine covers. They wonder if they will become women or look like the boy down the street. Will a prince come sweep them off their feet someday? Maybe you are that frustrated boy or girl. If, however, you are secure in who God made you, be compassionate and encouraging to those who struggle. *If you miss everything in this chapter, don't miss this —* GOD MAKES NO MISTAKES. If He gave you a Y chromosome on the day of your conception, He meant you to be a unique boy, bold and brave in Him.[372] If He gave you an X chromosome, He meant for you to be a unique, beautiful girl, precious in His sight. He will be with you every step to help you grow into the man or woman He wants

---

372 Unfortunately, our fallen world suffers from disease, disabilities, and deformities. You might be surprised to learn that some babies' sex organs (1 in 2000) are not fully or distinctly formed in the womb, just as some babies' fingers or toes don't fully form. This doesn't make these babies any less valuable or loved by God or their parents! It just means the parents need to make some careful, very challenging decisions with their doctor, pastor, and ultimately with God about how the baby should be helped and raised.

you to be. Someday, Jesus will be the One to sweep you off your feet when He returns. God rejoices in you, my boy or girl! Rejoice in Him and who He made you to be.

THINGS TO THINK ABOUT AND TALK OVER:

- *What are some traits you have as a boy or girl that "fit" your sex? What are some traits you wish were different? Is there anything you can do to change some of those (for example, exercise, diet, clubs, sports, or your circle of friends) that would help you become more like the person God wants you to be? Share your ideas with someone you trust.*

- *Do you know a boy who looks or acts more girlish? Do you know a girl who acts more like a boy? Instead of avoiding them like some kids do, how can you befriend them? If they confide in you that they feel out of place as a boy or girl, how might you encourage them?*

- *Are there some stereotypes in our culture about boys or girls that you think should be challenged? Do you see God's plan for boys and girls being confused or rejected by our culture? Have you seen hurting kids and adults as a result of that confusion?*

THE PERSON IN THE MIRROR

# SPORTS AND EXERCISE

*Or do you not know that your body is a temple of the Holy Spirit within you, whom you have from God? You are not your own, for you were bought with a price. So glorify God in your body.*[373]

"Coach Stone, I can't run as fast as all the other kids!"

"Gary, why do you think we run? Do you think those fast kids will be in the Olympics someday?"

"I'm not sure. Probably not."

"Then why should we run? So we can be popular? Maybe to be good-looking? Do you think God cares more about someone becoming a popular sports star or a person of character? Tell me something, Gary. Where does God live?"

"In my heart, I think."

"And if He lives in your heart, your body is His temple. That's a pretty awesome thought. The God of the universe has made His home in you. You think He wants a flabby temple? Or does He want you to have the most energy and feel the best you can so that you can better serve Him and care for other people?"

Paul wrote to his sports-minded friends in Corinth,"*I run in such a way, as not without aim; I box in such a way, as not beating the air; but I discipline my body and make it my slave, so that, after I have preached to others, I myself will not be disqualified.*"[374]

Paul was smart. He wasn't looking for a Nike endorsement. He chose a sport that put his body under the command of his mind and spirit to gain an eternal crown.

No one wants to win a race and then get disqualified for breaking the rules. After training hard and running a difficult race in life,

373   1 Corinthians 6:19-20
374   1 Corinthians 9:26-27

how can we get disqualified and lose our crown before God? Easy!
We can cheat! We cut corners when no one is looking. We look at
erotic images on the internet when we think no one else is watching.
Fasting or praying in public can be only for show.[375] In other words,
we let the desire for pleasure (sometimes the Bible calls that our
"flesh") run our lives. We eat too much. We sit on the couch and
watch entertainment on TV rather than use our time for God's
kingdom.

So how can running or another sport help us? Like Paul knew,
exercise is a powerful way we can discipline our body and make it
our slave for God's purposes, instead of allowing our body or physical
desires to call the shots. Can a disabled person discipline their body?
Of course! They can fast. They can pray at hours when others are
asleep. They can also push themselves physically. Nick Vujicic was
born with no arms or legs. But instead of being confined to a bed or
a wheelchair, he has learned to swim, play soccer, ride a horse, surf
and probably has done a dozen other things that most "normal" people
never have. With great joy in the life God has given him, no wonder
Nick has a tremendous ministry called "No Limbs, No Limits."

Naturally, disciplining your body can be taken in a wrong direction.
Sadly, many people make sports the center of their lives. Some
families spend far more time going to sports practices, games, and
camps than they do reading God's Word, enjoying good fellowship,
and serving others. Of course, you can do a good deal of ministry in
sports. But any honest person can quickly tell if their primary focus
in life is sports itself or serving God through sports. Which one do
you think about when you wake up in the morning? Which one do
you usually talk about over breakfast or dinner? Do you ask God
more often to help you win or help you witness?

In the same way, we should train our bodies mainly to be obedient
to God's will, not for our appearance or praise. How much time do
you spend in front of the mirror, either in admiration or derision?
Contrast that with how much your physical discipline enables you to
press on spiritually. Where is your focus?

Test yourself. See if your physical discipline is impacting your
spiritual and mental discipline. Do you make yourself get out of

---

375 Of course, praying and fasting are important for all of us. However, if we are doing these
things for show, the real purpose is lost.

bed, wash your face, and read your Bible in the morning? Do you share your love for God with someone as His Spirit leads?

Okay, so what if I've been slacking? I know God has been telling me to get disciplined. My diet and exercise are a sad affair. Where do I begin?

First, pray and ask for forgiveness and for God to make your heart right. He is always calling, waiting with delight to pour out His power when you turn to Him for help. But check your primary motivation. *Strive to do everything in life because you love God, not because you feel guilty or disgusted with yourself.*

Second, start slow! Don't try to run a marathon the first day. Build slowly, maybe adding just one extra lap of swimming a day. Or try five minutes of running and five minutes of walking each day this week. Then do seven minutes of each next week. Set a reasonable goal of three to five 30-minute sessions per week.

Third, if possible, find someone you will enjoy exercising with. If that's not possible, try to find someone who can help you be accountable and encourage you. "Did you go to your exercise class today? How long did you run?[376] What time are you going tomorrow? What are your goals for tomorrow?" The best exercise partner I've found will also engage in a spiritual discipline with you at the same time like prayer or Scripture memory.

My dad — your grandpa — is a lifelong runner. Just to spend time with him, I joined him on runs as a teenager. I was never that fast and don't remember ever winning any ribbons in track or cross country. But I was faithful and kept running. Even when I was doing chemotherapy thirty years later, I felt like God wanted me to get out and run. So I ran as best I could for about one mile in the winter snow to work, even though I was terribly slow and weak. Later in life, exercise and fresh air can only help your immune system. Disciplining my body to do something difficult also helped me to fight depression during chemotherapy treatments. As hard as it

376   This is a better question than "How far did you run?" Remember: your goal is lifelong fitness and discipline for God's kingdom. Twenty or thirty minutes a day of intense physical activity is probably optimum for most people. Knowing how fast you went, how far you made it, and how many points you scored might help motivate you to keep going sometimes, but a bad day in those areas can make you want to hang it up. How many people after 60 are still actively sprinting or playing basketball, football, or baseball? Very few! However, many still jog, swim, or do aerobics.

was to inject myself with Interferon every week that year, physical determination in sports helped give me grit to not give up. However, I did give up desserts and soda that feed cancer. Discipline also helped me to pray and keep ministering to others when I felt like passing out or throwing up during chemotherapy.

Exercise will be a great asset in your life, as long as your main reason in doing it is to serve God better.[377] You are His temple. Although I found running to be the simplest and fastest way to keep my body in shape, you may prefer another activity. I found I could run almost anywhere in the world. I just need a pair of shoes. Sometimes you don't even need those! Even better, I could use my time spent running to feed my soul by listening to worship music or good teaching through earphones. Find exercise that you will still be able to do when you're an adult. Biking, aerobics, soccer, and swimming are good options, but are dependent on weather, friends, or having the right facilities. Use wisdom to not overly focus on sports that can cause excessive injuries or are not demanding enough (sorry, chess is not a sport.) The good habits of self-discipline and exercise that you establish in your youth will often be the same ones which will help you the rest of your life. May God be glorified in your disciplined body!

THINGS TO THINK ABOUT AND TALK OVER:

- *Do you think God is telling you to get into a regular exercise program? What, if anything, is holding you back? What is the most helpful and realistic plan for you? Who should you share your plan with?*

- *Gluttony is a sin (Philippians 3:19). Why? Would a healthy diet make sense for a person who wants to honor God with their body?*

- *How can you tell if your discipline (exercise or diet) is mainly for you or mainly for God? What if God impressed on you, "Your sport or food is distracting you from the ministry I've given you." Would you give whatever it was up? If a physical injury,*

---

377  Injuries or physical limitations are exceptions, of course. God may also direct abstinence from sports or exercise for a season  so you can focus on fulfilling His purposes in another area.

*ministry demands, or financial limits took away your sport or your healthy food, would you still have your joy?*

- *Team sports can teach you many things that you will miss in individual sports. What do you think are some good benefits to playing team sports? If you are not involved in one, what do you think you might like to try? Tell someone who can help you learn more or help get you onto a team. Soccer is a great sport that is almost universal, and is a great way to meet new friends. I've seen barefoot kids playing in Africa who don't even have a real ball! They made one with plastic bags and string. Imagine what their joy would be like if you gave them a real soccer ball.*

THE PERSON IN THE MIRROR

# HEALTHY COMPETITION

*". . . let us run with perseverance the race marked out for us, fixing our eyes on Jesus, the pioneer and perfecter of faith."*[378]

"I won!"

"No, you didn't! That wasn't fair!"

Your mom and I can't count the times we've heard those words from each of you since you were old enough to walk and talk. There's something inside of every human that loves competition, especially when we win! But if you are anything like me, the jitters and butterflies during competition drive you crazy. Losing after trying very hard can be really hard to handle in a civilized way. From grades, popularity, and sports to clothes, toys, and money, competition can drive you to the edge of sanity. There is a tremendous difference between healthy, helpful competition and the kind that is unhealthy or destructive.

My good friend, Marty Louthan, came from and married into very competitive, athletic families. The Hull family had several sisters and one brother. They were all excellent students and gifted musicians who radiated the joy and love of the Lord. I was privileged to eat at their enormous dining room table on the night of an important basketball game (there were always extra seats for any guests the kids wanted to bring home.) I remember their Uncle Bill praying for his niece that she would reflect the joy and love of God when playing later that evening. I can say with certainty that of the many ball games I've been to in my life, I've never seen anything like it. This young girl bounced up and down the court, beaming the whole time, especially when she looked up into the stands at her cheering family. She wasn't a "ball hog," and helped her teammates and opponents who fell on the floor. But she scored — by far — more points than any other girl. In short, this was the most "healthy" competition I'd ever seen. It was fun, almost magical, for everyone to watch. Her team won. But I have a strong suspicion that her joy would have been the same if the other team had won instead.

378   Hebrews 12:1b-2a

On the other hand, you've probably seen or have been in the middle of unhealthy competition. Maybe you've seen tennis players who throw their racquets when they lose a game, or a father who curses at an umpire or a referee when they make a bad call. Even if we don't act that badly, but scowl and fume inside or smile while cussing quietly to ourselves, we sense is isn't right. Every normal person recognizes they would prefer to be like the Hull's daughter on or off the court.

To make that healthy transition, we need to be transformed on the inside. The secret? Fall in love with God. Were you expecting that? I've seen some friends do some insane things showing off to a girl that they had a crush on. On any normal day, they would probably never consider doing a double backflip off the diving board . . . until some gorgeous girl walked into the pool area! If your affections are so high for the God who saved you, went to the cross for you, and loves you, that you would do anything to bring Him joy, it will transform how you train, play chess, and study for your exams. Let the peace and joy of God consume your heart. When your treasure is in heaven, you won't be shaken when you lose a hard-fought tournament, and your pride will remain in check when you get the best grade in class. Everything we do should be for God and we should leave the results in His loving hands. He made our minds and our bodies and deserves the credit. We should do our best for Him and let Him determine the outcome.

You've may wince when someone says, "It doesn't matter if you win or lose. It just matters how you play the game." Honestly? I don't think I've ever met anyone who completely doesn't care if they lose. Sure, we should play by the rules and have good sportsmanship, but the desire to win is normal. If our hearts are right with God, we should do everything we can to win in a contest of peers. What is good sportsmanship? Compete in a way that builds up your team and your opponents without drawing excessive attention to yourself. If the meanest kid on the other team has a good move or scores a goal, compliment him! You might be surprised at how it takes the mean edge off him. Whether or not we win the local softball or debate championship doesn't matter in the big scheme of the universe. When the dust settles, can you look at your teammates or your neighbor on the opposing team and smile, knowing your friendships were completely honored?

Of course, not all the stakes are equally important. The outcome of World War II was on a totally different level than when I played checkers with you when you were five. (Yes, I did let you win most of the time!) Let God help you decide the level of importance of your current engagement. I would be making a good guess to say that 95% of our current competition is on the level of checkers in contrast to the impact on relationships. Consider carefully "how" you play the game that can impact others. Only 5% of competition would place winning as supreme over relationship (for example World War II, the understanding of essential truth, the protection of others, and helping people gain eternal life.

But what happens when we lose? Whether on the level of global peace or a district basketball championship, how should I react to losing a challenging struggle? In 2012, I ran for a political office during an intensely hot summer. The temperature was over 100 degrees for about a month straight. I visited thousands of homes, going door-to-door to explain who I was and what my vision was. I felt God was leading me to run and I really wanted to win. I also felt that no matter what the outcome was, I wanted to use the time to minister to others. Whether in conversations following speeches or visiting shut-in seniors, I was thrilled to meet people, hear their stories, and pray with those who were willing. Even though we did well in the election, I came in second of four. Was I disappointed? Sure! Honestly, it took time to come to full peace with the final tally, but I knew God was ultimately in charge of the outcome.[379]

Remember the two chapters for "When You Fail"? Two facts have helped me enormously:

1.  God is sovereign over every detail of our lives[380]
2.  God will work every loss for our good if we are in Christ[381]

That means you will always win, even when you lose! But to actually rest and fully enjoy those two powerful intentions of God, we must put our trust in Him. He has the power, the love, and the

379 Romans 13:1, "Let everyone be subject to the governing authorities, for there is no authority except that which God has established. The authorities that exist have been established by God."
380 Total sovereignty means having absolute power and the will to govern even the smallest things in the universe; Matthew 10:29-31, "Are not two sparrows sold for a penny? And not one of them will fall to the ground apart from your Father. But even the hairs of your head are all numbered. Fear not, therefore; you are of more value than many sparrows."
381 We know that all things work together for those who love God and are called according to His purpose. - Romans 8:28

intent to bring blessing into our lives no matter what outcome challenges our desires. We just have to love and trust Him.

Someday soon, we will each leave behind all the trophies, diplomas, riches, and fame this life may offer. In the day your race ends, your "accomplishments" will become absolutely meaningless if you did them for your own glory. The only thing you can take to heaven is a faithful testimony and others who became citizens of heaven because of your testimony. Run a healthy, joyful race with your eyes fixed on Jesus.

### THINGS TO THINK ABOUT AND TALK OVER:

• *Good sportsmanship is a skill. It takes time to develop. How can you improve your ability to encourage classmates, teammates, and even opponents?*

• *Try to remember a time when you were playing a game and didn't have the best attitude or behavior. Maybe you are even embarrassed as you remember how you acted. Think about the verse at the opening of this chapter, Hebrews 12:1-2. How did Jesus "let" Himself be overpowered and put on the cross for a much greater purpose? How would His example help you "do over" that game?*

• *Nobody likes a sore loser. How might you teach your younger siblings or friends to lose with grace and joy? (Remember that the best lessons are usually caught, not taught.)*

• *People love a gracious winner. How can you prepare your heart ahead of time to humbly accept the praise of victory?*

# A LETTER FROM MY GREAT-GREAT-GREAT GRANDMOTHER IN 1854

The following letter was foundational in my desire to write this book. I remember reading her letter as a young man and being profoundly moved at the depth of her writing and insight, even though I was not yet a Christ-follower. Obviously, my great-great grandfather was also moved because he kept the letter, passing it to my great Aunt Lucille, through whom we came into a possession of a copy. Passing the depths of the knowledge of God's grace from generation to generation is a tremendous privilege and joy.

Excerpts below are from the original letter written by Lucy Caroline Webb, widow of Dr. Joseph Thompson Scott the first to her third son Dr Joseph Thompson Scott II when he was studying in Paris France with his older brother dr. Isaac Webb Scott. He was 22 years old and had received a medical degree from Transylvania in 1852. He took his mother's advice to heart and lived to be a credit to his profession and to his family. He preserved his mother's letter all his life and gave it to his son Dr Joseph Tilford Scott who in turn left it to his daughter Lucille Scott Munstead.

*Lexington, November 1854*
*My dear Joe,*

*For weeks now I have intended answering you're very affectionate and gratifying letter, the acknowledgement of wrongdoings with a determination of future amendment on your part, as such as a mother is ever ready to receive and forgive. But I would not be so unfaithful to my God, my child, nor myself, as to remind you and endeavor to impress it upon you, that whenever you sin, you sin against a higher power and stronger love than that of a mother. And could your confession for past sins be made in the sincerity and language of David (expressed in the 51st Psalm) then indeed my heart would run over with joy, for I should be confident that although you were not able to resist temptations of yourself, yet in the language of the Great Apostle, you could do all things in Christ strengthening you.*

*This my dear son is our only safety, a firm on shaken reliance in all his blessed promises which are yea and amen in Christ Jesus our*

*Lord. And now in particular, surrounded as you both are, by all the temptations of a Parisian life do you, most especially need his protecting care and direction of you.*

*I shudder to think few of those that have trusted themselves within her borders have escaped without making shipwreck of their Immortal Souls, and when I reflect that I have two sons exposed to similar temptations and that with my own consent, conceive if you can imagine this anguish I sometimes feel that I too, may be instrumental in your eternal destruction.*

*Think, Joe. How transitory are the riches and honors of this life and yet how eager men pursue them to the destruction of their immortal spirits. True, I have hoped to see my son's eminent and distinguished in their professions, but God forbid it should be the first consideration with me or either of you. My most earnest wish and fervent prayer is that you both may seek first and Immortal crown of glory, which the Lord and the righteous judge has promised to place upon the heads of all those that love his appearing.*

\*\*\*

*The Whigs are again defeated in their candidate for president— Kentucky goes for Scott—all returns have not come in but sufficient to know Pierce is elected. So much for allowing the rabble of Europe to control our elections.*

*We have had the most exciting time in Lexington I ever saw. Mr. Brown was arraigned before Presbytery to answer charges in Goodlow's pamphlet. Bob Breckiaridge has taken throughout an active part against him, also Joe Bullock. I certainly never saw two men who had disgraced themselves as they have done in this and brought disgrace on the cause of Christ . . .*

\*\*\*

*And now I must tell you that they are not done laughing at me for sending you to Paris to break you off from bad company, but I bear it pretty well and tell them I don't regret it. I hope that you will be able to prove to them that I did the best for you and taking your brother's advice, in whom I feel the most entire confidence.*

*Write often, study hard and above all study the scriptures, take them as a light to your feet and a lamp to your path, it will prevent you from entering many a dark hole.*

*My best love to you both my dear sons,*
*Your Mother*